PEER SUPPORT IN MENTAL HEALTH

FOUNDATIONS OF MENTAL HEALTH PRACTICE

The Foundations of Mental Health Practice series offers a fresh approach to the field of mental health by exploring key areas and issues in mental health from a social, psychological and a biological perspective. Taking a multidisciplinary approach, the series is aimed at students and practitioners across the people professions- including student nurses, social workers, occupational therapists, psychiatrists, counsellors and psychologists.

Thurstine Basset worked as a community worker and social worker before becoming involved in mental health training and education in the 1980s. He is an independent training and development consultant and has experience of working with a number of universities, statutory and voluntary mental health organisations, service user and carer groups. He has published widely across the mental health training and education field. In collaboration with Theo Stickley, he is a Co-editor of '*Learning about Mental Health Practice*' (Wiley 2008). He is also a Board Member for the *Journal of Mental Health Training, Education and Practice.*

Theo Stickley is Associate Professor of Mental Health Nursing at the University of Nottingham. He has authored and edited many books and journal articles about mental health. Each represents his interest in promoting a fair, just and genuinely caring way in which to think about and deliver mental health care. His area of research is promoting mental health through participatory arts and he advocates a creative approach to care delivery.

Available now:

Working with Dual Diagnosis: A Psychosocial Perspective by Darren Hill, William J Penson and Divine Charura

From Psychiatric Patient to Citizen Revisited by Liz Sayce

Models of Mental Health by Gavin Davidson, Jim Campbell, Ciaran Shannon and Ciaran Mulholland

Values and Ethics in Mental Health: An Exploration for Practice by Alastair Morgan, Anne Felton, Bill Fulford, Jayasree Kalathil and Gemma Stacey

PEER SUPPORT IN MENTAL HEALTH

EDITED BY EMMA WATSON
AND SARA MEDDINGS

First published 2019 by
RED GLOBE PRESS

Red Globe Press in the UK is an imprint of Springer Nature Limited,
registered in England, company number 785998, of 4 Crinan Street,
London, N1 9XW.

Red Globe Press® is a registered trademark in the United States,
the United Kingdom, Europe and other countries.

ISBN 978–1–352–00506–6 paperback

This book is printed on paper suitable for recycling and made from fully
managed and sustained forest sources. Logging, pulping and manufacturing
processes are expected to conform to the environmental regulations of the
country of origin.

A catalogue record for this book is available from the British Library.

A catalog record for this book is available from the Library of Congress.

Contents

List of figures and tables

Editor Biographies

Emma Watson began working as a peer support worker in Nottinghamshire NHS Foundation Trust in 2010. During this time she also worked as a peer researcher, completed an MSc in Mental Health and Social Inclusion and worked at the Institute of Mental Health as a peer trainer for their accredited peer support provision. Emma has co-produced training and published several papers drawing on her academic and lived experience of peer support and recovery. She is now peer support development lead for Nottingham NHS Trust, a role which involves supporting and growing a peer workforce, facilitating training and working with services to embed peer ways of working within the organisation. She is also undertaking a PhD to explore the mechanisms that underpin peer support, and how peer support is affected by the context it takes place within.

Sara Meddings is psychology and psychological therapies consultant lead for recovery and well-being at Sussex Partnership NHS Foundation Trust. She has over 25 years' experience working with people with mental health challenges and their families. She is a member of the advisory group for Recovery Partners and a consultant with ImROC. She has developed a number of hearing voices self-help groups. She co-led the development of Sussex Recovery College and co-facilitates the ImROC Recovery College learning network. She has co-produced trainings in recovery and family inclusive practice and developed an accredited family interventions course in partnership with Surrey University. She is published in the areas of recovery, psychosis and family work. She draws on her personal experiences regarding mental health and well-being in her work and manages her own recovery from ME/chronic fatigue.

Emma and Sara met through their work as ImROC consultants where they use their experiences to support other organisations wishing to develop systems, services and cultures that support recovery and well-being for all.

List of Contributors

Shazia Ali is an intersectional feminist, peer support specialist/trainer and a campaigner of mental and emotional distress.

Jacqueline Clarke-Mapp is a coach, mentor, trainer and the founder of Confident Carers. She works with people to improve mental health services for people with lived experience and their family, friends and unpaid carers.

Mirika Flegg is a researcher at the Centre of Resilience for Social Justice at the University of Brighton. She lectures in Public Health and Clinical Research and has worked in peer-led organisations in the UK, New Zealand and Canada.

Eleanor Hope is a life coach, peer support specialist/trainer and the founder and director of Hope Matters, a Black and Minority Ethnic personal development and well-being social enterprise.

Sandra Jayacodi is a service user advisor and representative for various NHS trusts on research, quality improvement and patient and public involvement and engagement projects.

Karen Machin works freelance in mental health and writes from the perspective of lived experience.

Phil Morgan is the lead for recovery and social inclusion for Dorset HealthCare University NHS Foundation Trust and co-lead of Dorset Well-being and Recovery Partnership.

Clare Ockwell has used mental health services since childhood and is chief executive of the CAPITAL Project Trust, a West Sussex-wide peer support charity.

Howard Pearce is a former mental health service user working in mental health recovery, peer support and suicide prevention. He is a founder and co-director of Recovery Partners.

Glenn Roberts worked in rehabilitation psychiatry in Devon and is a past lead on recovery for the Royal College of Psychiatrists.

Waldo Roeg is a senior peer recovery trainer in Central and North West London NHS Foundation Trust and an ImROC consultant.

Anna Stratford lives and works in mental health recovery, peer support, suicide prevention and social work education. She is a founder and co-director of Recovery Partners.

1 Introduction

Emma Watson and Sara Meddings

Have you ever felt as if no one in the world could possibly understand how you're feeling or what you are living through? Have you ever felt so alone that even to be in the presence of other people is a painful reminder of the uniqueness of your own internal world? Maybe you have found yourself opposite a person who is trying to help you, maybe even paid to help you, and wondered how they could possibly understand. Worse still, have you ever sat opposite somebody who is telling you they know how you feel when they clearly don't?

We have both experienced this sense of isolation when life has brought us to particularly challenging places. My (Emma) experiences of mental distress have often been lonely and frightening. These experiences coloured my world and made it feel as if it was slightly (or sometimes wildly) different from the world that people around me lived in. My experiences of trying to explain my world to others have been, at times, incredibly shaming, reminding me of my difference; my inferiority even.

Throughout history people have found solace in meeting others who have had similar experiences to them, whether this be of parenthood, culture, education, grief, profession, emotional or physical pain. This has come to be known as peer support and many have described the profound impact that this has on their sense of self. In her book *Madness Made Me*, Mary O'Hagan describes the experience that meeting other 'peers' had on her:

> *Over the years I met many good people who were mad like me. Their madness
> had taken them to a foreign land where only mad people could go to ... Mental
> health professionals stood at the border trying to pull people out of the mad
> land, even the ones who wanted to stay. They knew the mad land as a bad place
> where people get lost, sometimes forever. But most of them had never been there.
> My peers showed me that the mad land, for all its perils, had some of the most
> enchanted scenery in the world. Like a land that has mountains and ravines, rivers
> and caves, blinding sun and swirling storms, the mad land could be a place of
> beauty as well as danger. My peers helped me to understand that I was not alone
> in the mad land, that there was a whole tribe of us who had been there and seen
> many of the same things. Things that other people did not easily understand.
> Things they feared and denigrated.* (O'Hagan, 2014, p. 111)

At its most simple, peer support is the coming together of two people who have walked along a similar path and who find comfort in each other's journey. But peer support is far more than that. Peer support rests on the assumption that a person's own experiences are a source of strength and the means to build connection with others. As such, it flips the narrative about where expertise lies on its head. It implies that we ourselves have the power to understand our experiences and are best positioned to direct our own path to well-being.

This is a powerful philosophical standpoint with far-reaching implications in terms of mental health service delivery and human rights. Traditionally we have seen people who experience distress as in need of professional, mostly medical, intervention. To locate expertise within the person, to name lived experience as a source of expertise, is disruptive.

In this way, peer support, which has at its heart a simple sharing relationship, is incredibly complex. Peer support is not an uncomplicated solution to the loneliness of mental distress. In fact, it seems that peer support in mental health is growing more complicated by the day. In recent decades, peer support has become more prominent in mental health policy and practice throughout the western world. More and more paid roles are being created within mental health services, as well as in community initiatives. Training courses in peer support are becoming more widespread and in the UK and Ireland the introduction of peer workers is understood to drive forward culture change within mental health services. The growth of peer support has taken place in decades that have been defined by austerity and often division, but this has not seemed to slow its growth in popularity in mental health. Perhaps there is something refreshing about the peer support standpoint that values the voice of the non-expert and locates strength within individuals and communities, that explores experience rather than seeking to 'fix' it.

It is with this standpoint that we have written this book, capturing a snapshot of the landscape of peer support in the UK and Ireland, with the understanding that it is ever expanding, distorting and evolving. Given the breadth of offerings, both formal and informal, that fall under the umbrella of peer support, we have chosen to focus on intentional peer support in mental health, but not solely in mental health services. Intentional peer support involves deliberately offering support based on shared experience, most often where one person is working (either paid or voluntarily) within a peer role. This focus has enabled us to consider several forms of peer support in greater detail. Given the diversity that exists within peer support, it is not possible to explore every context in which it takes place, such as online, parenting groups, or in offending, prison or homeless populations. Nonetheless, we hope that the content of the book is helpful in understanding peer support as a concept and offering guidance, challenge and ideas which go beyond specific contexts.

We bring to this book a number of different identities and both of us have been defined, or have chosen to define ourselves, differently in our working lives. I (Emma) was employed and trained as a peer support worker in 2010, at a time when I was still very much swimming in my own experiences of distress, and using mental health services. Like so many other peer workers, the role helped transform my sense of self and I began to understand that I needn't see my experiences as failure or weakness. The role also brought my lived experience into the foreground; it was (and perhaps still is) what defined me and how others understood me.

I (Sara) am employed and trained as a clinical psychologist. However, my first experience of mental health services was of being sent to see a psychiatrist in my adolescence. The kind of psychologist I am is influenced by my life experiences, including of traumas, distress and disability, of using mental health services and of having close relatives use mental health services. Working alongside other recovery-oriented practitioners and professionals and peers who used their lived experience helped me integrate these two forms of learning. Working with the peers at the Recovery College, and in writing this book, has profoundly inspired me, helping me to see my lived experience as an asset and to bring my dual identities more into the foreground.

There are both positive and negative consequences to the foregrounding of different expertise and experiences. Both of us have lived experience, and academic backgrounds, but the way the world sees us, and the way we experience the world, is very different. Within this book we draw on our experiences, lived and professional, academic and lay, and take every opportunity to invite the experiences of others. We are sharply aware of the privileges we have enjoyed as well as the challenges, and that as white, educated women, with our unique experiences of the world of mental health, we can only know so much.

This book is a coming together of people with diverse lived and life experience to explore the concept of peer support from different angles, to present the debates that exist in the literature, as well as those that they personally have experienced. The first part of the book introduces the concept of peer support; we go on to explore some of the specific settings where peer support occurs; and then the practicalities of providing peer support. We have learned much from developments in peer support in the USA, New Zealand, Canada and around the world. We hope that this book provides opportunities to learn from experience in the UK.

Chapter 2 provides an introduction to peer support, beginning with its history which is rooted in a civil rights movement, among other things. It also describes the evidence and values that underpin peer support, so that readers can hold on to these as they read later chapters, using them to develop their own perspectives on some of the debates that exist within peer support.

Chapter 3 places these debates under the microscope, in particular exploring the tensions that exist when peer workers are introduced into statutory mental health services, which use approaches that are often at odds with the philosophy of peer support. This chapter is by no means the only place where debates are explored. In each chapter the authors provide critical thinking points in relation to the subject at hand. Chapter 4 broadens the focus once more, beyond mental health services to describe and unpack some of the many ways that peer support is formally offered in the UK, including in group settings and within charities. Recovery Colleges are becoming more popular across the UK and we have dedicated Chapter 5 to these, to allow space to fully explore the peer support that is offered and received by students, tutors and staff in these settings.

Equally important and distinct in identity is the peer support that is offered between carers, family and friends, and peer support in communities that have traditionally been marginalised. Chapters 6 and 7 provide space for the uniqueness of peer support in different communities to be considered, and to explore who is a peer to whom. Debates surrounding identity and stigma are well articulated here, and the distance that peer support must still travel in order to appreciate the many different lived experiences which people define themselves by is clear.

Chapter 8 provides an overview of the learning that has emerged around peer support training. This includes a consideration of the values which must underpin training, and some of the common components of training courses, both in the UK and across the western world. Training, unsurprisingly, places emphasis on the use of lived experience, how a peer might go about this, and the boundaries which accompany peer support relationships. This is well positioned alongside Chapter 9, written by mental health professionals who consider how they and other professionals might use and share lived experience in their work. It includes a weighing up of the benefits and challenges that come with sharing personal experiences, especially when this is not expected within professional identities. This consideration draws attention to the huge amount of lived experience which exists within the mental health workforce, raising the questions of what support is consistently offered for mental health workers, and what additional support might be helpful in relation to lived experience?

Chapter 10 goes some way towards answering these questions as the authors describe best practice approaches to employing peer workers, and the support structures which are needed within organisations to offer these. The authors draw on the available evidence as well as their own experiences of employing peer workers and of working with organisations where the peer support role has presented a challenge to existing employment structures. Finally, Chapter 11 describes a world where the balance of peer workers and professional is tipped the other way. In 'peer-led' organisations, rather than having a seat at the table, people with lived experience have control over the design, delivery and evaluation of services. We end the book with the peer-led message as a means of inviting the reader to think radically about the way in which mental health support is currently offered, and what it could become if lived experience was as valued as professional expertise.

We have thought carefully about the language choices we make within this book, particularly the language we use to describe people and their experiences. Language is incredibly important; it demonstrates the value and meaning we place on ideas. We have strived to use language that represents the philosophy of peer support, that values whole people (not patients) and human experience (not illness). Given the history of peer support, rooted in campaigns against the medicalisation of madness, we have particularly avoided using the language of illness or medicine. This is not language which fits with our personal understanding of these experiences and does not fit with the philosophy of peer support.

It is unlikely that agreement will ever be reached on the most helpful language to use in the context of mental health. While some prefer the term madness, having reclaimed it within the Mad Pride movement, others find it offensive. While some prefer mental health problems, others believe this still implies illness and biomedical approaches. As much as possible we have chosen to use the terms 'lived experience', 'mental distress' and 'mental health challenges' to describe these experiences. We believe these are most in keeping with the philosophy of peer support (and our own personal values). They honour the very human nature of these experiences and encompass the broad spectrum on which they exist.

For similar reasons we have shied away from describing people as patients or service users, instead choosing terms such as people receiving peer support and people who use services, as this is less reductive. There may be points within the book where authors make other language choices based on their own perspectives and experiences or the literature and people they are citing, and we have not policed this too heavily; everybody has the right to choose how they describe themselves and how they understand their own experiences.

REFERENCES

O'Hagan, M. (2014). *Madness Made Me.* Wellington: Open Box.

2

What Is Peer Support? History, Evidence and Values

Emma Watson

Chapter Summary

- **Peer support** has become a formalised approach within mental health services but has its roots in self-help, advocacy and the survivor movement, where it began as a form of alternative support and a place of activism

- As peer support has become more widely accepted, it has appeared in policy documents in the UK, and there are growing recommendations for it to be included in mental health service provision

- Peer support benefits the person providing it, the person receiving it and the services within which the **peer worker** is based. Higher quality research is needed, as well as a clearer understanding about what peer support is and what should be measured

- Peer support can be understood in terms of the values and principles which underpin it. These values include mutuality, shared learning, agency and valuing strengths and experience. The mechanisms which underpin peer support are thought to include the use of personal experience but this is an under-researched area

- As peer support has become embedded in mental health services, debates have emerged about what this means for the approach, given its history, how to support peer workers and what this means for staff members with **lived experience**

Introduction

In mental health, 'peer support' is the support provided and received by people who have their own experiences of distress and recovery. It is considered to be a 'mutual' approach, in that it doesn't invite the overt power hierarchies that are involved in professional helping relationships, where one person has expertise over the other. This chapter provides an introduction to the concept of peer support in mental health services by reviewing its complex historical roots. We will see that peer support has grown from self-help and activism to become an evidence-based, formalised approach.

The chapter includes a variety of definitions of peer support which provide the opportunity to consider the different language that is used to describe the approach. There is also growing interest in what processes are involved in peer support and what benefits it brings. A growing body of evidence has focused on these questions, providing us with an emerging understanding of the multiple benefits of peer support and the reasons why these benefits come about.

Any account of the history, research or processes of peer support will be partial. In particular, voices from black and minority ethnic and lesbian, gay, bisexual and transgender communities have often been absorbed into the wider history of the service user movement, reducing the prominence of the unique history of peer support in these settings. This is explored further in Chapters 3 and 6, and in the case example in Chapter 8. Rather than attempting to provide a comprehensive history, in this chapter we focus on some of the key developments in the peer support movement in mental health and use these to understand how current peer support practices have been informed by, or distorted from, the original vision of early pioneers.

The roots of peer support

The roots of peer support reach far back into the histories of psychiatry, social change movements, self-help and **survivor**-led initiatives. Davidson and colleagues (2012) describe an early example of the employment of people who had been committed in asylums as staff members (or 'servants') occurring in the late eighteenth century in Bicêtre Hospital in Paris where, 'As much as possible, all servants are chosen from the category of mental patients. They are at any rate better suited to this demanding work because they are usually more gentle, honest, and humane' (1793, Jean-Baptiste Pussin, cited in Weiner, 1979, p. 1132). Other examples of former patients being employed in caring roles also exist, highlighting that the value of peer support has been acknowledged in previous centuries. A review of patient records from 1870 to 1940 from a Canadian asylum identified numerous cases where inmates offered both formal and informal assistance to other patients (Reaume, 2000). While this shows that 'fertile ground' exists within mental health services for peer support to take root, we do not understand these examples to represent the birth of peer support, or to have had a significant impact on peer support in the present day. Like others (e.g. Beales & Wilson, 2015; Elias & Upton-Davis, 2015; O'Hagan, 2011) we argue that the roots of peer support lie most deeply in the self-help and service user movements which predominantly unfolded during the twentieth century and continue to thrive.

The Alleged Lunatic Friends Society (ALFS) is considered to be one of the earliest documented peer support and advocacy organisations in the world. It was founded in England in

1845 by Richard Paternoster, John Perceval, William Bailey, Richard Saumarez and Dr John Parkin, all of whom had experienced admissions to asylums, during which time they experienced maltreatment from those in charge (Hervey, 1986). ALFS argued that mental distress often arose from difficult life circumstances such as rejections and disappointments. They campaigned against confining individuals away from their family and loved ones, calling instead for people to be treated as adults, capable of making their own decisions. ALFS supported legal action taken by current and ex-patients against those who had incarcerated them. Similar campaigning groups also formed across the UK and Europe in the late nineteenth century.

The roots of peer support within community settings are largely unrecorded in history, perhaps because self-help at the grassroots level can take many forms and is hard to identify and define (Doughty & Tse, 2005). It was not until the early twentieth century, as professional services began to take an interest in community-provided services, that **peer-led** service groups began to define themselves as such (Beales & Wilson, 2015; Elias & Upton-Davis, 2015). In the arena of addiction, self-help and peer support groups have been identified as early as the eighteenth century (Robertson, 2009). The most notable of these is Alcoholics Anonymous (AA), founded in 1935 in Ohio, USA, before reaching the UK in 1947 (Borkman, 1999; Bill W., 2002). AA continues to thrive and has been adapted for use with other addictions and mental health experiences. Similar self-help programmes have been established by and for mental health communities throughout history. These forms of support have generally avoided political campaigning and adopted 'illness models' to understand distressing experiences. Nonetheless, the emergence of these groups often helped to meet needs which mental health services had not. For example, the Mental Patients Association (MPA) was formed in Canada in the early 1970s so that people could help each other to prevent suicides over the weekends when support from services is harder to access (Choi & Boschma, 2017; citing Vancouver Mental Patients' Association Society, 1983). In Ireland the mutual help movement GROW, which began in Australia, was established in 1969 (GROW in Ireland, 1994).

Later forms of peer support have had a more political presence, informed by the service user/survivor and hearing voices movements. The birth of the UK service user movement is considered to have taken place in the 1970s with the conception of the Scottish Union of Mental Patients (SUMP) and the Mental Patients Union (MPU) (Crossley, 1999). Within the context of a decade which witnessed the birth of the women's movement, the gay rights movement, and disability rights movements, former and current service users began to organise their own networks. They were united by the shared goals of campaigning against compulsory treatment, stigma and discrimination, and in favour of civil rights and approaches run by and for people experiencing mental distress.

The establishment of SUMP and the MPU acted as a catalyst for other similar organisations which added diversity to the movement and increased its publicity. Although activities varied between groups, these early networks provided peer support in crisis houses as well as campaigning for mental health service change at national and local levels. Mind began in 1946 as the National Association for Mental Health (Crossley, 1998) and by the 1970s it had rooted its philosophy in civil rights, actively campaigning for the rights of people using mental health services. It was in this decade that the name Mind was adopted and its ambitions began to overlap with those of the survivor movement leading to mutual influence.

By 1999 other survivor groups had been established such as Survivors Speak Out, Aware in Ireland and the United Kingdom Advocacy Network (UKAN). In their 1998 annual report UKAN recorded 246 groups across its network, mostly small peer support groups while others were national campaigning groups. The hearing voices movement was started in 1987 by Marius Romme, Sandra Escher and Patsy Hage.

The development of the hearing voices movement established an alternative understanding of 'auditory hallucinations', arguing that these are not merely a symptom of mental illness, but a meaningful human experience. Like the survivor movement, it rejected the medical understanding of human issues and campaigned for social justice. The Hearing Voices Network (HVN; see Chapter 4) was founded in England in 1988, offering peer support self-help groups for people, based on mutual respect and empathy. HVNs have since been established in countless other countries (Romme & Escher, 1993). Other survivor-run alternatives to medical treatment also began to emerge in the second half of the twentieth century, including Soteria houses in the USA and survivor-run crisis houses in the UK, based on medication- and restraint-free approaches.

The anti-psychiatry movements and service user movements influenced and shaped each other's campaigns. The service user/survivor movement is often conceptualised as a 'revolt from below' in psychiatry, highlighting the position within the power hierarchy that service users are seen to occupy. This 'revolt' was slightly preceded by the anti-psychiatry movement which is conceptualised as a 'revolt from above'. Like the service user/survivor movement and the hearing voices movement, the anti-psychiatry movement, led by psychiatrists including R. D. Laing, questioned the basic premises which underpin psychiatry; the concept of 'mental illness'; and that madness and sanity cannot be clearly distinguished. The movement also drew attention to the controlling function that psychiatry has within society, arguing that the treatment approaches used by psychiatrists cause more damage, and are more 'false', than the realities and experiences of those they treat. Despite differences in illness experiences and advocacy positions, what was collectively being called for was the opportunity for people using services to be included in decisions which concerned them. This is illustrated by the disability slogan of the 1990s 'Nothing About Us Without Us', made popular by a book of the same name published by James Charlton (1998).

The growth of the survivor and hearing voices movements has created an influx of narratives of service use, abuse, trauma and recovery and these present an ever-growing resource which can be drawn on. Notions of consumer power within health services has provided survivor voices with their own symbolic power. This is an important development in the history of peer support; by using personal narratives survivors have transformed their experiences into a form of power and capital (see Chapter 3). Judy Chamberlin's account, titled *On Our Own*, provided an important influence on the survivor movement when it was published in 1978. Within it, Chamberlin shared her experiences of mental health services alongside a critique of the approaches she encountered and the argument that patient-controlled alternatives are essential. Mad Pride, started by Pete Shaugnessy, and Survivors' Poetry further developed narratives of recovery, survival and positive self-identities where experiences are a source of pride. It is this vein of service and social change that led to the reclamation of the concept of recovery.

'Recovery' and the formalisation of peer support

Since its inception, the survivor and hearing voices movements have challenged the assertion that recovery is something that professionals effect, something that can be done to an individual, and argued that recovery is something that individuals must do for themselves (Chamberlin, 1978). The understanding of **recovery** which has emerged from the narratives of people who have lived through experiences of distress and madness has a radically different focus from clinical recovery. The centrality of hope, identity and personal responsibility has replaced the focus on functioning, symptoms and interventions (Ralph, 2000).

Pat Deegan, an American survivor and psychologist, has been central to developing the concept of recovery. In 1988 she published a paper entitled 'Recovery: The lived experience of rehabilitation'. Within it she defines recovery as 'the lived or real life experiences of people as they accept and overcome the challenge of the disability' (Deegan, 1988, p. 55). After defining recovery, Deegan (1988) continues to outline the rehabilitation approaches which are most supportive of personal recovery. She highlights the importance of 'consumer-run mutual support and self-help groups, self-help networks and advocacy/ lobbyist groups' in supporting recovery (Deegan, 1988, p. 58). The importance of support from those who have also experienced mental distress has become a common theme within survivor narratives. This early message has since been reiterated by countless others who describe the helpfulness of informal (peer) support from other survivors (e.g. O'Hagan, 2014).

Formal peer support within UK mental health services must, in part, credit the developments within North American consumer-provided services for its origins. For example, the employment of 'lay professionals' (or people with experiences of mental distress) became more popular during the 1960s within mental health (Carkhuff & Truax, 1965). The popularisation of recovery in North America grew throughout the 1990s and into the twenty-first century with the establishment of 'recovery organisations' employing people with lived experience in their hundreds alongside policies of zero physical restraint and moving away from medical understandings of distress. In America the turn of the twenty-first century saw the birth of formalised 'Intentional Peer Support'. This approach was developed by Shery Mead, a survivor who worked in peer support settings for a number of years before establishing this approach as a means of protecting the integrity and unique identity of peer support. She defines peer support as:

> a system of giving and receiving help founded on key principles of respect, shared
> responsibility, and mutual agreement of what is helpful. Peer support is not
> based on psychiatric models and diagnostic criteria. It is about understanding
> another's situation empathically through the shared experience of emotional and
> psychological pain. (Mead, 2003, p. 1)

In 1995 the Pathfinder User Employment Service was developed in south-west London by Rachel Perkins (Perkins et al., 2010). This was the first example of an NHS Trust developing roles where lived experience was an essential, as well as valued, prerequisite. Initially, support worker and Occupational Therapy Assistant posts were created in rehabilitation and occupational therapy services. The service then developed to include people with lived experience in a range of roles in mainstream mental health services. In the first four years of the service 72 people with lived experience of mental health challenges obtained posts in the Trust, and 39 were supported by the user employment service. A number of other Trusts and **voluntary sector** organisations then created posts where lived experience was an essential prerequisite. The Scottish Recovery Network (SRN) was founded in 2004 with the aim to raise awareness of recovery, promote recovery-orientated approaches and influence training and research. It placed a strong emphasis on the value of lived experience, and helped develop the first peer worker (or Expert by Experience) roles in the Scottish mental health sector in 2006, largely within a short-term pilot project across five NHS Trusts (McLean et al., 2009).

Exercise

Consider the area where you live – do you know when jobs were first created where lived experience was advertised as a prerequisite? What peer support organisations do you know of? Does your local mental health trust employ peer support workers? If you don't know the answer to these questions, how might you go about finding out?

Case Example: The Scottish Recovery Network and Peer Support

Lesley Smith, Scottish Recovery Network

The Scottish Recovery Network (SRN) was launched in 2004 as an initiative designed to raise awareness of recovery from mental health problems. This was a pivotal point in Scotland where people were increasingly drawing on their personal experiences to inform, inspire and challenge for change.

Our vision is of 'A Scotland where recovery is real for everyone in every community'. To deliver this SRN work with people and their networks to develop innovative, collaborative approaches and share learning. Our work is underpinned and informed by valuing, learning from and sharing the lived experiences of people who are affected by mental health problems. Locally and nationally, today recovery is a guiding principle for both service design and mental health improvement initiatives up to and including Scotland's 2017–2027 Mental Health Strategy. SRN, within this context, has been described as a catalyst, bridge-builder, facilitator and collaborator.

Peer support is a key theme throughout our work. SRN believe that recovery-focused services should involve people and use all available expertise – including lived experience. It is only by doing this that we ensure that the help and support available best meet the needs of people to lead their own recovery and develop a fulfilling and satisfying life. SRN initiated and supported the development of peer working roles across the mental health sector. From our collaborations and learning we have contributed to a growing evidence base and resources to develop understanding of the peer worker (paid and voluntary) role, ensure its ethos and inform future developments. We have developed resources which include 'Experts by Experience Guidelines' to support organisations to develop and implement peer roles; a 'Values Framework for Peer Working' to increase understanding and maintain efficacy of the role; training in Mental Health Peer Support accredited by the Scottish Qualifications Authority; and Peer 2 Peer, a free to access, adaptable training resource developed through a European collaboration (see further resources at the end of the chapter).

Alongside this, SRN has supported development of different peer approaches through Wellness and Recovery Action Planning and Write to Recovery groups.

A valuable lesson we have learned is that having a wealth of experience, resources and national policies doesn't ensure development. The expected growth in peer working has been limited with more within the third than the statutory sector.

Peer working roles developed from the grassroots activism of people demanding change in mental health services. In Scotland we embraced the international learning, though as with any development that you endeavour to scale up/replicate the starting points are different – it took us so far! Peer workers are inspirational and incredibly valued where they are but competing priorities and interests have limited development.

At SRN we responded and adapted with the 'Making Recovery Real' partnership work, a community development approach that ensures people living with mental health problems and providers are brought together to develop local approaches and resources. Working this way has created opportunities for people with lived experience to become partners and co-produce solutions. It is as if we have come full circle in relation to peer support – from providing opportunities to meet with others who share your experience to groups, learning opportunities and the more formalised peer worker (voluntary and paid) roles. Pat Deegan describes peer support as a 'disruptive innovation' – we see this in action when investment in time and opportunities encourages people with lived experience to become involved and empowered to be part of the solution and the future!

The first peer support workers in England were trained and employed in 2008–2009 by Cambridgeshire and Peterborough, Nottingham, and Sussex Partnership NHS Foundation Trusts, predominantly on fixed-term contracts with limited funding. Between 2010 and 2013, three NHS Trusts (Nottinghamshire Healthcare, Cambridgeshire and Peterborough, and Central and North West London NHS Foundation Trust) grew their peer workforce, employing 68 peers in total by 2013 (Repper, 2013). In other areas, including Sussex, the peer workforce expanded through peer-led organisations, such as CAPITAL and Recovery Partners. In Ireland the first peer support workers were employed in 2011 in County Mayo with the support of ImROC, an organisation established to support the development of recovery-orientated approaches within mental health services. ImROC also supported the development of the Advancing Recovery in Ireland (ARI) project 2013 which aims to communicate ideas about recovery and improve mental health services in collaboration with those that use and work in them. Given the roots of peer support within a movement that campaigned against psychiatric services and the medical understanding they impose upon recovery, the development of formal peer worker roles has not been without controversy and debate.

The increase in peer support workers has been accompanied by the development of peer support worker training (see Chapter 8) to help prepare peers for this role. It has also been paralleled by the increase of policy recommendations supporting the employment of peer workers.

Exercise

Think about a recent time when you have faced challenges (e.g. divorce, bereavement, starting university, becoming a parent). Did you prefer to get support from someone who had also been there or a professional or both? What do you think the benefits of each type of support (peer and professional) are?

Peer support in UK and Republic of Ireland policy

In the last decade the concept of peer support, and the employment of peer support workers, has been described within UK and Republic of Ireland mental health policy. The concept of recovery has shifted from the periphery of policy to a more central position, and peer support has begun to follow in its wake. In 2001 the Department of Health issued its first policy statement in relation to recovery:

> We need to create an optimistic, positive approach to all people who use mental health services. The vast majority have real prospects of recovery – if they are supported by appropriate services, driven by the right values and attitudes. The mental health system must support people in settings of their own choosing, enable access to community resources including housing, education, work, friendships or whatever they think is critical to their own recovery. (DoH, 2001, p. 24)

In Ireland, the Department of Health and Children issued a similar policy directive in 2006 (Department of Health and Children, 2006). Government policy relating to peer support was preceded by publications from influential institutions, including the Mental Health Commission of Ireland (Mental Health Commission, 2008), ImROC (Shepherd et al., 2008), Together (2010), the SRN (2011), the Mental Health Foundation (2012a, 2012b) and The King's Fund (2014a, 2014b, 2015), all of whom recommended the introduction of formal peer support worker roles into mental health services.

Ireland's 2006 'Vision for Change' (Department of Health and Children, 2006) proposal for mental health services communicated a strong commitment to peer support and recommended that peer workers should form part of every community mental health service provision. The national mental health service's 2016 operational plan laid out the intention to introduce peer support workers into Irish Mental Health services as a priority (HSE, 2016).

Similarly, in England and Wales in 2016 the independent mental health task force acknowledged that previous policy initiatives had been largely unsuccessful in their goals of transforming mental health services and improving outcomes for people who use them (NHS England, 2016). This report offered a Five-Year Forward view for mental health services based on the views of care leaders and people using and working in mental health services. The report contained nine references to peer support, including:

> Everybody in mental health services should be able to say ... I am provided with peer support contact with people with their own experience of mental health problems and of using mental health services. I can find peer support from people who understand my culture and identity. Peer support is available at any point in my fluctuating health – in a crisis, during recovery, and when I am managing being well. (p. 37)

The Scottish government expressed a commitment to peer support in their 2012–2015 mental health strategy. Yet there was little uptake, leading to calls for more direct action to increase peer worker roles in Scottish mental health services.

The evidence base for peer support

Reviews describe the positive impact of peer support on the person providing it, the person receiving it and for the service that they work within (Davidson et al., 2012; Repper & Carter, 2011). These reports used evidence from both randomised controlled trials (RCTs) and qualitative studies. Peer workers can reduce readmission rates and provide a range of positive outcomes for people receiving peer support, including increased levels of empowerment and social functioning and decreased stigma. Research also shows that working as a peer worker can increase self-esteem and support a person's continuing recovery.

The benefits for people receiving peer support range from decreased hospital admissions and relapse rates as well as increased early discharge from inpatient settings (Chinman et al., 2001; Clarke et al., 2000; Forchuk et al., 2005) to emotional benefits such as increased empowerment and hope and social functioning (Corrigan, 2006; Ochocka et al., 2006; Salzer & Mental Health Association of Southeastern Pennsylvania Best Practices Team, 2002). This could be attributed to the new ways of thinking and behaving that occur when reciprocal peer relationships are developed (Davidson et al., 1999; Kurtz, 1990). In both cross-sectional and longitudinal studies members of peer support initiatives have reported greater community integration, more social support and an increased sense of control, compared with participants not receiving peer support (Davidson et al., 2012; Forchuk et al., 2005; Lawn et al., 2008; Ochocka et al., 2006; Trainor et al., 1997).

The social support provided by a peer relationship promotes feelings of empathy, hope and acceptance through a sharing relationship (Davidson et al., 1999, 2006). People receiving peer support have reported greater feelings of being accepted and liked compared with individuals receiving traditional care (Sells et al., 2006; Mowbray et al., 1998). In a review of the experiences of 52 people offering and receiving peer support across five organisations in England, Faulkner and Basset (2010) found that peer support benefited people by offering them a sense of shared identity, increasing their confidence, breaking down stigma, as well as signposting them to other opportunities and giving them the opportunity to help others by sharing skills and experience.

More recently, work in the UK has investigated the cost-saving potential of employing peer support workers into the inpatient care pathway. Trachtenberg and colleagues (2013) identified six studies which provided information about the relationship between peer support and inpatient bed use. By using the cost of an average day for an inpatient bed in the UK and the salaries of peer support workers reported by each study, they created a ratio of pay cost versus money saved. Although there was a high level of variability between studies, the average ratio was found to be 3.81:1. So, for every £1 spent on peer support, £3.81 can potentially be saved.

However, more work is required to assess the relative value of peer versus professional services and to understand its underlying mechanisms (Watson, 2017). Many have expressed challenges in synthesising data across studies due to differences in the way peer support is provided and evaluated (Lloyd-Evans et al., 2014; Repper & Carter, 2011).

Recent reviews of solely quantitative evidence have presented more conservative findings of the benefits of peer support, in general concluding that peer support leads to the same or slightly better outcomes than traditional mental health services. A recent review, based on meta-analyses and systematic reviews of studies on peer services in the last 25 years (Bellamy et al., 2017), found that peer support results in at least equivalent outcomes to traditional mental health services, providing increased hope, recovery and empowerment and decreased hospital admissions. This review concludes with a call for more rigorous research. It is also difficult to establish an evidence base for peer support in part due to a lack of clarity about what exactly distinguishes it from the care provided by 'non-peer' staff. Reviewers have noted an absence of information about what peer workers do, in what way it is 'unique' and how it might facilitate positive outcomes (Lloyd-Evans et al., 2014; Pitt et al., 2013).

Despite this, a recent RCT exploring the use of peer support for people discharged from mental health crisis teams across the UK found that readmission rates were lower and the time in between admissions was longer for people who received peer support compared with the control group who received a wellness planning workbook in the post. The research also found that those who received peer support rated their satisfaction with mental health services more highly and scored higher on self-rated measures of recovery (Johnson et al., 2018). In line with previous research, the authors call for a better understanding of the mechanisms that underpin peer support, as well as a clearer understanding of how to embed and sustain peer support approaches within mental health services.

More attention must be paid to understanding the process and values that underpin the approach, what makes it unique and the mechanisms of change which underpin peer support relationships. Examination of these factors is essential for three reasons. First, to better understand what can be meaningfully measured within peer support as evidence of its impact. Second, what exactly is meant by peer support and thus whether what is being measured is actually peer support, or whether peer workers are merely emulating existing approaches to providing care. Finally, to understand what elements of peer relationships are powerful which could inform other helping professions and our understanding of how, and by whom, support can best be provided. There is also a need to understand the concept of 'peer'. This is often narrowly defined as being based on shared lived experience; however, who is a peer to each of us differs depending on other factors including race, culture, age, gender and class. A clearer understanding of this is important so that peer support and peer workers are not defined by their experience of mental distress alone (see Chapter 6):

> if peer workers are going to be introduced into mainstream mental health
> services anyway, irrespective of whether we think that is desirable or not, is it
> not morally important to somehow ensure that peer support is delivered in a way
> which is potentially as beneficial as possible for those involved? (Gillard et al.,
> 2017, p. 136)

Case Example: My Experience of Receiving Peer Support

Jodie Thomas

I met Aimee, a peer support worker, in August of 2013. At the time I knew very little about peer support. I had no idea what I should expect because I had never heard of it before. On our first meeting Aimee asked me what I thought peer support was, and then explained that it meant that she had lived experience of mental health struggles. Straight away, this made me feel completely at ease. Just knowing that she also struggled, and was now working and supporting others who were going through difficult times, immediately made me feel more hopeful that maybe I, too, could get through this and make a life for myself. I think it also helped that she was honest in telling me that she also felt nervous when meeting new people which made me feel like we were on a similar level, that she was human.

Throughout the time that she was working with me, she supported me through every challenge that arose in that time (and it was a lot) both good and bad. Having Aimee supporting me through things such as court hearings, being told I couldn't go back to sixth form, moving house (twice) and generally with the things that I faced daily, made everything so much easier to bear.

Aimee was so different in the ways that she supported me than what I was used to with my Community Psychiatric Nurse (CPN) and psychiatrist. Where they were rather practical and gave information and 'facts', Aimee listened to my thoughts and validated my feelings. She seemed to understand what I was saying in a way that no other professional had done before. When she didn't understand, she would ask questions to gain more of an understanding and seemed to want to know how things were for me personally, rather than assuming based on my diagnosis. I remember one particular professional handing me a list of 'coping strategies', many of which didn't relate to me at all. There were so many things on that list that just looking at it sent me into a panic and made me feel completely overwhelmed. Aimee had experience of something similar and so shared what she did in that situation. I tried it the next time I felt that way and it helped.

We spoke about so many different things, and it wasn't always completely about recovery or difficult things. While we did talk about these things, we also shared jokes and laughed a lot, too. With Aimee, there was a connection between us and our experiences, that wasn't there with other professionals. I never felt like I was pressured into talking about something that I didn't want to, and this made talking about really difficult things much easier.

I don't think I will ever forget anything Aimee taught me. She was such a huge part of the beginning of my acceptance of recovery. On our last meeting she gave me a card, with quotes and a letter. I still have these almost four years afterwards. I have them in a folder and I still read them sometimes. I read them a lot in the time straight after stopping seeing her. Gradually I have stopped reading them so often, maybe because I remember her words automatically, or maybe because I started believing them for myself. I still struggle with things sometimes, but now I know that I am strong enough to get through them.

Exercise

Shery Mead defines peer support as:

> a system of giving and receiving help founded on key principles of respect, shared responsibility, and mutual agreement of what is helpful. Peer support is not based on psychiatric models and diagnostic criteria. It is about understanding another's situation empathically through the shared experience of emotional and psychological pain. (Mead, 2003, p. 1)

Davidson defines peer support as:

> involving one or more persons who have a history of mental illness and who have experienced significant improvements in their psychiatric condition offering services and/or supports to other people with serious mental illness who are considered to be not as far along in their own recovery process. (Davidson et al., 2012, p. 444)

These are two very different definitions, using different language and placing emphasis on different important components. What do you think of each definition? How would you define peer support?

The principles and processes involved in peer support

There is a growing argument that the distinctiveness of peer support is due to a unique set of values which have emerged from the organic support offered to and by people with experiences of emotional distress (Mead & Macneil, 2004). As peer support has grown into a more formal approach, there have been many attempts to describe and define these values.

In New Zealand survivor and activist Mary O'Hagan and her colleagues (2009) established three values which they believe are central to peer support:

- A commitment to consumer/survivor choice and control over peer support, at individual and organisational levels
- Identification with each other – a sense of mutuality, camaraderie and acceptance between peers, reciprocal roles of helping and learning, and minimal distinction between 'staff and clients'
- A holistic understanding of madness – emphasising the whole of life, a strengths rather than illness focus, and confirming the validity of personal experience.

In the USA the Intentional Peer Support programme has defined peer support as (Filson & Mead, 2016):

A shift in focus from:

- Helping (problem solving or fixing) to Learning Together
- The individual to the relationship
- Fear-based responses to Hope-based responses.

From their work in supporting organisations wishing to employ, support and evaluate the impact of peer workers, ImROC (https://imroc.org/), a not-for-profit organisation, developed eight 'core principles' of peer support (Repper, 2013):

- **Recovery-focused** – supporting people to have hope, control and opportunities in their recovery
- **Mutual** – through shared experience of service use and recovery, peer support relationships are non-hierarchical
- **Reciprocal** – both people in a peer relationship share experiences and benefit from the other person's experiences rather than claiming expertise over each other
- **Strengths-based** – viewing experience as a source of strength and exploring a person's skills and assets which they can use in their recovery
- **Non-directive** – not prescribing solutions or courses of action but allowing an individual to find the solutions and understandings which work for them as experts in their own experiences
- **Safe** – cultivating emotional safety through negotiation of boundaries, a non-judgemental attitude and respect
- **Inclusive** – of different experiences and circumstances, helping a person to connect with the communities which are important to them using a shared understanding of stigmatised identities
- **Progressive** – rather than being a static friendship, peer support enables people to build further connections and move forward in their recovery.

The core principles established by O'Hagan, Filson and Mead, and ImROC are three attempts to articulate the values base which underpins peer support. Values have also been identified by charity-, government- and consumer-led services in the USA, Europe and the UK. The resulting frameworks have been used to evaluate and understand peer support projects. One of the most recent and comprehensive attempts to establish a values base which underpins peer support has been the 'ENRICH' project (Gillard et al., 2017). This used an extensive literature review alongside consultation with peer support providers and experts in the field to establish five 'fidelity criteria' by which peer support can be evaluated, and as a tool for reflection (Figure 2.1; Gillard et al., 2017).

A clear understanding of the values which underpin peer support relationships is helpful in communicating the approach a peer worker may take. Rather than focusing on specific tasks and responsibilities of a peer worker, focusing on how these are undertaken, using particular values and principles, offers a deeper understanding of the varied roles a peer worker may fulfil – it's not what you do but the way you do it.

Exercise

What are your core principles?

The core principles of peer support emphasise the importance of mutual relationships, the value of personal (or 'lived') experience and self-determination based on individual strengths. What would you select as your own core principles? Does your profession or field have core values or principles? How do you identify with them and what would you add or take away?

ENRICH Peer Support Principles

The development, delivery and evaluation of peer support services should:

1. Support the building of **safe, trusting relationships** based on **shared lived experience**

2. Ensure that the values of **mutuality** and **reciprocity** underpin peer support relationships

3. Promote the validation and application of **experiential knowledge** in the provision of peer support

4. Enable peers to exercise **leadership, choice and control** over the way in which peer support is given and received

5. Empower peers to discover and make use of their own **strengths**, and to build and strengthen **connections** to their peers and wider communities

In delivering on all these principles, peer support should respect and support the full **diversity** of experiences, language, culture, identity and background that people bring, enabling peers to build connections and relationships, and access resources and strengths found in the range of communities with which they identify and belong.

Figure 2.1 Fidelity criteria for peer support developed by Gillard et al. (2017)

Mechanisms underpinning peer support

A small amount of research has taken place to explore the components or processes which may explain the approach and why it works. Solomon (2004) suggests five possible mechanisms underpinning peer support: social learning theory, the helper-therapy principle, experiential knowledge, social comparison theory, and social support. Qualitative studies provide some evidence for the importance of all of these.

The sharing of personal experiences (experiential knowledge) of recovery can largely explain the powerful impact of peer support both for the speaker and for the person listening to them. For the person receiving support, the sharing of emotions such as anger and guilt in relation to particular experiences enables peers to build connections and feel 'normal', as others had also experienced these emotions (Gigudu et al., 2015; Gillard et al., 2015; Rebeiro Gruhl et al., 2016). For peer workers, the process of using experiences of recovery in a formal role transforms that which is most stigmatised into an asset. This allows a shift in identity from one rooted in shame to one rooted in pride (Moran et al., 2011).

The helper role has been used to explain a range of positive effects for the peer worker, including feeling useful to others, reducing internal stigma, feeling looked up to, and shifting focus away from oneself to others (Austin et al., 2014; Moran et al., 2011; Mourra et al., 2014; Proudfoot et al., 2012). Further research is needed to explore the mechanisms that underpin peer support to better understand the processes which make it so powerful (Rogers, 2017; Watson, 2017).

CONCLUSIONS: PEER SUPPORT IN THE PRESENT DAY

Peer support has evolved from its roots within the service user movement to become a formalised approach to offering and receiving support. The introduction of peer workers into mainstream mental health services has moved from being a rarity to a commissioning recommendation (NICE, 2016), and is understood to be a powerful way of driving forward culture change within mental health services towards 'recovery-focused' ways of working. Many (if not most) mental health trusts in the UK now employ and provide training for peer workers in an ever-increasing range of roles and service contexts, and the role of peer support in community initiatives is well recognised (Crepaz-Keay, 2017).

However, there are ongoing risks associated with the growth of peer support. These are described in detail in the next chapter. Given the history of peer support, as one which has campaigned for alternative understandings of distress and against the abuse of medical systems, many are concerned that peer support within mental health services will become compromised, that peer support will lose its identity and that peer workers will be expected to conform to controlling, risk-focused ways of working. As the growth of peer support continues to unfold, new platforms, most notably online forums, are being created which offer accessible ways of connecting with people who share experiences.

ACKNOWLEDGEMENTS

With thanks to Jodie Thomas and Lesley Smith for their case examples, and Mirika Flegg, Gordon Johnston, Michael Ryan and Mike Watts for their contributions.

FURTHER READING AND RESOURCES

Stories of recovery and living with voices: Romme, M., Escher, S., Dillon, J., Corstens, D. and Morris, M. (2009). *Living with Voices: 50 Stories of Recovery*. Ross-on-Wye: PCCS Books.

Alcoholics Anonymous:

• https://www.alcoholics-anonymous.org.uk/

Shery Mead describes Intentional Peer Support in the USA:

• https://www.youtube.com/watch?v=Q1w_HGQWTiU

Ron Coleman's personal narrative: Coleman, R. (1999). *Recovery: An Alien Concept*. Gloucester: Handsell.

ImROC website:

• https://imroc.org/

Scottish Recovery Network website:

• https://www.scottishrecovery.net/

Survivor history website:

• http://studymore.org.uk/mpu.htm

Pat Deegan's blog about peer support:

• https://www.patdeegan.com/blog/posts/peer-staff-disruptive-innovators.

REFERENCES

Austin, E., Ramakrishnan, A. and Hopper, K. (2014). Embodying recovery: A qualitative study of peer work in a consumer run service setting. *Community Mental Health Journal*, 50, 879–885.

Beales, A. and Wilson, J. (2015). Peer support: The what, why, who, how and now. *The Journal of Mental Health Training, Education and Practice*, 10(5), 314–324.

Bellamy, C., Schmutte, T. and Davidson, L. (2017). An update on the growing evidence base for peer support. *Mental Health and Social Inclusion*, 21(3), 161–167.

Bill, W. (2002). *Alcoholics Anonymous: The Story of How Many Thousands of Men and Women Have Recovered from Alcoholism* (4th edn). New York: Alcoholics Anonymous World Services.

Borkman, T. (1999). *Understanding Self-Help/Mutual Aid: Experiential Learning in the Commons*. New Brunswick, NJ: Rutgers University Press.

Carkhuff, R. R. and Truax, C. B. (1965). Lay mental health counseling: The effects of lay group counseling. *Journal of Consulting Psychology*, 29(5), 426.

Chamberlin, J., (1978). *On Our Own: Patient-Controlled Alternatives to the Mental Health System*. New York: McGraw-Hill.

Charlton, J. I. (1998). *Nothing About Us Without Us: Disability Oppression and Empowerment*. Berkeley: University of California Press.

Chinman, M. J., Weingarten, R., Stayner, D. and Davidson, L. (2001). Chronicity reconsidered. Improving person-environment fit through a consumer-run service. *Community Mental Health Journal*, 37(3), 215–229.

Choi, R. and Boschma, G., (2017). *The Emergence of Survivor Groups in B.C.: A Historical Perspective*. On Our Way: Recovery News. https://peerwork.wordpress.com/on-our-way-recovery-news/history-of-mental-health-survivor-groups-in-b-c/ [Accessed 20 July 2017].

Clarke, G., Herincks, H., Kinney, R., Paulson, R., Cutler, D. and Oxman, E. (2000). Psychiatric hospitalizations, arrests, emergency room visits, and homelessness of clients with serious and persistent mental illness: Findings from a randomised trial of two ACT programs vs. usual care. *Mental Health Services Research*, 2, 155–164.

Corrigan, P. W. (2006). Impact of consumer-operated services on empowerment and recovery of people with psychiatric disabilities. *Psychiatric Services*. 57(10), 1493–1496.

Crepaz-Keay, D. (2017). Peer support in community settings: Getting back to our roots. *Mental Health and Social Inclusion*, 21(3), 184–190.

Crossley, N. (1998). Transforming the mental health field. *Sociology of Health and Illness*, 20(4), 458–488.

Crossley, N. (1999). Fish, field, habitus and madness; on the first wave mental health users in Britain. *British Journal of Sociology*, 50(4), 647–670.

Davidson, L., Bellamy, C., Guy, K. and Miller, R. (2012). Peer support among persons with severe mental illnesses: A review of evidence and experience. *World Psychiatry : Official Journal of the World Psychiatric Association (WPA)*, 11(2), 123–128.

Davidson, L., Chinman, M., Kloos, B., Weingarten, R., Stayner, D. and Tebes, J. K. (1999). Peer support among individuals with severe mental illness: A review of the evidence. *Clinical Psychology Science and Practice*, 6, 165–187.

Davidson, L., Chinman, M., Sells, D. and Rowe, M. (2006). Peer support among adults with serious mental illness: A report from the field. *Schizophrenia Bulletin*, 32(3), 443–445.

Deegan, P. E. (1988). Recovery: The lived experience of rehabilitation. *Psychosocial Rehabilitation Journal*, 11(4), 11.

Department of Health and Children (2006). *A Vision for Change: Report of the Expert Group on Mental Health Policy*. Dublin: Stationery Office.

DoH (Department of Health) (2001). *The Journey to Recovery*. London: HMSO

DoH (Department of Health) (2006). *Supporting People with Long-Term Conditions to Self-*

Doughty, C. and Tse, S. (2005). The effectiveness of service user-run or service user-led mental health services for people with mental illness. *A Systematic Literature Review*. Wellington: Mental Health Commission.

Elias, P. and Upton-Davis, K. (2015). Embedding peer support using social work values. *The Journal of Mental Health Training, Education and Practice*, 10(5), 304–313.

Faulkner, A. and Basset, T. (2010). *A Helping Hand. Consultation with Service Users about Peer Support.* London: Together.

Filson, B. and Mead, S. (2016). Becoming part of each other's narratives: Intentional peer support. In Russo, J. and Sweeney, A. (eds), *Searching for a Rose Garden: Challenging Psychiatry, Fostering Mad Studies.* Monmouth, OR: PCCS Books, 109–117.

Forchuk, C., Martin, M. L., Chan, Y. C. L. and Jensen, E. (2005). Therapeutic relationships: From psychiatric hospital to community. *Journal of Psychiatric and Mental Health Nursing*, 12, 556–564.

Gigudu, V., Rogers, E. S., Harrington, S., Maru, M., Johnson, G., Cohee, J. and Hinkel, J. (2015). Individual peer support: A qualitative study of the mechanisms of its effectiveness. *Community Mental Health Journal*, 51, 445–452.

Gillard, S., Foster, R., Gibson, S., Goldsmith, L., Marks, J. and White, S. (2017). Describing a principles based approach to developing and evaluating peer worker roles as peer support moves into mainstream mental health services. *Mental Health and Social Inclusion*, 21(3), 133–143.

Gillard, S., Gibson, S. L., Holley, J. and Lucock, M. (2015). Developing a change model for peer worker interventions in mental health services: A qualitative research study. *Epidemiology and Psychiatric Sciences*, 24(5), 435–445.

GROW in Ireland (1994). *GROW in Ireland: A Celebration and a Vision of Innovations in Community Mental Health*, Kilkenny: GROW in Ireland.

Hervey, N. (1986). Advocacy or folly: The Alleged Lunatics' Friend Society, 1845–63. *Medical History*, 30(3), 245–275.

HSE (2016). *Mental Health Dvision: Operational Plan.* https://www.hse.ie/eng/services/publications/serviceplans/serviceplan2016/oppls16/mtlhthtoppls16.pdf [Accessed 27 June 2018].

Johnson, S., Lamb, D., Marston, L., Osborn, D., Henderson, C. et al. (2018). Peer supported self-management for people discharged from a metnal health crisis team: A randomised controlled trial. *The Lancet*, 392, 409–418.

The King's Fund. (2014a). *People in Control of Their Own Healthcare.* Briefing Paper, November 2014, The King's Fund, London.

The King's Fund. (2014b). *Supporting People to Manage their Health.* Briefing Paper, May 2014, The King's Fund, London.

The King's Fund. (2015). *Mental Health Under Pressure.* Briefing Paper, November 2015, The King's Fund, London.

Kurtz, L. F. (1990). The self-help movement: Review of the past decade of research. *Social Work with Groups*, 13, 101–115.

Lawn, S., Smith, A. and Hunter, K. (2008). Mental health peer support for hospital avoidance and early discharge: An Australian example of consumer driven and operated service. *Journal of Mental Health*, 17(5), 498–508.

Lloyd-Evans, B., Mayo-Wilson, E., Harrison, B., Istead, H., Brown, E., Pilling, S. ... and Kendall, T. (2014). A systematic review and meta-analysis of randomised controlled trials of peer support for people with severe mental illness. *BMC Psychiatry*, 14(39), 1–12.

McLean, J., Biggs, H., Whitehead, I., Pratt, R. and Maxwell, M. (2009). *Evaluation of the Delivering for Mental Health Peer Support Worker Pilot Scheme.* Edinburgh: Scottish Government.

Mead, S. (2003). *Defining Peer Support. Intentional Peer Support: An Alternative Approach.* http://www.Intentionalpeersupport.org/what-is-ips/ [Accessed 8 July 2017].

Mead, S. and Macneil, C. (2004). *Peer Support: What makes it unique?* http://www.Intentionalpeersupport.org/articles/ [Accessed 8 July 2017].

Mental Health Commission (2008). *A Recovery Approach within the Irish Mental Health Services: A Framework for Development.* Dublin: Mental Health Commission. https://www.mhcirl.ie/File/framedevarecov.pdf [Accessed 27 June 2018].

Mental Health Foundation (2012a). *Developing Peer Support in Long Term Conditions.* London: Mental Health Foundation.

Mental Health Foundation (2012b). *Peer Support in Mental Health and Learning Disability.* London: Mental Health Foundation.

Moran, G. S., Russinova, Z., Gidugu, V., Yim, J. Y. & Sprague, C. (2011). Benefits and mechanisms of recovery among peer providers with psychiatric illnesses. *Qualitative Health Research*, 30, 1–16.

Mourra, S., Sledge, W., Sells, D., Lawless, M. and Davidson, L. (2014). Pushing, patience and persistence: Peer providers; perspectives on supportive relationships. *American Journal of Psychiatric Rehabilitation*, 17, 307–328.

Mowbray, C. T., Moxley, D. P. and Colllins, M. E. (1998). Consumer as mental health providers: First person accounts of benefits and limitations. *The Journal of Behavioural Health Services and Research*, 25(4), 397–411.

NHS England (2016). *The Five Year Forward View for Mental Health. A Report from the Independent Mental Health Taskforce to the NHS in England.* London: NHS England.

NICE (National Institute for Health and Care Excellence) (2016). *Nice Guideline 53: Transition between Inpatient Mental Health Settings and Community or Care Home Settings.* Manchester: NICE.

O'Hagan, M., (2011). *Peer Support in Mental Health and Addictions: A Background Paper.* Wellington: Kites Trust.

O'Hagan, M., (2014). *Madness Made Me: A Memoir.* Wellington: Open Box.

O'Hagan, M., McKee, H. and Priest, R. (2009). *Consumer Survivor Initiatives in Ontario: Building for an Equitable Future.* Toronto: Ontario Federation of Community Mental Health & Addiction Programs.

Ochocka, J., Nelson, G., Janzen, R. and Trainor, J. (2006). A longitudinal study of mental health consumer/survivor initiatives: Part 3 – A qualitative study of impacts of participation on new members. *Journal of Community Psychology*, 34(3), 273–283.

Perkins, R., Evenson, E. and Davidson, B. (2010). *The Pathfinder User Employment Programme. Increasing Access to Employment within Mental Health Services for People Who Have Experienced Mental Health Problems.* London: South West London and St George's NHS Trust.

Pitt, V., Lowe, D., Hill, S., Prictor, M., Hetrick, S. E., Ryan, R. and Berends, L. (2013). Consumer-providers of care for adult clients of statutory mental health services. *Cochrane Database of Systematic Reviews*, Vol. 3.

Proudfoot, J. G., Jayawant, A., Whitton, A. E., Parker, G., Manicavasagar, V., Smith, M. and Nicholas, J. (2012). Mechanisms underpinning effective peer support: A qualitative analysis of interactions between expert peers and patients newly diagnosed with bipolar disorder. *BMC Psychiatry*, 12, 196–207.

Ralph, R. O. (2000). Recovery. *Psychiatric Rehabilitation Skills*, 4(3), 480–517.

Reaume, G. (2000). *Remembrance of Patients Past: Patient Life at the Toronto Hospital for the Insane, 1870–1940.* Toronto: University of Toronto Press.

Rebeiro Gruhl, K. L., LaCarte, S. and Calixte, S. (2016). Authentic peer support work: Challenges and opportunities for an evolving occupation. *Journal of Mental Health*, 25(1), 78–86.

Repper, J. (2013). *PSWs: Theory and Practice.* London: ImROC and Sainsbury Centre for Mental Health.

Repper, J. and Carter, T. (2011). A review of the literature on peer support in mental health services. *Journal of Mental Health*, 20(4), 392–411.

Romme, M. and Escher, S. (1993). *Accepting Voices.* London: Mind Publications.

Romme, M. A. J., Honig, A., Noorthoorn, E. O. and Escher, A. D. M. A. C. (1992). Coping with hearing voices: An emancipatory approach. *British Journal of Psychiatry*, 162, 99–103.

Robertson, R. (2009). *Consumer and Peer Roles in the Addiction Sector.* Wellington: Matua Raki.

Rogers, E. S. (2017). Peer support services: State of the workforce-state of the field in the USA. *Mental Health and Social Inclusion*, 21(3), 168–175.

Salzer, M. S. and Mental Health Association of Southeastern Pennsylvania Best Practices Team (2002). Consumer-delivered services as a best practice in mental health care and the development of practice guidelines. *Psychiatric Rehabilitation Skills*, 6, 355–382.

The Scottish Government (2012). *Mental Health Strategy for Scotland: 2012–2015.* http://www.gov.scot/resource/0039/00398762.pdf [Accessed 27 June 2018].

The Scottish Government (2017). *Mental Health Strategy: 2017–2027.* http://www.gov.scot/Resource/0051/00516047.pdf [Accessed 27 June 2018].

Sells, D. L., Davidson, L., Jewell, C., Falzer, P. and Rowe, M. (2006). The treatment relationship in peer-based and regular case management for clients with severe mental illness. *Psychiatric Services*, 57(8), 1179–1184.

Shepherd, G., Boardman, J. and Slade, M. (2008). Making Recovery a Reality. London: Sainsbury Centre for Mental Health. https://www.centreformentalhealth.org.uk/Handlers/Download.ashx?IDMF=e94d8999-4010-4a5e-a5d8-0c3f1eb2d0e6 [Accessed 1 July 2018].

Solomon, P. (2004). Peer support/peer provided services: Underlying processes, benefits, and critical ingredients. *Psychiatric Rehabilitation Journal*, 27(4), 392–401.

SRN (Scottish Recovery Network). (2011). *Experts by experience: Guidelines to support the development of peer worker roles in the mental health sector.* https://scottishrecovery.net/wp-content/uploads/2011/09/srn_exe_form.pdf [Accessed 27 June 2018].

Trachtenberg, M., Parsonage, M., Shepherd, G. and Boardman, J. (2013). *Peer Support in Mental Health Care: Is It Good Value for Money?* London: ImROC and Sainsbury Centre for Mental Health.

Trainor, J., Shepherd, M., Boydell, K. M., Leff, A. and Crawford, E. (1997). Beyond the service paradigm: The impact and implications of consumer/survivor initiatives. *Psychiatric Rehabilitation Journal*, 21, 132–140.

Vancouver Mental Patients' Association Society (1983). *Head On: Into the Eighties.* Vancouver: Carolina Publications.

Watson, E. (2017). The mechanisms underpinning peer support: A literature review. *Journal of Mental Health*, 20, 1–12.

Weiner, D. B. (1979). The apprenticeship of Philippe Pinel: A new document, observations of Citizen Pussin on the insane. *The American Journal of Psychiatry*, 36, 1128–1134.

3

The Politics of Peer Support

Emma Watson

Chapter Summary

- This chapter considers some of the debates relating to power and status within peer support

- Peer support is built upon the idea that experiential knowledge is valuable, in particular that a person has the right to define their experiences for themselves, and that they are the expert in these. This is often at odds with medical or psychiatric understandings of human experience, which conceptualises these as forms of mental illness. Psychiatric understandings are used to inform mental health service delivery and are enshrined in law through mental health legislation. This affords them a powerful position within western societies

- When peer support workers are introduced into psychiatric services, peer relationships are no longer equal, and some argue that this introduction compromises the way that peer support is offered. As peer support in mental health services becomes more widely recognised, research into the outcomes and cost effectiveness of peer support has increased. This research prioritises economic and service outcomes over outcomes relating to social change which lie at the heart of peer support and the survivor movement

- Working in mental health services, which can create conflict between mutual ways of working inherent in peer support and expert-based approaches, has been found to affect individual peer workers.

Introduction

In this chapter, we examine the politics of peer support, that is, the current tensions and debates surrounding peer support, particularly relating to power and status. We begin by exploring the sources of knowledge and power that underpin peer support, as well as those underpinning mental health services in the western world. This provides a backdrop to consider the debates relating to the economic case for peer support and how research into peer support may serve (and do a disservice to) different groups.

We explore whether the role of the peer worker has been adapted to suit the needs of healthcare services; does the introduction of peer support into mental health services change, compromise or 'co-opt' the way that peer support is offered? It has certainly led to a greater focus on its effectiveness, including cost-effectiveness, and how it might save mental health services money. We explore debates relating to how evidence for peer support is collected and how the focus of this prioritises certain forms of knowledge over others. Using the accounts of peer workers, we consider how these critical, political issues translate to everyday working practice for peer workers.

Competing forms of knowledge and power

Many of the political issues surrounding peer support have emerged, or have at least been amplified, by the introduction of peer support worker roles into mainstream mental health services. The history of peer support, described in Chapter 2, located its roots within the service user/survivor movement, a movement which challenged the power of the psychiatric system and its approach, underpinned by 'treatment' of 'mental illness'. We explore this conflict further in this chapter as a means of highlighting the relationship between psychiatry and peer support, and their often competing value bases and positions within society. In doing so it is not our intention to criticise professional groups or survivors, or to polarise what is, in reality, a complex, changing social picture.

Survivor knowledge and power

Peer support is explicitly underpinned by the belief that it is the individual that holds the key to understanding and living alongside their own experiences of distress. This is sometimes referred to as experiential or **survivor knowledge**, that is, 'specialized knowledge, grounded in an individual's lived experience' (Borkman, 1990, p. 3). In the context of peer support, experiential knowledge may include the knowledge of service use, oppression, poverty and inequality as well as mental distress. The service user/survivor movement was influential in amplifying the personal accounts of people who had experienced distress, as it documented peoples' recoveries from a broad spectrum of experiences, including abuse from mental health services. Partly as a result of this and partly due to the establishment of 'consumer power' in health services, the service user/survivor voice has become powerful in its own right. As Crossley (2004) describes:

> Survivors have been able to convert their experiences of mental distress and (mis)treatment into a form of cultural and symbolic capital. The disvalued status of the patient is reversed within the movement context. Therein it constitutes

authority to speak and vouches for authenticity. The experience of both distress and treatment, stigmatized elsewhere, has become recognized as a valuable, perhaps superior knowledge base. Survivors have laid a claim, recognized at least within the movement itself, to know 'madness' and its 'treatment' with authority, on the basis that they have been there and have survived it. (p. 167)

It is important to note Crossley's emphasis that the experiential authority of survivors has symbolic capital *within the movement context.* Outside of this, experiential knowledge has long been marginalised in favour of scientific, expert understandings.

The use of experiential knowledge is central to peer support and the authentic sharing of personal experiences is thought to be one of the reasons for its success (Faulkner & Basset, 2010). Survivors, service users and peer supporters have used their 'experiential authority' (Borkman, 1990) to demonstrate the creative and personally meaningful ways that an individual can interpret their experiences outside and often in spite of psychiatry and the medical model. Peer support is understood to be characterised by mutual (equal) relationships, reciprocity in giving and receiving support, and connection/communities built on shared experience.

The power of personal accounts of recovery has been recognised within teaching settings and healing relationships, as well as a means to change the culture of mental health systems. Even the use of the term survivor, with its connotations of defiance, strength and courage, to replace the term patient, with its connotations of sickness and dependency, demonstrates the evolution of a more powerful portrayal of lived experience. However, writer and trainer Peter Campbell (2010), himself a survivor, warns of the 'potential tyranny of personal experience that can pre-empt disagreement and make fruitful discussion and debate ... very difficult' (p. 29). Although he also testifies to the benefits of its use, this exemplifies the point that personal experience has reached in acquiring a form of symbolic power, based in experiential authority and individual accounts. But how far does this power reach?

Suddenly, and in very new ways, those of us with experience of madness and/or the mental health system are working both within and outside of mental health fields of power to contribute, disrupt, and complicate how and what knowledge about us is produced ... Yet, unlike most fields, we have yet to engage openly with the hard questions on the possibilities, limits, and conditions of relying on experiential knowledge to authorize our standing. (Voronka, 2016, p. 191)

Professional (psychiatric) knowledge and power

Mental health systems in the western world are underpinned by a biopsychosocial model of understanding mental distress. That is, mental health problems are caused by chemical abnormalities, alongside the experience of negative life events and environmental factors, which in turn affect psychological functioning. While professionals working within mental health services may hold alternative beliefs, structurally, these services are established to diagnose, treat and provide care using a medical paradigm. Although, for many, medical understandings of distress have lost their credibility in light of the poor evidence for the current classification systems (Bentall, 2004) and for the use of pharmaceutical treatments

(Whitaker, 2010), psychiatry continues to occupy a powerful position within society, and psychiatric understandings of distress dominate our social world.

Psychiatry has economic power, being funded by government and endorsed by the pharmaceutical industry, reinforcing the use of medication and expert-based approaches. Psychiatric knowledge is also enshrined in the law. For example, in England and Wales, the Mental Health Act (1983) affords mental health professionals power to detain a person in hospital against their will if they are deemed to be a risk to themselves or others. The 2007 revision of the act added Community Treatment Orders (CTOs) which made it possible for people to be recalled to hospital if they did not follow certain conditions – in effect obliging people to take medication once discharged from hospital.

The use of a medical classification system within the law and within mental health services affords power to mental health professionals with training in identifying and classifying behaviours. It means that professionals have a role in assessing and managing the risk of the people they support. The scientific paradigm means that scientific (quantitative) methods which focus on the effectiveness of clinical interventions, whether they are chemical or psychological, are highly prized within research and by the National Institute for Health and Care Excellence (NICE) which produces guidelines for practice.

The conceptualisation of distress which underpins mental health services in the western world locates expertise within professional knowledge. From an objective standpoint, a mental health professional supports and treats a patient using their training to offer guidance and advice. In contrast, peer support locates expertise within the individual who experiences distress. Although, in reality, the distinction is more blurred than these science–art, professional–lived, objective–subjective distinctions, in general, different forms of knowledge are valued by psychiatric services than those by the survivor movement.

Two different conversations about peer support

Mead et al., 2001

'Peer support can offer a "culture" of health and ability as opposed to a culture of illness and disability. (Curtis, 1999) The primary goal is to responsibly challenge the assumptions about 'mental illness' and at the same time to validate the individual for who they really are and where the have come from. Peer support should attempt to think creatively and non-judgmentally about the way individuals experience and make meaning of their lives in contrast to having all actions and feelings diagnosed and labeled.'

Dark et al., 2017

'[peer support is] an innovative model of service that has arisen from the growth of the consumer movement and research on how people with lived experience can enhance recovery from mental illness. Patient outcomes from current care are suboptimal particularly on measures of psychosocial functioning and recovery of premorbid functioning potential. There is a need for new ways of delivering care that champion service-user engagement and evaluation of these interventions.'

Figure 3.1 Two different conversations about peer support

The differences between psychiatric understandings and survivor understandings become clear when looking at the language used in publications about peer support. Figure 3.1 presents two such publications placed next to each other. The first is written by Shery Mead, the founder of Intentional Peer Support in the USA and a survivor who advocates for the preservation of mutuality in peer support. The second (Dark, Patton & Newton, 2017) is an academic publication presenting the 'case for' peer support written by a psychiatrist. While Mead and colleagues (2001) describes the primary goal of peer support as responsibly challenging assumptions about illness, Dark and colleagues (2017) focus on patient outcomes and service user engagement and describes peer support as a *model of service* which can enhance clinical recovery from *mental illness*. These two examples highlight the different ways that peer support is described and how these serve different agendas – Mead's using the language of the survivor movement, and Dark's the language of service delivery.

Exercise: The Language of Peer Support

Language choices are carefully considered within peer support. One skill of a peer support worker is to 'reframe' negative or unhelpful language choices. For example, the words 'victim' or 'sufferer' might be reframed to 'survivor', or a person described as 'non-compliant' might better be described as 'not finding a certain medication or service helpful'. Look at the language below and try to reframe the phrases using a strengths focus:

Non-engaging
Attention seeking
Emotionally unstable
Refusing to accept help

Peer support and the psychiatric system: Mutuality meets hierarchy

It is unsurprising, given the conflicts described above, that when peer support approaches are introduced into psychiatric systems it causes controversy, disagreement and often confusion. While some have welcomed the introduction of peer workers as a sign that cultures are becoming more open to valuing lived experience, others have viewed it as 'co-option' or misuse of survivor knowledge to serve mental health systems, leaving their controlling practices intact (Penney & Prescot, 2016). Concerns have been raised about how peer support may be misused within mental health services, so that peer workers will be expected to conform to the practices that the survivor movement continues to campaign against. Voronka (2017) questions: 'to what effect are we [peers] deploying our work to orient clients toward feelings and responses that actually encourage compliance and cooperation with dominant conceptual models of mental illness?' (p. 335).

Survivors have argued that when peer support becomes intentionally offered (as opposed to informal peer support) there needs to be support in place to maintain the values of the approach (Mead et al., 2001; O'Hagan et al., 2009). Many survivors have questioned how possible it is to maintain these values within highly structured organisations such as the NHS, especially where no peer supervision is available (Faulkner & Kalathil, 2012).

Mead and Filson (2016, p.114) argue: 'peer support has more often than not ended up looking like clinical support. The inequality of one-way helping relationships has become the norm. By default, mental health organisations contradict the principles of peer support through the following:

- Mandatory reporting
- Policies regarding diagnosis and treatment
- Contractual/funding constraints around who I can see
- Agreements about how long we can have a relationship for
- Policies directing boundaries around peer relationships'

We would add to this list 'the use of chemical and physical restraint' as this has emerged in recent years as a highly contentious area in peer support. Where peer workers are employed in inpatient wards, their role sometimes requires them to be prepared to be involved in physically restraining a person. Some argue that the presence of peer workers will lead to reduced restraint, that no staff member wishes to be, or enjoys being, part of restraining a person in distress, and that peers may be able to 'de-escalate' situations by building trusting relationships with people (see 'Further Reading and Resources' at the end of the chapter). Others believe that the use of peer workers in physical restraint is a stark example of how the mutuality of peer support in mental health services becomes compromised. This issue is illustrated in Andy White's account of working as a Peer Healthcare Assistant (or HCA) on an inpatient ward, a role where he is expected to be involved in physical restraint.

Case Example: Peer Support and Physical Restraint

Andy White, Peer Healthcare Assistant

As a peer, or as a HCA, the prospect of restraint is not something I look forward to. However, working in an acute setting, restraint can occur, whether this is due to aggression and frustration, self-harm, or issues regarding medication. The 'no force first' principles and post-restraint review are critical for my own personal acceptance of my role as a peer/HCA, and as such it is imperative that I seek all opportunities to avoid and mitigate restraint. It is important to emphasise that as well as actively restraining a person, restraint can be passive, i.e. walking someone away from a situation. There is an argument also, that where we encourage an individual to do something they don't want to do we are affecting their liberty.

In terms of positives regarding my role, and based on five years' experience, I do not believe I have damaged the therapeutic relationships I foster with people using services. Firstly, as a peer I believe I should provide constant and consistent support to people throughout their time on the ward in good, bad or indifferent health. To only be around people in their settled times, is not providing holistic support. I cannot simply say 'I'll come back in a couple of hours when you're more settled or less distressed.'

'Further, when I am with an individual in distress, I am using my peer skills and showing empathy and understanding. The ability to actively listen and support the individual can and frequently does lower stress and distress and can actually reduce levels of restraint. It can build trust and understanding which can help prevent future incidents. Even when restraint is used, the quality and compassion of the interactions as a peer is not lost on the person being restrained. I have countless examples where having a peer involved enhances outcomes and, working with Service Users, minimises distress.

On a personal note my peer skill set has a significant and quantifiable effect in lowering and minimising distress. The culture that other staff experience when they see peer support workers interacting and working with service users throughout their admission also helps to create a positive environment for people on the ward.

In terms of cons, on an individual level, there is a stress and toll on myself that managing conflict on a regular basis creates. There is a need to debrief and reflect. It is standard practice for us to debrief and reflect with the person who has been restrained afterwards, but this can also be personally demanding. I recognise that not all peers would want to be employed in this capacity, and believe that peers' working opportunities should be diverse.

If you accept the premise that a person can face intense distress, at times, shouldn't a peer support worker be there, to help alleviate and minimise such distress, even if this means entering into the possibility of physical restraint? The premise of a 'pure peer role' on a ward fails to completely meet a service user's needs.

Exercise

As Andy White describes in the example above, peer workers are sometimes employed in roles where they may be involved in physically restraining a person. Make a list of the advantages and disadvantages of peer workers working in these roles. Think about these in relation to:

- People who use services
- The peer worker and
- Staff who work alongside peer workers
- The service as a whole.

Scott and Doughty (2012) and Scott and colleagues (2011) explore similar arguments relating to record-keeping procedures and risk assessments. They describe how peer workers may be drawn in two directions, having to report and manage risk using clinical frameworks while drawing on their own understandings to support another person to feel in control of their own 'risk'. The mutuality of peer support is inevitably compromised when one person is employed and their role involves risk assessment and note-keeping. Peer support is gradually transformed from a relationship between two people with shared experience to an intervention provided by one person to support the other:

> By becoming part of mental health services, which continue to use practices which are at odds with its philosophy, peer support walks a delicate tightrope between being part of the solution and becoming part of the problem. (Watson, 2017, p. 130)

The economics of peer support

> Of course, as long as psychiatry maintains its power, 'recovery' will mean compliantly taking one's drugs, and 'peer support' will mean supplying the system with cheap labor. (Chabasinski, 2012)

In 2013, an ImROC briefing paper written to support the introduction of peer support workers into the mental health workforce listed ten 'myths and misconceptions' relating to peer support (Repper, 2013). The first of these was that 'peer support is just a way of saving money' (p. 7). Because peer workers are usually, but not always, employed at lower pay grades than staff with professional qualifications (often at the same grade as healthcare assistants or support workers), they can be seen as a way of increasing the mental health workforce at a relatively small cost. ImROC argue that peer workers are better equipped to support people to make sense of their experiences, and that the professional domain need not be extended beyond its original remit of providing specialist expertise. They conclude: 'It is therefore clearly not simply a case of "saving money"; rather ensuring services optimise value for money, and the added value, of all staff groups' (p. 7).

Since this argument was put forth, interest in the economics of peer support has continued to grow, and its potential to reduce the costs of providing mental health services has led to the regular inclusion of peer support alongside economic arguments in reports and policy guidance. For example, while The King's Fund has consistently advocated for greater use and access to peer support, often its reports contain the implicit assumption that peer support would help relieve the financial burden that mental health services face. For example, peer support is discussed alongside online resources and the use of volunteers (The King's Fund, 2014a, 2014b). The focus on cost-saving and cost-effectiveness is part of a wider context within mental health services which affects the whole workforce. For example, NICE explicitly looks at how many 'qualiyears' (years with good quality of life) interventions including cognitive behavioural therapy (CBT) or family therapy offer for a particular amount of money. In joining the mental health workforce, peer workers are subject to the same level of scrutiny as any other intervention.

The cost-saving benefits of peer support (Trachtenberg et al., 2013) have been used to provide an explicit business case for the employment of more peer workers. Rethink's 'Investing in Recovery' (Knapp et al., 2014) argued that co-designing and delivering services with people who use them is among the approaches which offers the biggest scope for cost-saving in mental health care.

The economic case for peer support will undoubtedly influence how widely peer support is introduced. While cost-effectiveness may not be the sole reason for the introduction of peer support, it seems to have taken precedence over the moral or ethical reasons. Peer workers themselves have described peer support as a form of cheap labour (Manning & Suire, 1996). This issue goes beyond pay to encompass wider issues about the value of peer support. Peer workers describe feeling used as a 'dogsbody' a 'fad' and a 'phase to phase out' (Dyble, 2012, p. 135).

While it is important to 'sell' peer support to those who may not understand its worth, and, while doing this, to speak in terms that will appeal to their needs, the focus on money overshadows the different values which underpin peer support and overlooks the many ways that mental health services contradict peer-based approaches. The use of research to understand peer support beyond its cost-saving ability is needed; however, this is not without critical issues of its own.

Understanding and measuring the impact of peer support

There have been calls for an understanding of the 'whole' value of peer support through research and evaluation, rather than focus on the cost-saving potential of the approach. Research into peer support is growing at a steady pace. Large organisations such as The Health Foundation and Mind have focused large research projects and provided funding streams to smaller projects, in order to understand the contribution and impact of peer support. There remains some difficulty in deciding what exactly should be measured if we are to understand the impact of peer support. Some have argued that randomised controlled trials (RCTs) have not measured outcomes which are relevant to peer support or that people report as the benefits they experience (Gillard et al., 2017).

Much of the difficulty of evaluating peer support relates to the arguments described above about different forms of knowledge: What type of knowledge matters? Service-level evaluations often focus on cost-saving and broad outcomes such as employment, symptom reduction and decreased service use/inpatient admissions. Quality of Life scales are also often included in evaluations of peer workers, requiring people receiving peer support to rate themselves on validated scales. These types of evaluation increase the likelihood for further funding based on clear evidence of the need for the service. However, for some, because recovery is a personally defined human experience, the search for broad outcomes flies in the face of what peer support should be about. Large trials of peer support focusing on quantitative service outcomes mean that the person-ally meaningful benefits experienced by people receiving peer support are not collected. Using the protocols required to conduct RCTs, assigning participants to peer support or 'control' groups runs the risk of altering the nature of peer support relationships by removing choice and control from the people taking part (Corrigan & Salzer, 2003), which is even more significant if choice is part of the mechanism for why peer support is helpful. Personal accounts of the experience of peer support would provide a more personal and detailed narrative of the benefits of the relationship, but these accounts will not provide evidence for the broad, replicable effectiveness of peer support which is necessary for NICE.

There is also a question about *who* should be researching peer support: Whose knowl-edge matters? Should research into peer support be carried out by professionals using the standards that are used to judge other interventions, or should peer support be looked at using the standards which it defines for itself? For many survivors, the object of peer support is social change, and this is what should be measured in order to understand the success of peer support:

> As peer support in mental health proliferates, we must be mindful of our
> intention: social change. It is not about developing more effective services, but
> rather about creating dialogues that have influence on all of our understandings,
> conversations, and relationships. (Mead, 2016)

Impact of politics on peer workers

The conflicts and critical issues in peer support impact on peer workers to different degrees. For some, the presence of other peers, a supportive working environment where they feel able to reflect and develop their own approach and the opportunity for training may minimise negative impacts. Penney and Prescot (2016) note that peer workers and the systems they work in may uncritically welcome the introduction of peer support if they are unaware of the history of the survivor movement or have a sincere belief in the validity and value of the medical model.

Despite this, there is a large amount of research which testifies to the difficulty experienced by peer workers working within mental health systems. Research consistently emphasises themes of feeling stigmatised by other staff, being viewed through a diagnostic lens, experiencing poor support structures, a lack of credibility in peer support and unclear working roles (e.g. Vandewalle et al., 2016; Walker & Bryant, 2013). One large-scale survey of almost 600 peer workers in the USA found that 64.3 per cent had experienced or witnessed stigmatisation or discrimination from their co-workers (Cronise et al., 2016).

These working environments, coupled with the pressure to maintain personal wellbeing, have been linked to burnout in peer workers (Mancini & Lawson, 2009). Irwin (2017) describes her reasons for leaving her peer role on an inpatient ward:

> I asked myself many times whether I would be able to, or even whether my conscience would allow me to, work within an existing system of psychiatric care that had essentially left me feeling disempowered, utterly hopeless, re-traumatised, passive beyond recognition and a great deal 'sicker' than when I first entered the system. If I worked within it, would I feel that I was condoning a system that had essentially harmed me? ... I left because I had reached a point where I felt I could no longer work in an environment which compromised my own values, and the values of peer support. (p. 153)

She goes on to describe other factors which influenced her decision to leave, including the difficulty of working in an underfunded system:

> During my time as a PSW, I witnessed a system that was over stretched and jaded by constant funding cuts. I witnessed compassionate staff with too little time to spend building relationships, and I witnessed frustrated and distressed people, who entered with hope that somebody would listen and left with so much less than they deserved (p. 155).

Exercise

Some peer workers describe feeling empowered by working in a role where they are able to use their lived experience freely. For others, being defined first and foremost by their lived experience feels stigmatising and obscures other parts of their identity. How would you feel if you were employed in a peer support role? Would you feel comfortable with the expectation that you will share your lived or life experience? How do you think the role might benefit and challenge you?

There are other problems facing peer workers relating to the concept of lived experience. For some, this phrase is meaningless as all experience is 'lived' (Penney & Prescot, 2016). For others, grouping people together by describing them as having lived experience removes the individuality of their experiences. This grouping is sometimes referred to as 'strategic essentialism' and has been used by other social change movements including feminism as a means of uniting under a shared identity to bring about social change. Strategic essentialism can be a powerful tactic for collective change, but defining a person using only their experiences of mental distress may serve to reinforce the stigma associated with this identity by failing to take into account the other, equally important, elements of a person's character. Some research has found that peer workers found that their 'peer' identity might impede their future progression in recovery and in their working roles (Dyble, 2012; Moran et al., 2013). Career progression is another critical issue in peer support, with few opportunities being provided for peer workers to access further relevant training or move into more senior roles. This is illustrated in the case example below, written by Tessa Rodgers who describes the lack of career progression within her peer role, and how her previous experiences as a Drug Support Worker were not taken into account. Nevertheless, there are some exceptions; in other NHS Trusts that employ peer workers, their management and leadership experience and responsibilities are taken into account, and there are posts at the same pay scale as team leaders or service managers.

Case Example: Peer Support – Costs and Balances

Tessa Rodgers, Peer Support Development Worker

Are Peer workers 'used' by services when they use their lived experiences of mental distress to support others? A massive question with philosophical and ethical undercurrents, and talking of ethics, I want to make it clear that I speak solely for myself, referencing my work and life history.

I came to Peer Support after having had a series of well paid jobs, but after a long period of being unable to work due to my mental health. I was so enthused about the role; it was the total reversal of what I had been going through having lost a job due being unwell. That had been turned on its head and I had been offered a job because of those very things. It was, and remains, wonderful that I do not have to conceal parts of me that are so important. There is no question at all that this job, in all its myriad locations, teams, restructures and all that follows in the slipstream of constant change, has helped me to positively redefine who I am.

Here comes the BUT, I have been on the same pay grade for well over five years now, and I use not only my lived experience, but my employment experience too. My experience of group facilitation, writing and delivering workshops, extensive training, and knowledge of working with substance use. In my working life prior to peer support, I have worked in commissioning, managed budgets, written strategies and policies and, as I became well, again those skills reawakened in me in my peer support role. It was very healing to realise that I still was that person; I could give presentations, write and deliver workshops. It's very interesting and I am never bored at work, but I do feel exploited and I can feel resentful too.

> I especially feel that resentment on behalf of my peer colleagues who are much younger than me. I see their shining intelligence, their passion and creativity, their total commitment to changing the culture and perceptions around the understanding and 'treatment' of mental distress. What I have yet to see is a clearly defined career pathway, a strategic vision of how to mentor and financially reward peer workers. Yes... I've just said the 'F' word! But finances are important and while my employer benefits from the extensive skill and talent base of the peers it employs and we as peers find our voices and our confidence again, we have bills to pay and lives to lead.

Making change: Abolition or evolution?

This chapter has provided an overview of some of the current debates in peer support, highlighting the sometimes conflicting approaches to working, measuring and understanding peer support relationships. The growing popularity of peer support within mental health services has meant that the values of mutuality and personal choice which lie at the heart of peer support have met with systems which favour expert-based approaches and are required to demonstrate clinical effectiveness.

The debates in peer support include a diverse range of people who believe in bringing about change. Conflicts arise in how people believe change should come about: Should peer support be introduced into mental health services as a means of evolving the culture, or should mental health services be abandoned in favour of peer-led approaches? Or, to put it another way, do we believe that mental health services can change (or even if they need to change) their philosophy, or should peer support remain outside of them?

Nevertheless, peer workers are being introduced in greater numbers into mental health services across the world. Pertinent questions relate to how we protect the identity of peer support as it is introduced, how we can support peer workers to cope and to progress within psychiatric institutions, and how we might measure the impact of peer support in a way which does justice to peer relationships rather than solely to build the economic case.

ACKNOWLEDGEMENTS

With thanks to Tessa Rodgers and Andy White for their contributions.

FURTHER READING AND RESOURCES

Mad in America website (science, psychiatry and social justice):

• https://www.madinamerica.com/

The work of Jijian Voronka around social justice and peer support:

• http://uwindsor.academia.edu/JijianVoronka

Iris Benson MBE from Mersey Care Trust describing her experiences of being restrained and working in the No Force First project:

*   https://www.youtube.com/watch?v=sTSPBNP_E2U

Read more about Mersey Care's No Force First project:

*   http://positivepracticemhdirectory.org/adults/no-force-first-2/

REFERENCES

Bentall, R. P. (2004). *Madness Explained: Psychosis and Human Nature*. London: Penguin.

Borkman, T. J. (1990). Experiential, professional, and lay frames of reference. In T. J. Powell (ed.), *Working with Self-Help*. Silver Spring, MD: NASW Press, 3–30.

Campbell, P. (2010). Surviving the system. In T. Basset and T. Stickley (eds), *Voices of Experience: Narratives of Mental Health Survivors*. Hoboken, NJ: John Wiley & Sons, 21–32.

Chabasinski, T. (2012). Our task is to take away the power of psychiatry. *Mad in America*. https://www.madinamerica.com/2012/10/our-task-is-to-take-away-the-power-of-psychiatry/ [Accessed 25 November 2018].

Corrigan, P. W. and Salzer, M. S. (2003). The conflict between random assignment and treatment preference: Implications for internal validity. *Evaluation and Program Planning*, 26(2), 109–121.

Cronise, R., Teixeira, C. and Rogers, E. S. (2016). The peer support workforce: Results of a national survey. *Psychiatric Rehabilitation Journal*, 39(3), 211–221.

Crossley, N. (2004). Not being mentally ill. *Anthropology and Medicine*, 11(2), 161–180.

Dyble, G. L. (2012). 'Going through the transition from being an end user to sort of the provider': Making sense of becoming a mental health peer support worker using Interpretative Phenomenological Analysis, unpublished doctoral dissertation, University of Nottingham.

Faulkner, A. and Basset, T. (2010). *A Helping Hand. Consultation with Service Users about Peer Support*. London: Together.

Faulkner, A. and Kalathil, J. (2012). *The Freedom to be, the Chance to Dream: Preserving Used-Led Peer Support in Mental Health*. London: Together for Mental Wellbeing.

Gillard, S., Foster, R., Gibson, S., Goldsmith, L., Marks, J. and White, S. (2017). Describing a principles-based approach to developing and evaluating peer worker roles as peer support moves into mainstream mental health services. *Mental Health and Social Inclusion*, 21(3), 133–143.

Irwin, S. (2017). Why I chose to leave mainstream psychiatric services: A peer supporter's personal perspective. *Mental Health and Social Inclusion*, 21(3), 153–160.

The King's Fund. (2014a). *People in Control of their own Healthcare*. King's Fund Briefing, November 2014.

The King's Fund. (2014b). *Supporting People to Manage their Health*. King's Fund Briefing, May 2014.

Knapp, M., Andrew, A., McDaid, D., Iemmi, V., McCrone, P., Park, A. L., Parsonage, M., Boardman, J. and Shepherd, G. (2014). *Investing in Recovery: Making the Business Case for Effective Interventions for People with Schizophrenia and Psychosis*. London: Rethink Mental Illness. http://eprints.lse.ac.uk/56773/1/Knapp_etal_Investing_in_recovery_2014.pdf [Accessed 20 November 2018]

Mancini, M. A. and Lawson, H. A. (2009). Facilitating positive emotional labor in peer-providers of mental health services. *Administration in Social Work*, 33(1), 3–22.

Manning, S. S. and Suire, B. (1996). Consumers as employees in mental health: Bridges and roadblocks. *Psychiatric Services*, 47(9), 939–940.

Mead, S., Hilton, D. and Curtis, L. (2001). Peer support: A theoretical perspective. *Psychiatric Rehabilitation Journal*, 5(2), 131–141.

Mead, S. (2016). 'What is IPS?', Intentional Peer Support (website). http://www.intentionalpeersupport. org/what-is-ips/ [Accessed 20 November 2018]

Mead, S. and Filson, B. (2016). Becoming part of each other's narratives: Intentional peer support. In J. Russo and A. Sweeney (eds), *Searching for a Rose Garden: Challenging Psychiatry*. Monmouth: PCCS Books, 109–117.

Moran, G. S., Russinova, Z., Gidugu, V. and Gagne, C. (2013). Challenges experienced by paid peer providers in mental health recovery: A qualitative study. *Community Mental Health Journal*, 49(3), 281–291.

O'Hagan, M., McKee, H. and Priest, R. (2009). *Consumer Survivor Initiatives in Ontario: Building for an Equitable Future*. Toronto: Ontario Federation of Community Mental Health & Addiction Programs.

Penney, D. and Prescot, L. (2016). The co-optation of survivor knowledge: The danger of substituted values and voices. In J. Russo and A. Sweeney (eds), *Searching for a Rose Garden: Challenging Psychiatry, Fostering Mad Studies*. Monmouth: PCCS Books, 35–45

Repper, J. (2013). *Peer Support Workers: Theory and Practice*. Briefing Paper, ImROC and Sainsbury Centre for Mental Health Research Report, London.

Scott, A., Doughty, C. and Kahi, H. (2011). 'Having those conversations': The politics of risk in peer support practice. *Health Sociology Review*, 20(2), 187–201.

Scott, A. and Doughty, C. (2012). 'Confronted with paperwork': Information and documentation in peer support. *Journal of Mental Health*, 21(2), 154–164.

Trachtenberg, M., Parsonage, M., Shepherd, G. and Boardman, J., (2013). *Peer Support in Mental Health Care: Is It Good Value for Money?* London: Centre for Mental Health.

Vandewalle, J., Debyser, B., Beeckman, D., Vandecasteele, T., Van Hecke, A. and Verhaeghe, S. (2016). Peer workers' perceptions and experiences of barriers to implementation of peer worker roles in mental health services: A literature review. *International Journal of Nursing Studies*, 60, 234–250.

Voronka, J. (2016). The politics of people with lived experience: Experiential authority and the risks of strategic essentialism. *Philosophy, Psychiatry, and Psychology*, 23(3), 189–201.

Voronka, J. (2017). Turning mad knowledge into affective labor: The case of the peer support worker. *American Quarterly*, 69(2), 333–338.

Walker, G. and Bryant, W. (2013). Peer support in adult mental health services: A metasynthesis of qualitative findings. *Psychiatric Rehabilitation Journal*, 36(1), 28–34.

Watson, E. (2017). The growing pains of peer support. *Mental Health and Social Inclusion*, 21(3), 129–132.

Whitaker, R. (2010). *Anatomy of an Epidemic*. New York: Crown Publishers.

The Many Faces of Peer Support: What Can It Look Like in Practice?

4

Emma Watson

Chapter Summary

- Peer support can be offered in a variety of ways in different settings, including within charity organisations, self-help groups, community groups, online and within statutory mental health services

- Peer support in each of these settings is offered in different ways, to different people, depending on the restrictions that an organisation might place on peer workers, ideas about boundaries, training and support for peer workers, accessibility and availability of services

- While there are benefits to peer support approaches within different settings, the values of mutuality and reciprocity might be compromised when peer support roles are formalised, particularly within mental health services

- The variety of peer support approaches indicates the widespread popularity for peer support but might also mean that peer workers and the people they work alongside might benefit from more clarity about the specific tasks and responsibilities of their role

Introduction

While peer support has been offered informally and in user-led organisations throughout history, recent years have seen a huge increase in the amount of formal peer support that is available across the globe. While the evidence base for peer support and its presence in mental health policy and commissioning guidance continue to grow, the nuts and bolts of peer support working remain undefined. Definitions of peer support are generally broad, emphasising components such as mutuality and reciprocity, but leaving room for the practicalities of the peer support role/approach to be defined in different ways depending on the context it is offered within.

We saw in Chapter 3 that there are issues surrounding the introduction of peer workers into traditional mental health service provision. Many people believe that this fundamentally alters the way in which peer support can be offered and compromises the ability for peer support to be mutual. In this chapter we explore some of the different ways that peer support is currently offered, including within mental health services, in community settings and using group approaches. This provides us with an opportunity to explore the benefits and challenges of different types of peer support and begin to understand the way in which context shapes the approach that is offered. It would be impossible to even come close to exploring all the ways that peer support is offered; instead, we have chosen to focus on some examples of peer support that have 'stood the test of time', including peer support in grassroots organisations and hearing voices groups. We also look at newer forms of peer support, including the 'peer healthcare assistant' role that has been introduced in some mental health trusts. We have refrained from exploring peer support in **recovery colleges** as this is covered in detail in the next chapter.

The many faces of peer support

Perhaps it is the power of shared experience which makes peer support such a commonplace part of the world we live in. Outside of mental health, peer support is the foundation of groups such as Weight Watchers, prison mentorship programmes, breastfeeding support and online platforms such as Mumsnet. Within mental health, there have been several attempts to categorise the ways in which peer support is offered. Davidson and colleagues (1999) used three broad categories to group peer support approaches:

- Naturally occurring mutual support of a similar fashion to friendship, based around shared experiences
- Consumer-run services, which include the Hearing Voices Network (HVN) and Alcoholics Anonymous (AA)
- Consumers as providers within clinical and rehabilitation settings, sometimes referred to as intentional peer support.

To add to the complexity of peer support we suggest that it can also be offered:

- as an activity within non–peer-led charity organisations such as Mind
- within communities including religious groups
- in non-clinical settings such as befriending services

- as part of other mental health support services such as advocacy and housing/employment support
- as a specific 'intervention' developed for research purposes
- within mental health services and by external agencies.

Furthermore, peer support can be offered by people in paid roles or by volunteers, and within one-to-one relationships or in group settings. In their meta-analysis of over 1,000 peer support studies, NESTA and National Voices (2015, p. 2) provided the overview given in Figure 4.1 of the different dimensions of peer support and their impact.

Components of peer support	Improves experience	Improves health behaviour and outcomes	Improves service use and costs
Who receives support	• people with long-term helath issues • people with mental helath issues • carers • people from certain age and ethnic groups and those with specific experiences • parents • at risk groups	• people with long-term helath issues • at risk groups	• people with long-term helath issues • people with mental health issues
Who facilitates support	• untrained peers • trained peers • paid peers • lay people • peers with professionals • professionals	• trained peers • lay people • peers with professionals • professionals	• lay people
How support is delivered	• one-to-one • small groups • larger groups • face-to-face • telephone • internet	• one-to-one • larger groups • face-to-face • telephone	• face-to-face
What support is provided	• education • emotional support • social support • discussion • befriending • activity-based • peer-delivered services	• education • physical support • discussion • activity-based • peer-delivered services	*(blank cells show there is insufficient research to draw conclusions)*
Where support is provided	• own home • hospital • other services	• own home • hospital • other services	
When support is provided	• one-off • up to six months	• weekly • up to six months	

Figure 4.1 Key findings about the impact of different types of peer support, developed by NESTA and National Voices (2015)

Exercise

What types of peer support have you offered or experienced? Which do you think are most helpful? Do you anticipate any challenges arising with any of the forms of peer support listed above?

In this chapter we explore three different forms of peer support using examples to compare the benefits and challenges of each:

- One-to-one peer support provided by **third sector** organisations including 'grassroots' initiatives
- One-to-one peer support provided within statutory (NHS) mental health services
- Peer support groups provided outside of formal mental health services.

Peer-led services, where all members have a 'peer' identity, offer another example of how peer support looks in practice. There are several fascinating examples of how peer-led services use the values of peer support at every level in their organisation. Peer-led services are described and explored in Chapter 11, with further examples in Chapter 10, so we have not covered them here. The two chapters combined provide a more complete picture of peer support approaches.

Peer support and 'third sector' organisations

'Third sector' is a term used to refer to organisations or collectives which sit outside of the public sector (which is made up of government-provided services such as the NHS) and the private sector (which is made up of profit-making businesses). The third sector includes independent organisations including charities, self-help services, community organisations and social enterprises. These may be peer-run, such as Recovery Partners in Sussex, or not, in the instance of charities such as Mind.

Poppy is Head of Operations and a PAL (Peer and Ally for Living) at Real Lives. The organisation provides peer support to people using personal budgets accessed through social care services. She has worked in these roles since the organisation was formed in 2012. She offers support and supervision to PALs, as well as setting and planning social care packages with clients. In the case example below she discusses peer support in the third sector organisation, Real Lives

---

Case Example: What Does Peer Support Look Like in the Third Sector?

Poppy Repper, Head of Operations, Real Lives

At Real Lives Community Interest Company (CIC), which provides 1:1 support to people in their homes and communities, we call our workers PALs. This stands for Peers and Allies for Living. When we were trying to find a name for our workers that reflected our vision and ethos we wanted to demonstrate that everyone would be treated as an equal, and that we would match worker and client on a whole range of experiences anyone can bring. PALs bring their whole life experience to the role and use it to work alongside someone. That might be parenthood, diagnosis, age, sex, cultural background, interests and skills.

Our training towards the PAL role is recovery-focused, person-centred, non-directive and constantly supports people to draw on their own experience and humanity to empathise with their client. By using this approach consistently, and building these skills, our PALs work alongside their client as a peer or an ally, and we feel both are as important as each other.

We can all remember a time we felt hopeless, overjoyed, sad, proud and that doesn't have to be following the same experience as our client, but it can put us next to them and equal to them, and therefore in a position to support them in a truly person-centred way.

This approach and way of working can be adopted by anyone; it doesn't say one person's experience is more important than another. It is more around how that person uses their experience. We have qualified staff in our company and it doesn't mean they are better PALs because of that. It means that is one of their many assets as with those who may not have a qualification, but have a plethora of amazing and rich life experiences.

We match workers and clients using a good knowledge of each person and recognising what might work best for consistent and growing healthy relationships. Obviously, there are times when matches don't go well and ending these positively is important for both parties. Also asking people who come with a professional identity to put that on the back seat and focus on their life experiences to provide genuine and meaningful support can be difficult for those individuals, but when the approach is mastered, it is magic.

Exercise

Look at the core principles of peer support outlined in Chapter 2. How do you think peer support in Real Lives encompasses these?

In Real Lives, anybody who has access to a personal budget is able to work with a PAL. While PALs are not required to bring lived experience to their role, they are expected to draw on their life experiences to build connections with people based on shared identities. Poppy Repper emphasises the 'matching process' which Real Lives uses to ensure that people are offered relationships where they can feel some sense of peer connection and experience being treated as an equal partner.

In other third sector organisations peer support may be free for anybody to access, and in others a referral from a health professional or funding may be required. Peer support might also be accessed informally during other activities such as walking or gardening groups. Online support may be offered. Mind's 'Elefriends' online forum is one such example of this. Here, peer support is available to anybody who can use a computer.

What are the benefits and challenges of peer support in the third sector?

Peer support approaches in the third sector may benefit from using a looser risk assessment structure and are required to keep fewer paper records than statutory services. Criteria for accessing peer support is generally related to age, geographical location and experience of mental health difficulties, although in some cases referrals may be required from mental health professionals or GPs. Peer support may be a 'by-product' of other activities, which provides the opportunity to develop skills and relationships with other people, and may make conversations about mental health occur more organically. The looser structures of third sector organisations may also present a challenge to peer workers, leading to poorly defined roles and lack of clarity about where to access support for their own development (Leamy et al., 2011).

Funding is often an ongoing challenge to third sector organisations. This may mean that peer support services rely on renewed funding or remain small despite high demand. Waiting lists for certain services such as peer befrienders might make these less accessible. In addition, there is an element of 'postcode lottery', as the services available will differ depending on where a person lives. The difference between the availability of support within large cities and rural areas is often stark.

Peer support and statutory services

Here we will explore peer support in formally provided NHS mental health services. These include community services and services which a person would be forced to use if they were sectioned under the Mental Health Act. Statutory services are often, but not always, underpinned by a therapeutic or medical paradigm, that is, a person's distress is understood to be a mental illness or the person has symptoms which require treatments by healthcare professionals, often with medication.

Kat works as a Peer Healthcare Assistant (HCA) on an inpatient ward in Nottingham NHS Foundation Trust. Kat has also written poetry and spoken at national conferences about her experiences of the peer HCA role.

Case Example: What Does Peer Support Look Like in an NHS Inpatient Service?

Kat Turner, Nottinghamshire Healthcare NHS Foundation Trust – Peer Support, Acute Care and Me!

I'm always looking for new and creative ways that I can offer peer support within our ward environment. I aim to work 'outside the box', fitting around individual people's needs, strengths, abilities, limitations, anxieties and trying not to squeeze them into the mould I have used previously. My hope is that I can provide peer support which is unique to each new person I meet and is constantly evolving with fresh ideas.

I aim to provide a space where, with the right support, people can identify their own needs, build hope for themselves and have the freedom to express their dreams for the future.

Working within the ward environment is a daily challenge. I juggle with a medical model, ward restrictions, staff shortages, unpredictable behaviour and the constant 'unknown' cloud looming over my head, but within the hustle and bustle of working on an acute ward I am embedded in a dedicated team of amazing colleagues who work to provide the highest level of care. I hope the way I work and the language I use can demonstrate the values and principles of peer support, challenging and changing the culture of the ward.

I feel the simple tasks I often do with people can have many layers and depth. For example, walking with someone to the shops may incorporate one-to-one time, freedom from the ward, fresh air, being within nature, the quietness to think and reflect on where they are at, how they are feeling, providing a space for them to share and work through trauma, distress or celebrate achievements, expressing fears and frustration, talking through solutions to barriers. Listening to someone can be very powerful, giving my time, attention, compassion, understanding and walking at someone's side 'literally' and hypothetically through their recovery journey.

I have offered peer support in many different ways, from sitting on someone's bedroom floor to chat when they can't face leaving their room, to going for coffee, taking someone home, into town, to the dentist or the hairdresser's. How I see my role is not so much about the task we are doing together but I tend to focus on connecting with someone, finding a way into their world, where they may have been so hurt they have shut everyone out as a way of protection and survival. I slowly and gently build trust and relationships with people which can take time and patience. I advocate for people or support them to find the confidence to have a voice for themselves. It has been a great privilege to see the transformation in people during their time on the ward.

Exercise

Look at the core principles of peer support outlined in Chapter 2. How do you think peer support on inpatient wards encompasses these?

Kat Turner has described her role as a peer HCA working on an NHS inpatient ward. In this context, she builds relationships with people who have been admitted, by fulfilling the duties of a Healthcare Assistant combined with her peer support skills. She describes using every opportunity to build trust and connection based on a person's hopes, strengths and unique struggles. Like any worker within a large organisation, peers are expected to work within policies relating to lone-working, professional boundaries and record-keeping.

What are the benefits and challenges of peer support in statutory services?

The employment of peer workers within mental health services provides people who use them with a different, more mutual form of support. It affords people greater choice as to the type of support they would like to access. In services which are underpinned by medical expertise, the presence of peer workers might help a person to feel more in control of their own well-being. Research suggests that peer workers in mental health settings are able to act as a bridge between staff and people using services by occupying the dual identities of staff member and 'service user' (Gillard et al., 2015).

In the case example above, Kat describes the challenge of working alongside the medical model, as well as the environmental limits created by the ward context. A challenge for peer support in NHS settings is the requirement to conform to the demands of service context. Kat's peer support relationships are time limited because of the ward environment. In other settings such as community teams, peer support relationships may be time limited according to the length of time a service is commissioned to provide care for.

For peer workers, working within a large organisation may bring benefits such as clear job descriptions, pensions, formalised processes relating to personal development and supervision, and adequate training. The challenges of working in mental health service environments for a peer worker are described in Chapter 3, and Kat is not alone in feeling that part of her role is to change the culture she works within. The benefits of peer support in statutory services go beyond the peer and person they are working with. The introduction of peer workers changes the culture of mental health services both by providing a different approach to understanding and working with people, and by talking to staff members about working practices (Repper & Carter, 2011).

Peer support in self-help groups

Peer support self-help groups can take many different forms. They can be run by professionals or large organisations such as the NHS or Mind, or they can be run by individuals within their own communities. Often, self-help groups use 'ground-rules' which are agreed by the group to help ensure it feels safe for each of its members. These may be devised within the group, and there may be a predetermined charter. Figure 4.2 is an example of this taken from the HVN groups.

Criteria For Affiliated Group Membership

The Group ...

- Accepts that voices and visions are real experiences
- Accepts that people are not any the less for having voices and visions
- Respects each member as an expert
- Encourages an ethos of self-determination
- Values ordinary, non-professionalised language
- Is free to interpret experiences in any way
- Is free to challenge social norms
- Sanctions the freedom to talk about anything not just voices and visions
- Is a self-help group and not a clinical group offering treatment
- Focuses primarily on sharing experiences, support and empathy
- Members are not subject to referral, discharge or risk assessment
- Members are able to come and go as they want without repercussions
- Members are aware of the facilitator's limits concerning confidentiality
- Is working towards fulfilling criteria for full membership

Figure 4.2 Hearing Voices Network (HVN) group charter

Eve Mundy is the manager of Voice Collective, a nationwide support service for children and young people who hear voices, and their families and supporters, at Mind in Camden. She is also leading on the development of the charity's Women's Voices Unlocked service, supporting women in prisons, secure units and Immigration Removal Centres. Eve is an experienced trainer and international speaker, and has launched and facilitated hearing voices groups in prisons, secure units, adolescent in-patient units and the community.

Case Example: What Does Peer Support Look Like in a Group Setting?

Eve Mundy, Voice Collective

It's difficult to capture in words the spirit of a Hearing Voices Group. In essence, they're safe, confidential spaces in which to share experiences of hearing, seeing or sensing things that others can't, be they positive, negative or neutral.

Groups offer the opportunity to connect with fellow voice hearers, to explore and make sense of experiences, including those that are overwhelming, distressing or taboo, to receive and offer support, and they serve as an important resource for helping people to cope.

For many, groups offer the first opportunity to share and reflect on the nature and meaning of their experiences on their own terms. Groups create sanctuaries that hold the stories of their members, honouring pain and despair, as well as joy, and making space for hopelessness, powerlessness and shame to be heard and validated. Through this, groups can facilitate self-acceptance, solidarity and hope, and for many they can be life-changing.

You can find over 180 groups throughout the UK, and they can help to build communities of trust and support in diverse and challenging environments. At Mind in Camden we've set up groups throughout the community, in hospitals and secure settings, and they are complementary to therapy and psychoeducation, although they bear little resemblance to groups with a fixed programme/structure, and many are open on a drop-in basis with no fixed end point.

Hearing Voices Groups hold the ethos of the HVN, an influential voice hearer and survivor-led organisation promoting peer support, self-determination, empowerment and hope. One of the many strengths of the HVN approach is its assertion of the diversity of the causes of hearing voices. No single causal explanation, be it psychological, religious or spiritual, environmental, paranormal, biomedical etc., is either explicitly or tacitly promoted by group facilitators, who can include voice hearers and peer supporters as well as those who don't hear voices.

No presumption of illness or wellness is made by facilitators; neither do they judge voices to be inherently positive or negative. A curious and empathetic approach to listening, sitting with and responding to experiences is modelled by facilitators, who serve to maintain safety within the group without directing it. Instead groups are led by their members, with facilitators ensuring that the group's agreement to maintaining confidentiality, mutual respect and a sharing of the space is upheld.

The challenges of developing and facilitating groups are numerous, and can arise at the personal, cultural and organisational level. For example, for some facilitators, the biggest challenge may be sitting with the pain, distress or trauma expressed within a group; for others, sitting with silence. Some may find introducing the HVN ethos within their setting challenging, while others may lack the confidence or support from within their host institution/organisation to respond to any breaches of the group's agreement effectively.

Specialist training and support is highly encouraged. We offer group facilitation training, providing trainees with clarity around boundaries and their role within a group. We also provide ongoing mentoring across multiple platforms, including email, telephone and an online forum, supporting facilitators to hone their skills, develop their reflexive practice and confidence.

Exercise

Look at the core principles of peer support outlined in Chapter 2. How do you think peer support in HVN groups encompasses these?

Eve Mundy has described the approach to group facilitation taken by the HVN. Groups are open to anybody who wishes to access them and who can attend at the arranged time. Facilitators may bring their own experiences of hearing voices, or use professional expertise. Rather than offering peer support themselves, their role is to facilitate peer support and emotional safety between group members. In other self-help groups, the facilitator may be more directive, providing specific information, or sharing their 'story' of recovery. There may also be an expectation that a person attends a set number of group sessions.

What are the benefits and challenges for peer support in self-help groups?

The beauty of self-help groups lies in the opportunity they provide to make connections, offer and seek support from a large group of people, rather than one staff member. Relationships formed within self-help groups have the potential to evolve into friendships, providing long-term connection for group members. Accessibility to groups may be more straightforward than for one-to-one peer support, given that there are more spaces available. Groups such as those described above are not underpinned by a specific explanation for distress, allowing individuals to find their own meaning in their experiences.

The challenges of group peer support include managing difficult dynamics between group members which might affect the emotional safety of the whole group. Group work might place pressure on the facilitators who, depending on levels of training, supervision and confidence, may struggle to manage the challenging situations which may unfold. Further challenges relate to availability, as groups may not be facilitated in every locality, and sustainability, as they rely on the availability of facilitators and sufficient numbers of participants regularly attending.

Common ingredients of peer support

Shared experience

It is no surprise that each of the different forms of peer support has at its core shared experience. In each setting peers use their experience either directly or indirectly to inform their approach to offering support. In the accounts above this is not the only means that peers use to build relationships with people. Poppy Repper describes how PALs draw on a range of emotional and life experiences in their peer relationships; Kat Turner describes her creative approach to finding points of connection. It is written into the Hearing Voices Group Charter that while the focus of the group is primarily sharing experiences of hearing voices, members should feel free to talk about whatever they wish to. While shared 'lived' experience is the seed of peer support, surrounding it are offshoots of different experiences which are equally important in building relationships.

Values

Each of the accounts above describe an approach to peer support which is built on a person-centred or recovery-focused values base. This involves not prescribing a particular approach but stepping back and trusting people to find their own meaning and solutions. This may not be a universal component of peer support. Within more structured groups such as AA there may be a defined process that a participant is expected to follow with the direction and guidance of more experienced peers.

Chapter 2 describes some of the work that has been undertaken to describe the values base which does (or should) underpin peer support. The ingredients of emotional safety, equality of experience and choice are all described above, although how these values are expressed may differ depending on the constraints of different contexts.

Common challenges

There seem to be common challenges which affect peer support across contexts. Perhaps because peer support is still relatively new to the world of mental health service provision (although it has occurred informally and within communities for centuries) the availability of peer support varies depending on geographical location and service setting. Although most NHS mental health trusts employ peer workers, this is usually still in small numbers and in particular services and not others. Some self-help groups such as AA and the HVN have well-established networks; peer support for other experiences may be less easy to access, and one-to-one peer support offered by third sector organisations faces this same challenge.

One exception to this challenge is online peer support which is becoming increasingly recognised as a valuable resource. While it is beyond the scope of this chapter to examine online peer support in detail, it is clearly one of the most accessible and least restrictive forms of peer support, being available to anybody who is able to create an account, at any time of day or night.

A further common challenge relates to the experiences of the peer workers or group facilitators themselves. Each of the accounts above described the support networks available to peer workers, in the form of training, supportive teams and facilitator networks. The use of personal experience within 'professional' roles has been found to be both profoundly beneficial and decidedly challenging for peer workers (Bailie & Tickle, 2015). This is particularly the case when peer workers are employed alongside professionals who may vary in how comfortable they are using their personal experiences in their working roles. The need for extra, or perhaps different, training and support for peer workers so that they may use and manage their experiences of well-being in a way that feels emotionally safe for them has been highlighted by several authors (e.g. Mourra et al., 2014).

How do the different forms of peer support differ?

Role, tasks and boundaries

The different forms of peer support described above differ on a number of levels. Most notably, the specific roles and tasks of peer workers are defined by their working context. So, on a ward, a peer worker may help serve meals, talk to people and accompany them on leave, while in a group the same peer worker would facilitate discussion and ensure the group charter is kept in mind. Beneath these differences peer workers may be operating with a different set of boundaries and responsibility for the people they support. The chance for these relationships to evolve into friendships or exist outside of working hours is small, and training often emphasises the importance of boundaries for the peer support worker (see Chapter 8).

In many mental health organisations there are strict boundaries about working relationships which describe the limits of when support can be provided, how long for and when this should come to an end. Commonly, the progression of working relationships into friendships is prohibited within codes of conduct and other elements of friendship, such as accepting gifts and communication on social media are prevented. In some organisations, however, peer support relationships are built with different boundaries, allowing for the possibility of friendships developing. In New Zealand, for example, some organisations see this as fundamental to the authenticity of peer support:

> If we had a policy that said you're not allowed to continue the friendship, then
> going into peer support with someone new, I would not be giving of my full self.
> If I knew that in a year's time I was going to have to back off. Whereas now
> I will go into it not knowing if it's going to develop into a friendship or not.
> (Peer supporter cited in Scott, 2011, p. 181)

Choice and control

The context where peer support unfolds affects the amount of choice and control that each person has within peer support relationships. In third sector and group peer support a person is generally free to decide whether or not they would like to access support. This is certainly true of group support such as that provided by the AA or the HVN. Within some third sector organisations (including Real Lives, described above) a person may need to be in receipt of a personal budget in order to access the support of a PAL. The concept of choice in formal mental health services is a contentious issue; most people access peer support in community services voluntarily where it is available, however many do not choose to access inpatient services, but are required to because they are deemed to be a risk to themselves or to another person. Kat Turner described peer support on a ward, where people are often admitted under the Mental Health Act. Within this environment of limited choice Kat's presence provides people with some option about whether or not they would like to talk to a peer worker. It is arguably at times like these, when people are in intense distress, that they might most benefit from being with a peer worker.

The highest levels of control over the degree of participation in peer support exists within peer support group settings which are most often freely available and accessible for as long as a person needs them. There may be threats related to funding and issues relating to demand for the service exceeding its capacity. In formal mental health services peer support processes may be established to help the person receiving support feel as in control as possible; however, they may not be able to choose how long they receive peer support for, who they receive it from and the boundaries which inform this relationship.

Reciprocity and mutuality

Although one of the core principles of peer support is reciprocity (Repper, 2013), within formalised peer support the relationship may have tipped into a more one-sided approach. Where the peer worker is providing support to a peer who is receiving mental health services, the shared benefits take on a different form. The peer worker may benefit financially from being in a paid role as well as benefiting from hearing about another's recovery, and from being in a helper role where they can share their experiences.

The direct practical benefits such as problem solving, making sense of personal experiences or housing support are the preserve of the peer or service user.

In addition, in many mental health services peer workers are privilege to personal information about the person they support, including their life history, family circumstance and diagnosis which are stored in their patient records. This places the peer support worker in a more powerful position and removes choice from the person they support about the information they would like the peer worker to know. Although some argue that mutuality and reciprocity remain in peer relationships within mental health services, others argue that in this context peer support becomes an 'intervention': 'Unlike mutual support and consumer-run programs, peer support [in mental health services] is thus defined as involving an asymmetrical – if not one-directional – relationship, with at least one designated service/support provider and one designated service/support recipient' (Davidson et al., 2006, p. 444).

CONCLUSIONS: WHAT DO THESE DIFFERENT APPROACHES MEAN FOR THE IDENTITY OF PEER SUPPORT?

In this chapter we have considered some of the differences, benefits and challenges involved in various types of peer support. To do this we have focused on three contexts in which peer support is offered. Even within each of these contexts it would be possible to draw out examples of contrasting approaches, informed by different values and operating with different understandings of peer support. We have tried to draw out broad themes and patterns which occur in each setting and this has led to some generalisations of each context.

Peer support is understood and offered in a wide spectrum of ways in the UK and across the world. Some of these are well established, such as the HVN groups, and others are newer and still developing their identity in relation to peer support values. So, what do all these different faces of peer support mean for its identity? They indicate the popularity of peer support; there seems to be an ever-growing appetite for peer support within mental health services, in community organisations and online, and this is exciting to see.

The popularity of peer support has contributed to a growing interest in the values of peer support, both defining and protecting them. There has been much debate in recent years about the different ways that peer support is offered, particularly as they have been introduced into statutory services, and how these may compromise the original values of peer support. National standards for peer support have been developed in other arenas, such as HIV support settings (Positively UK, 2017) as a means of protecting the identity of peer support and ensuring the original values of mutuality and reciprocity do not become diluted beyond recognition.

The variety of ways that peer support can be defined and offered might also have led to continued confusion about what peer support workers actually do among staff groups. There is a large body of evidence which attests to the ill-defined nature of peer worker roles in mental health services (Bailie & Tickle, 2015) and the ways that these can lead to distress, low job satisfaction and failure of peer support projects in mental health services (Gillard & Holley, 2014). While there should be room for peer support to flourish in as many contexts as possible, there is work to be done in each of these settings to ensure that values and specific activities of peer support are defined sufficiently to ensure its success.

ACKNOWLEDGEMENTS

With thanks to Poppy Repper, Kat Turner and Eve Mundy for their contributions. Thanks also to Simon Betts for his support developing ideas for the chapter.

FURTHER READING AND RESOURCES

Real Lives video by Waldo Roeg:

- https://www.real-lives.co.uk/

Elefriends online support group:

- https://www.elefriends.org.uk/

Hearing Voices Network website:

- https://www.hearing-voices.org/

Kat Turner reading a poem about physical restraint:

- https://www.youtube.com/watch?v=da55ss5HsL0

REFERENCES

Bailie, H. A. and Tickle, A. (2015). Effects of employment as a peer support worker on personal recovery: A review of qualitative evidence. *Mental Health Review Journal*, 20(1), 48–64.

Davidson, L., Chinman, M., Kloos, B., Weingarten, R., Stayner, D. and Tebes, J. K. (1999). Peer support among individuals with severe mental illness: A review of the evidence. *Clinical Psychology: Science and Practice*, 6(2), 165–187.

Davidson, L., Chinman, M., Sells, D. and Rowe, M. (2006). Peer support among adults with serious mental illness: A report from the field. *Schizophrenia Bulletin*, 32(3), 443–450.

Gillard, S., Gibson, S. L., Holley, J. and Lucock, M. (2015). Developing a change model for peer worker interventions in mental health services: A qualitative research study. *Epidemiology and Psychiatric Sciences*, 24(5), 435–445.

Gillard, S. and Holley, J. (2014). Peer workers in mental health services: Literature overview. *Advances in Psychiatric Treatment*, 20(4), 286–292.

Leamy, M., Bird, V., Le Boutillier, C., Williams, J. and Slade, M. (2011). Conceptual framework for personal recovery in mental health: Systematic review and narrative synthesis. *The British Journal of Psychiatry*, 199, 445–452.

Mourra, S., Sledge, W., Sells, D., Lawless, M. and Davidson, L. (2014). Pushing, patience and persistence: Peer providers; perspectives on supportive relationships. *American Journal of Psychiatric Rehabilitation*, 17, 307–328.

NESTA and National Voices (2015). *Peer Support: What Is It and Does It Work?*. London: NESTA and National Voices. [Accessed 10 November 2018]

Positively UK (2017). *National Standards for Peer Support in HIV*. http://hivpeersupport.com/. [Accessed 10 November 2018]

Repper, J. (2013). *PSWs: Theory and Practice*. London: ImROC and Sainsbury Centre for Mental Health.

Repper, J. and Carter, T. (2011). A review of the literature on peer support in mental health services. *Journal of Mental Health*, 20(4), 392–411.

Scott, A. (2011). Authenticity work: Mutuality and boundaries in peer support. *Society and Mental Health*, 1(3), 173–184.

Recovery Colleges and Peer Support

5

Sara Meddings, Waldo Roeg and Sandra Jayacodi

Chapter Summary

- Recovery Colleges bring together lived and professional expertise to **co-produce** educational courses about recovery and well-being
- There is growing evidence for the benefits of Recovery Colleges
- All aspects of the college are co-produced by mental health professionals, **peer trainers** and students
- Students value the **lived expertise** of peer trainers and the support they receive from them
- Students also benefit from co-learning and the informal peer support from each other
- Recovery Colleges need to reach out to people from a range of backgrounds so that they are truly open to all

Introduction

Recovery Colleges are one way of learning about self-management and gaining peer support both formally from peer trainers and informally from students. They share many of the values of peer support and are based on an understanding that: 'Recovery is about building a meaningful and satisfying life, as defined by the person themselves, whether or not there are ongoing or recurring symptoms or problems' (Shepherd et al., 2008, p. 1). Although they are a relatively new development within UK mental health systems, Recovery Colleges have become central to many people's recovery.

The first Recovery College was piloted in 2009 and officially opened in 2011 in South West London. This was followed by Nottingham, Central North West London (CNWL) and then Sussex. By 2017 there were over 75 Recovery Colleges in the UK and around the world (Perkins et al., 2018). Recovery Colleges draw on the ideas of initiatives such as the Expert Patient Programme in the UK (Department of Health, 2001) and recovery education centres in the USA, yet are different from these. The majority in the UK are funded by the NHS, either through direct commissioning or by NHS mental health Trusts as part of their overall contract (Anfossi, 2017) but follow recovery education paradigms different from mainstream services. Recovery Colleges bring together the expertise of mental health professionals and experts by lived experience through co-production in an adult learning environment. Initially they focused on mental health but now include a range of long-term conditions.

In this chapter we outline what a Recovery College is, the principles behind it and how they are run. We discuss the growing evidence base for Recovery Colleges, how they reduce stigma, open doors to employment and improve quality of life. We consider the particular role of peer trainers in supporting recovery through inspiration, role modelling and mutual support. We also discuss peer support between students. We explore critical debates about how we can achieve co-production and engage under-represented groups. We illustrate the chapter with our own experience and quotes from Recovery College students.

What is a Recovery College?

The defining features or critical dimensions of Recovery Colleges were originally outlined in the ImROC briefing paper by Perkins and colleagues (2012) and McGregor and colleagues (2014). Over the past ten years these have been refined. Perkins and colleagues (2018) suggest six principles define Recovery Colleges.

Recovery Colleges are:

1. **Based on educational principles** – there is a prospectus offering a range of courses relating to recovery and well-being, and clear structure for lesson plans, learning plans, courses and terms. They do not replace therapy or mainstream education. People are not patients, but students who bring their own experience and knowledge and are self-directed
2. **Founded on co-production, co-facilitation and co-learning** – everything about the college is co-produced, with lived and professional expertise valued equally. Decisions about enrolment processes, what courses to include and the content of courses are

made valuing the expertise of students and staff. Trainers and students learn from one another

3. **Recovery-focused, strengths-based and person-centred** – students choose courses they want to attend rather than being referred. The achievements, skills and strengths of staff and students are valued. Hope and possibility is conveyed throughout the college including the prospectus, physical environment and courses. Space is provided for learning rather than information being delivered didactically

4. **Progressive** – students work towards their own goals at college and in life. The college helps students build connections to move forward in their recovery. Individual learning plans help students identify their goals and the support they need to achieve them

5. **Integrated with the community and mental health services** – active engagement with mental health services, community organisations and further education colleges. Partnership working harnesses different types of expertise and fosters links with employers and mainstream colleges. They promote recovery-focused service transformation and communities which accommodate mental distress

6. **Inclusive and open to all** – welcomes students of all cultures and educational achievement, offers reasonable adjustments and reaches out to diverse groups. Relatives, friends, **carers** and staff attend the college, with students learning from each other, helping to break down barriers between people with mental health challenges, staff and the wider community.

These principles mirror what students say they value about Recovery Colleges (Meddings, Guglietti et al., 2014):

- *Learning from other students* – 'we are all in the same boat'; 'realise you're not the only one'
- *Co-production and the valuing of lived experience* – 'it was the equality, learning from peer trainers' lived experience and professionals that helped'
- *A safe supportive environment and the personal qualities of staff* – 'empathy, warmth and a welcome'
- *Learning new knowledge* – 'it was helpful to learn techniques that help me manage my anxiety'; 'learning something new gave me confidence'
- *Social opportunities* – 'I have met people I will continue to meet up with'
- *Structure* – 'I learned that I need to have a structure to the week'
- *Choice and control* – 'choice is empowering – you choose what course from a prospectus, instead of professionals assessing and referring'
- *Progression* – 'I feel more prepared to tackle voluntary work'.

Exercise

Compare the principles of peer support described in Chapter 2 and the defining features of Recovery Colleges.

The introduction of Recovery Colleges in the UK offers a radical departure from treatment-based approaches to supporting mental health. The recovery educational paradigm enables students to choose courses which they find helpful, positioning them as the experts in their own needs. The educational approach used within Recovery Colleges does not reflect traditional 'psycho-educational' approaches where information is offered to people about their illnesses. Instead, classes are underpinned by the understanding that everybody has something to offer. Just as shared learning is central to peer support, it is fundamental to Recovery Colleges. Students learn from each other as well as from facilitators, but, most importantly, they are encouraged to acknowledge their own expertise and develop their own understanding about their experiences. In this way courses are not facilitated on the assumption that students will learn the 'right' answers, but that students will reach their own understandings of recovery and living well, which may or may not be in agreement with established treatment approaches.

Support is offered to students throughout their learning process. Recovery Colleges aspire to offer all students Individual Learning Planning (ILP) meetings to consider their personal goals in attending the college and what adjustments they might need to enable them to access courses. These adjustments are unique to each student's physical and mental health needs; some students ask to sit near the door to ease their anxiety, others for support with reading and writing, others for help in travelling to class. Where it is not possible to offer ILPs, colleges may find other ways of understanding students' needs and ambitions, for example asking about reasonable adjustments on the registration form or considering personal goals in the first session. Students who attend courses provide feedback to improve the college and may go on to co-produce future courses, highlighting that everyone has something to learn and something to offer others. Student representatives and student unions are commonplace within Recovery Colleges, providing feedback on student experience, courses and college processes. Students also receive certificates of attendance after they complete a course, and most colleges have graduation ceremonies to celebrate students' success.

Case Example: Sussex Recovery College

Louise Patmore, Lead Peer Trainer, Sussex Recovery College

Sussex Recovery College is based on the south-east coast of the UK. It is a partnership between Sussex Partnership NHS Foundation Trust, Southdown and other voluntary sector organisations. The first courses were advertised and facilitated in spring 2013. The college operates with separate campuses in East and West Sussex and in Brighton and Hove city.

Sussex Recovery College offers educational courses about mental health and recovery which aim to increase knowledge and skills and promote self-management. Over 2,000 students register with the college each year. Of these, two-thirds are new with one-third comprising returning students. The majority of students are people with serious mental health challenges who use secondary mental health services. The rest are their relatives, friends and carers, staff of partner organisations and people with milder mental health challenges.

Students view information about the college and courses in termly prospectuses. They complete a registration form which includes information about reasonable adjustments and support needs. Individual Learning Planning meetings are offered to those who want them. Courses are held in a range of local venues such as libraries. Courses last an average of 5–6 weeks with each session being about two hours long – students say this length is best. Students receive text reminders as recommended by students to help improve attendance. Seventy-five per cent of those who start a course complete more than 70 per cent classes and go on to graduate at the annual graduation ceremony. The most popular courses include *planning your recovery, understanding psychosis, managing anxiety, happiness* and *skills for emotional well-being.*

The college employs three part-time senior peer trainers, a lead peer trainer and more than 40 sessional peer trainers. Subject area expertise is mostly provided by clinicians working for Sussex Partnership who co-produce and co-facilitate courses as part of their wider clinical roles. Other trainers come from partner organisations including MindOUT, Sussex Wildlife Trust and Recovery Partners. Each campus has a student union with student representatives.

All aspects of the college are co-produced (Meddings, Byrne et al., 2014). For example, decisions about how to measure outcomes and quality are made by a group comprising peer trainers, student representatives, researchers and Recovery College managers. The college is overseen by an academic board which meets termly. The board is chaired by the Trust Director of Education and Training and again includes Recovery College managers, senior peer trainers, clinicians, student representatives, researchers and voluntary sector partners.

Sussex Recovery College has demonstrated that after attending the college students make progress with their recovery (Meddings et al., 2015). More than 95 per cent of students say they would recommend the course they did. Students use mental health services less after attending the college (Bourne et al., 2018).

For more information, see www.sussexrecoverycollege.org.uk

Quality and outcomes

How each Recovery College measures quality and outcomes may be defined through co-production with students, peer trainers, clinicians, managers and commissioners. Commonly, this might include measures of:

- Inputs – who uses the college, demographics, learning support needs and attendance
- Quality indicators – presence or not of the key defining features described above, course feedback, curricular review, surveys
- Outcome measures – measures completed as part of an ILP, or at the beginning and end of courses.

Quality assurance

A quality assurance group of peer trainers, students and mental health professionals may review courses. This might include how courses meet the defining features such as how much courses were co-produced or whether they are open to everyone; how courses relate to the evidence base; registration numbers; and student feedback.

It is essential to balance the value of learning about the quality and effectiveness of courses and college with the potential burden this might place on students and staff. ILPs offer an opportunity for students to set their own goals and assess their progress; trainers to gauge how to adapt lessons to meet their needs; *and* for the college to collate this information to see how students as a group have progressed and assess the effectiveness of the college as a whole.

Outcomes

While there are yet to be any formalised controlled trials, local audits and evaluations show the benefits of Recovery Colleges. Recovery Colleges are popular and students are highly satisfied. More than 95 per cent of students say they would recommend the course they did to others (Rennison et al., 2014 and Meddings, Guglietti et al., 2014 in the UK; and Gill, 2014 in Australia). Recovery Colleges have quite high attendance rates, generally around 60–70 per cent, consistent with mainstream adult education (e.g. Meddings et al., 2015; Rennison et al., 2014). Students feel they have greater knowledge, skills and understanding after attending Recovery College (Burhouse et al., 2015; Meddings, Guglietti et al., 2014).

Recovery College students make progress towards their own personal recovery goals (Burhouse et al., 2015; Meddings et al., 2015; Rinaldi & Wybourn, 2011; Sommer, 2017). After attending Recovery College they have more contact with education, employment, volunteering, the arts, and social interactions with family and neighbourhood; they have larger social networks with people they can confide in (Hall et al., 2016; Meddings et al., 2015; Rennison et al., 2014; Rinaldi & Wybourn, 2011).

When students have completed standardised measures of recovery, their mental health has been found to improve (Meddings et al., 2015; Nurser et al., 2017). They also report less self-stigma (Nurser et al., 2017); feeling more hopeful about the future (Rennison et al., 2014); having greater self-confidence and self-esteem (Skinner, 2015); and experiencing improved well-being and quality of life after attending Recovery Colleges (Meddings et al., 2015; North Essex Research Network, 2014).

Attendance at Recovery Colleges is associated with reduced hospital and community service use (Barton and Williams, 2015; Bourne et al., 2018; Mid-Essex Recovery College, 2014; Rinaldi & Wybourn, 2011). Bourne and colleagues (2018) found that people spent half as many days in hospital after than before registering with the Recovery College, equating to non-cashable cost-savings of £1,200 per student.

Recovery Colleges are also a resource for training and developing skills of staff who work within mental health services to support recovery more effectively. After attending Recovery College as students, staff report a positive impact on how they support others and on their own well-being and job satisfaction. They feel more positive about mental health and recovery, understand the meaning of recovery better, feel more hopeful and empathic, and feel a sense of reduced barriers between 'us' and 'them' (Perkins et al., 2017; Sommer, 2017).

However, we need more robust research. Evaluations show correlations between positive outcomes and attending Recovery College but we do not know whether attendance causes this. For example, students may already be at a place in their recovery journey where they would have been making progress whether or not they had attended. Again, we do not know whether gains were maintained a year after attendance. Assuming that something is helpful about Recovery Colleges, we need to explore what this may be. It might be gaining hope and reducing stigma due to co-production, peer support and valuing lived experience. It may be being a student rather than a patient and new relationships with other students, trainers and with mental health services. It might be the recovery-oriented environment and choosing what courses to take or what works for you. It might be the content of the courses and learning from trainers and each other. Toney and colleagues (in press) identify three mechanisms of action for Recovery Colleges: empowering environment, enabling different relationships and facilitating personal growth.

Exercise

What Recovery College course might you like to attend? And what would you hope to gain from it? Take a look at a local Recovery College prospectus.

The role and experience of peers

A peer trainer is someone with lived experience of mental health challenges or a long-term condition, and training in teaching and using their lived experience to help others. They are employed to co-produce and co-facilitate courses, and use their lived experience to help others, modelling that recovery is possible. They also bring knowledge of literature written by people with lived experience and about what different people find helpful. They work alongside staff who are employed for their professional qualifications and skills.

Peer trainers are integral to helping students feel empowered and that not only is recovery possible, but they can be equally valued for what they contribute. It might be the first time they have seen someone using their lived experience of services or a diagnosis formally. Peer trainers specifically share their lived experience in the design and delivery of courses – hearing about the peer's experience is one way that Recovery College courses differ from other self-management courses.

Students value this co-production. Meddings, Guglietti and colleagues (2014) report that 94 per cent of students say it was helpful that the training was facilitated by both peer trainers with lived experience and trainers with professional expertise. Students report feeling empowered by being taught by someone who has had a similar experience or has been there themselves. It also shows in practice what it means to work collaboratively within a service. This helps break down the power dynamics that exist between services and people who use them. Shepherd (2015) argues that it is this changed power relationship and reduction in stigma and self-stigma that makes Recovery Colleges effective by rediscovering a sense of control and empowerment, bringing hope, possibility and a re-evaluation of self.

Students say:

> *Hearing the personal stories from the trainers created a safe environment to share honest opinions from both service users and staff members.*

> *It was the equal contribution of peer trainers and professionals that helped.*

> *After seven years of being unemployed following my diagnosis of mental illness, hearing the lived experiences of peer trainers and how they have taken back control of their life, moved forward in a positive way, and been employed once again has inspired me and given me hope that I also can move forward in my life and be employed one day.*

Recovery Colleges also have a positive impact on the trainers. CNWL Recovery College surveyed 16 peer trainers and 17 practitioner trainers (Skinner, 2015). Both sets of trainers reported greater self-confidence and self-esteem. They valued the experience of co-production and the learning opportunities this afforded. Their well-being improved as they became more aware of the need to look after themselves and the importance of health and well-being at work. The Recovery and Wellbeing College supported them in this with regular supervision. All the peer trainers reported positive effects of moving into employment. They felt less stigma and more self-worth. Peer trainers also reported that their use of services had reduced and their material well-being improved.

Case Example: The Experience of a Senior Peer Trainer

Waldo Roeg, Senior Peer Trainer, CNWL Recovery College

After spending a long time using services I believed I would never work again. I had lost any hope that I'd ever be able to have the opportunity to work. Working for CNWL as a Senior Peer Trainer is beyond any expectations I had when I was unwell, and has proved to be at the heart of my recovery. Rediscovering what it is like to be a valued member of a team. Moving from being helpless to being helpful, being an inspiration and catalyst of hope by modelling my own recovery. Seeing the impact of this on students has been extremely empowering and rewarding. I am constantly learning things from the students' experiences that help me in my own recovery. I feel privileged to be part of an initiative that I believe has and will continue to have an invaluable impact on mental health services. Doing this work gives me a sense of purpose, and has given meaning to the difficulties that I went through in the past. I believe that my role keeps me motivated to keep well and look after myself, in order to support others in doing the same and this responsibility has added huge value to my daily life and future aspirations. Becoming a contributing citizen rather than a burden has given me back a sense of purpose and value, and being connected to colleagues and people because of my peer work has been invaluable. These have and continue to play a huge part of what has kept me in recovery over the last five years.

Critical debate: How can we get real co-production at all levels?

Co-production is about 'doing with' rather than 'doing to or for' people, building on people's existing capabilities, valuing their assets and working together to achieve a mutual goal in equal partnership. It requires sharing decision-making power. In mental health this involves those who traditionally use mental health services working together with those who traditionally provide that service to discover new solutions:

> *Co-production means delivering public services in an equal and reciprocal*
> *relationship between professionals, people using services, their families and*
> *their neighbours. Where activities are co-produced in this way, both services and*
> *neighbourhoods become far more effective agents of change.* (Boyle & Harris,
> 2009, p. 11, emphasis in original)

Co-production has been rated one of the most important features of Recovery Colleges, second only to recovery principles (King, 2015). Service user, carer and staff students all find co-production to be one of the most helpful aspects (Meddings et al., 2014; Perkins et al., 2017; Zabel et al., 2016).

Co-producing courses involves lived expertise by peers, expertise in education and training, and subject matter expertise of mental health professionals. It is an ongoing, iterative process which students become part of through course feedback and review.

However, Recovery Colleges need to include their students more in co-producing college systems. Anfossi (2017) found that only 26 per cent of colleges had student representatives. Only two of 23 respondents in King (2015) mentioned co-production involving students, indicating that, in reality, co-production often only includes peer trainers and mental health professionals.

To co-produce all aspects of the Recovery College we need to include the expertise of students who use the service as well as peers and professionals. For co-production to be meaningful we need to consider what is being co-produced and who brings lived expertise of that element. While a peer may bring lived experience of anxiety to co-produce and co-facilitate an anxiety management course, if they have never been a Recovery College student they are unable to bring experience of college processes such as registration. Equally, it would be tokenistic to expect them to co-produce courses relating to experiences they have not encountered such as drug use or being a carer.

Peer trainers, students and mental health professionals need to work together to co-produce staff recruitment, curricula, paperwork and quality and outcomes processes. It is essential that students as well as peers are represented on the academic or management board that oversees the running of the college (Figure 5.1).

There are inherent organisational and structural inequalities between mental health clinicians, managers and people who use services, which makes co-production challenging. Peer trainers and student representatives are usually paid less than other college staff and have less inherent power. There may also be inequalities based on gender or ethnicity. Recovery Colleges strive towards reducing inequalities and transforming these into valued resources. However, in many colleges the ultimate power and responsibility for overseeing the college, and its budget, lies with a mental health professional who sits on an NHS board. Co-production requires genuine power sharing. It is questionable whether real co-production can happen if the budget is controlled only by managers and mental health professionals.

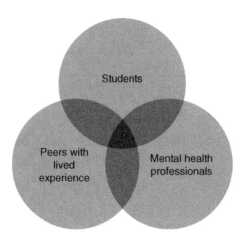

Figure 5.1 Co-production in Recovery Colleges

Co-production can be enhanced where:

- Student representatives and peers receive training in leadership and how the mental health and social care system works
- Student representatives have people to represent through a student union
- Student representatives are paid expenses and for their time
- Training in co-production and recovery is provided, alongside ongoing supervision and support, not only for student reps but also for peer trainers, clinicians and managers
- People are included who bring the range of expertise required for this particular task and all their assets are recognised
- There are clear expectations of what is required of each person
- Time and resources are dedicated to co-production
- Senior management support and Trust policies promote co-production
- The assets and strengths of the whole student or service user community are harnessed
- Attention is paid to co-production from the start and as the college grows.

Exercise

What has been your experience of co-production? Can you think of any aspects of your work setting that could be improved by co-production? How might you go about starting this process?

Students supporting each other

Recovery Colleges provide peer support not only from trainers, but also from co-learning with other students. In interviews with students about the best aspects of Recovery Colleges more students mentioned learning from other students than any other factor (Meddings,

Guglietti et al., 2014). Meeting others who had experienced similar challenges helped them realise they were not alone. They valued talking with people who had been in a similar situation, seeing one another's strengths and contributions, and supporting each other with challenges. A Recovery College is a space to share experience without being judged. People get support from the group. Some may not speak but are helped by listening to others:

It made me realise I wasn't alone.

Before I attended the Recovery College I had no clue about how other people with mental health illness were coping with their lives. Hearing other students' coping strategies and crisis plan helped me to put together my own and that they are not set in stone. I learnt from my peers how not to be judgemental and trivialise other people's coping strategy.

Building relationships with other students helps people to feel less isolated and make social contacts and friends. Students might share phone numbers with each other, go for coffee after class and stay in touch after the course:

There is a bond that is created amongst the students. That goes beyond the classroom.

Staff who attend a Recovery College as students also find the co-learning experience valuable. 'Learning alongside service users as equals appeared to encourage staff students to understand and appreciate their perspective, recognise commonalities, and reduce barriers' (Perkins et al., 2017, p. 22). For students who use mental health services, hearing mental health professionals open up about their own difficulties breaks down perceived differences and helps to see commonality – not them versus us – not those who are well versus those who are ill.

The college creates space for informal peer support to happen. Feeling comfortable and safe is increased by learning agreements (ground rules):

You might feel more comfortable speaking with someone from your own culture when you are in this environment whereas at other times you might feel stigmatised.

It is a place to exchange ideas with other students – what's worked, what others have tried and progress made.

One of the original principles for Recovery College was to have a physical base with classrooms and a library (Perkins et al., 2012). Although many colleges do not have them, in such bases students can meet people from other courses and have increased opportunities for informal peer support and building social networks. The student union is another opportunity where students can meet and gain informal peer support while also influencing the running and development of the college.

However, meeting other students is not all positive. It is sometimes difficult to support students who are struggling, and trainers need good classroom management skills to enable everyone to get the most from class when one student may be experiencing difficulties. Dunn and colleagues (2016) found one of the reasons students missed classes was owing to worries about other students and potential disruption in class.

Case Example: One Student's Experience

Sandra Jayacodi

I was introduced to the Recovery College by my psychologist and I am so grateful to her for doing that. The courses helped me to take back control of my life. Being in a classroom with other students who have mental health conditions gave me a platform to talk about my own illness without being afraid of the stigma. I also learnt that my stigma was more internalised. The peers were non-judgemental and it felt very easy to share. The more I shared in the classroom the easier it became to share outside the classroom. I also realised that the peers were in a similar boat to me, afraid to talk about their mental illness in the beginning.

The Recovery College was a place for a great support network, be it in the classroom or outside the classroom. I have made friends and found it easier to engage with my peers than my old friends who were finding it very hard to fit around me or could not understand why I wasn't engaging with them.

There have been times when I have seen other students who would not engage at all in the class or even make eye contact and I would have been quick to judge and criticise them for not making an attempt to engage. Then I found out that for that student just turning up to the class was like reaching the mountain top. That was when I realised that I was judging people by my standard. In fact what I learnt from that particular event helped me when I relapsed and would not get out of the house and engage with anyone.

Hearing other students and peer trainers' stories about their recovery and getting back into employment inspired me to want to go back to work. Hearing how they have retrained and used their lived experiences to become peer trainers and peer support workers led me to take up relevant courses to become one. In the classrooms you can always hear other students sharing the opportunities that are out there. It was also a place of resources.

Exercise

Think of a time when you have been a student. What peer support did you gain from your fellow students?

Engaging under-represented students

One of the principles of Recovery Colleges is that they are inclusive and open to all. Some colleges have inclusion criteria due to funding arrangements which may mean, for example, that they focus on people using secondary mental health services. Few have further exclusion criteria; however, the students of many colleges are largely white women in middle age – being inclusive requires a more proactive approach.

Statutory organisations are required to monitor protected characteristics: age, gender, sexual orientation, gender reassignment, ethnicity, religion and disability (in England,

Wales and Scotland, Equality Act, 2010). Recovery Colleges additionally aim to reach staff, carers and people with a range of mental health challenges. Information from the registration process may be audited against local mental health and population data. Where a college is not reaching these groups, they can take further steps. Inclusivity is improved if the prospectus, often people's first contact with the college, includes images of people from different cultural backgrounds; the course descriptions make clear they are for staff and relatives as well as people who use services; and EasyRead versions are promoted. Prospectuses can be available, not only in mental health buildings but also online, in voluntary sector and GP settings, and in places where different groups are more likely to go such as faith centres.

Colleges need to discuss and action reasonable adjustments to enable individuals to attend, such as particular lighting for someone with epilepsy, a buddy to reduce anxieties or wheelchair accessible classrooms. In order to reach people who are detained some courses might be held on acute wards, forensic units or in prisons (see, for example, Frayn et al., 2016). Courses may be developed for specific groups such as women who have been abused or LGBT (lesbian, gay, bisexual and transgender) students. Voluntary sector partners might be better placed to reach out to specific groups, for example MindOUT has co-produced and co-delivered courses for people who identify as LGBT in Sussex.

Case Example: Recovery Colleges in the West of Ireland

Donal Hoban, Recovery College Director, Mayo Recovery College

The County Mayo Recovery College was the first Recovery College in the Republic of Ireland, opening in 2013. It serves a predominantly rural population of 130,000 people in an area of 2,000 square miles.

Our approach from the outset was to position the colleges as resolutely community facing and to disassociate the Recovery College phenomenon from secondary mental health services. To achieve this we co-located Mayo Recovery College with a higher education institution, Galway Mayo Institute of Technology (GMIT). The Recovery College operates as a faculty within GMIT and has attracted an eclectic membership from the community inclusive of families, service users, students and health/social care professionals. The Recovery College contributes co-produced and co-delivered inputs to the social care and psychiatric nursing undergraduate programmes and is responsible for one entire final-year undergraduate module.

Owing to the rural area and spatial spread of students we initially offered a spoke and hub approach with 'pop-up' or peripatetic courses using community spaces. This approach enables reach and presence in the community and solves transport issues but proved challenging in terms of sustainability and resourcing. We also found that students were more willing to travel to GMIT than community or mental health spokes. We noticed the value and kudos enjoyed by students who could now attend a 'real' hub college (GMIT) and the experiential dividend of enjoying an identity beyond that of patient or service user in an institute of higher learning.

> The college has flourished in terms of student numbers, engagement and a diverse student population. Students report increased self-esteem, feel less lonely and form friendships. There have been gains in health promotion, population health, community development and anti-stigma identity. The college has a strong fidelity with adult education and there is less risk of it becoming an adjunct to mental health services with para-therapeutic interventions. However, the dividend in terms of organisational change within mental health services has been less evident and clinical practitioners have been slower to engage. While reaching the wider community, care needs to be taken not to inadvertently exclude people with significant mental health and recovery needs.
>
> For more information, see: www.recoverycollegewest.ie

Finally, Recovery Colleges need to give attention to how they can reach people in rural areas. There may be issues associated with transport and the distance to travel to class. Transport or expenses may be provided. Partnerships might enable courses to be held nearer to people. In rural areas of Northern Ireland, partnerships have been formed between Health and Social Care Trusts and the Library Service and courses are held within libraries – this has enabled greater reach into rural areas (Perkins et al., 2018). In the Republic of Ireland, Recovery Colleges partner with higher education institutions and students have been more willing to travel to mainstream college than to local community or health venues (Donal Hoban, personal communication, 25 June 2018). Again virtual or online classes might be considered (e.g. Working to Recovery Online Open Recovery College, https://www.workingtorecovery.co.uk/recovery-college.aspx) although care would need to be taken to be inclusive of people who might need help with literacy or using computers.

CONCLUSIONS

Recovery Colleges are becoming established across the UK, Ireland and beyond. They are reaching large numbers of people with mental health challenges and other long-term conditions along with their relatives, carers and staff. There is growing evidence that Recovery Colleges are effective. Students particularly value co-production, the role of peer trainers and the learning and mutual support they get from other students.

Recovery Colleges are at the forefront of bringing peer support into the delivery of services. Peer support and co-production when combined together are a force for undermining the stigma that exists around mental health in mental health services. Recovery Colleges open up possibilities and hope. Not only people who use services but their relatives, carers and staff all benefit. This may be one of the reasons for the growing evidence that Recovery Colleges improve recovery and well-being.

However, true co-production in Recovery Colleges needs to recognise the value and role of students as well as staff. Unless students' expertise is harnessed they might not reach their full potential. Recovery Colleges need to ensure they are truly inclusive and reach out to the range of people who might benefit. If they can do this then peer support and Recovery Colleges may transform the narratives around mental health, not only in mental health services but in society more broadly.

ACKNOWLEDGEMENTS

With thanks to Louise Patmore, Lead Peer Trainer, Sussex Recovery College; Donal Hoban, Recovery College Director, County Mayo; and to the students whose anonymous quotes we have included.

FURTHER READING AND RESOURCES

Briefing paper exploring in more detail the defining features of Recovery Colleges, what a Recovery College is and is not, their effectiveness and development:
Perkins, R., Meddings, S. Williams, S. and Repper, J. (2018). *Recovery Colleges: Ten years on.* Nottingham: ImROC.

An introduction to Recovery Colleges with a focus on co-production:
Shepherd, G., McGregor, J., Meddings, S. and Roeg, W. (2017). Recovery Colleges and Co-production. In Slade, M., Oades, L. and Jarden, A. (eds), *Wellbeing, Recovery and Mental Health.* Cambridge: Cambridge University Press.

A key paper on the meaning of co-production and potential benefits for public services:
Boyle, D. and Harris, M. (2009). *The Challenge of Co-production: How Equal Partnerships between Professionals and the Public Are Crucial to Improving Public Services.* London: NESTA. http://b.3cdn. net/nefoundation/312ac8ce93a00d5973_3im6i6t0e.pdf

Videos about Recovery Colleges:
Cambridge: https://youtu.be/I6cV9DvTk_E
CNWL: https://youtu.be/JqzbXUtHX-g
Health Foundation: https://youtu.be/TqV0nFt_POM
Sussex: https://youtu.be/QFc_9nZNy_k

REFERENCES

Anfossi, A. (2017). *The Current State of Recovery Colleges: Final Report.* Nottingham: ImROC.
Barton, S. and Williams, R. (2015). *Evaluation of 'The Exchange' (Barnsley Recovery College).* Barnsley: South West Yorkshire Partnership Foundation Trust.
Bourne, P., Meddings, S. and Whittington, A. (2018). An evaluation of service use outcomes in a Recovery College. *Journal of Mental Health*, 27(4), 359–366.
Boyle, D. and Harris, M. (2009). *The Challenge of Co-production: How Equal Partnerships between Professionals and the Public Are Crucial to Improving Public Services.* London: NESTA.
Burhouse, A., Rowland, M., Niman, H. M., Abraham, D., Collins, E., Matthews, H., Denney, J. and Ryland, H. (2015). Coaching for recovery: a quality improvement project in mental healthcare. *BMJ Quality Improvement Reports*, 4(1). https://doi.org/10.1136/bmjquality.u206576.w2641
Department of Health (2001). *The Expert Patient: A New Approach to Chronic Disease Management for the 21st century.* London: Department of Health.
Dunn, E. A., Chow, J., Meddings, S. and Haycock, L. J. (2016). Barriers to attendance at Recovery Colleges. *Mental Health and Social Inclusion*, 20(4), 238–246.
Frayn, E., Duke, J., Smith, H., Wayne, P. and Roberts, G. (2016). A voyage of discovery: Setting up a Recovery College in a secure setting. *Mental Health and Social Inclusion*, 20, 29–35.
Gill, K. (2014). Recovery colleges, co-production in action: The value of lived experience in 'learning and growth for mental health'. *Health Issues*, 113, 10–14.

Hall, T., Brophy, L. and Jordan, H. (2016). A report on the early outcomes of the Mind Recovery College. University of Melbourne.

King, T. (2015). An Exploratory Study of Co-production in Recovery Colleges in the UK. MSc Dissertation in Mental Health, University of Brighton.

McGregor, J., Repper, J. and Brown, H. (2014). 'The college is so different from anything I have done'. A study of the characteristics of Nottingham Recovery College. *Journal of Mental Health Education Training and Practice*, 9, 3–15.

Meddings, S., Byrne, D., Barnicoat, S., Campbell, E. and Locks, L. (2014). Co-delivered and co-produced: Creating a Recovery College in partnership. *Journal of Mental Health Training, Education and Practice*, 9, 16–25.

Meddings, S., Campbell, E., Guglietti, S., Lambe, H., Locks, L., Byrne, D. and Whittington, A. (2015). From service user to student – the benefits of Recovery College. *Clinical Psychology Forum*, 268, 32–37.

Meddings, S., Guglietti, S., Lambe, H. and Byrne, D. (2014). Student perspectives: Recovery college experience. *Mental Health and Social Inclusion*, 18, 142–150.

Mid Essex Recovery College (2014). *Hope Health, Opportunity and Purpose for Everyone. Evaluation Report.* Chelmsford: North Essex Partnership University NHS Foundation Trust.

North Essex Research Network and South Essex Service User Research Group (2014). *Evaluation of the Mid Essex Recovery College October-December 2013.* Anglia Ruskin University. http://hdl.hand.lenet/10540/347125. [Accessed 10 February 2015].

Nurser, K., Hunt, D. and Bartlett, T. (2017). Do Recovery College courses help to improve recovery outcomes and reduce self-stigma for individuals who attend? *Clinical Psychology Forum*, 300, 32–37.

Perkins, R., Meddings, S., Williams, S. and Repper, J. (2018). *Recovery Colleges: Ten Years On.* Nottingham: ImROC.

Perkins, R., Repper, J., Rinaldi, M. and Brown, H. (2012). *Recovery Colleges*, ImROC, Briefing No. 1. Centre for Mental Health, London.

Perkins, A., Ridler, J., Hammond, L., Davis, S. and Hackmann, C. (2017). Impacts of attending Recovery Colleges on NHS staff. *Mental Health and Social Inclusion*, 21(1), 18–24.

Rennison, J., Skinner, S. and Bailey, A. (2014). *CNWL Recovery College Annual Report.* London: Central and North West London NHS Foundation.

Rinaldi, M. and Wybourn, S. (2011). *The Recovery College Pilot in Merton and Sutton: Longer Term Individual and Service Level Outcomes.* London: South West London and St George's Mental Health NHS Trust.

Shepherd, G. (2015). Possible mechanisms of change in Recovery Colleges: individual and organisational. Paper given to the Recovery Colleges International Community of Practice, London, Thurs 5 June.

Shepherd, G., Boardman, J. and Slade, M. (2008). *Making Recovery a Reality.* London: Sainsbury Centre for Mental Health.

Skinner, S. and Bailey (2015). *CNWL Recovery and Wellbeing College Annual Report.* London: Central and North West London NHS Foundation Trust.

Sommer, J. (2017). *South Eastern Sydney Recovery College Preliminary Evaluation Report. The First Three Years: July 2014–2017.* Sydney: South Eastern Sydney Recovery College.

Toney, R., Elton, D., Munday, E., Hamill, K., Crowther, A., Meddings, S., Taylor, A., Henderson, C., Jennings, H., Waring, J., Pollock, K., Bates, P. and Slade, M. (in press). Mechanisms of action and outcomes for students in Recovery Colleges, *Psychiatric Services.*

Zabel, E., Donegan, G., Lawrence, K. and French, P. (2016). Exploring the impact of the recovery academy: A qualitative study of Recovery College experiences. *Journal of Mental Health Training, Education and Practice*, 11(3), 162–171.

6

Peer Support, Intersectionality and Socially Excluded Communities

Eleanor Hope and Shazia Ali

Chapter Summary

- This chapter focuses on the experience of **socially excluded communities** which experience the poorest health outcomes. These communities are over-represented in mental health services and under-represented in formalised peer support

- Although peer support has long existed in marginalised communities, the concept of lived experience often fails to take into account the multiple different kinds of lived experience a person has, including the experiences of racism, sexism, heterosexism, oppression and discrimination and their intersection

- Barriers to peer support for socially excluded groups include a lack of transcultural understanding within the recovery approach and peer support, the lack of trust of mainstream mental health services, use of language and communication, stigma, and lack of funding

- Best practice in developing peer support with and for socially excluded communities involves first acknowledging and accepting their current and historical experience, recognising their involvement as central to peer support development as part of inclusionary practice, encouraging and supporting BME (Black and Minority Ethnic) and LGBT (lesbian, gay, bisexual and transgender) contribution to the development of peer support services, developing processes that support this and co-producing services which take into account a diverse range of needs and identities

Introduction

Peer support by many other names has long existed in community-led, self-help, grass-roots projects, often with little or no funding, taking the form of supporting people by listening to each other over a cup of tea. This type of support continues to the present day in communities across the UK and a similar, more formalised, model is being used in mental health services. Socially excluded communities are over-represented in mental health services and under-represented within formalised peer support. This suggests that a deeper understanding of inclusion is necessary within peer support. In this chapter we explore some of these inherent inequalities within the recovery and peer support approach and their impact on socially excluded communities. We reflect on the need for a recovery and peer support approach that benefits socially excluded communities, communities that have long benefited from self-help models.

The focus of this chapter is on peer support provision for people from communities who are seldom heard such as the BME (black and minority ethnic) and LGBT (lesbian, gay, bisexual and transgender). Such characteristics are protected in England, Wales and Scotland under the Equality Act 2010. We have largely emphasised racialised communities as this is where our own personal experiences of recovery as BME/LGBT activists lie, and it is these communities that experience the poorest health outcomes (Sewell, 2013).

This chapter begins by examining the current state of mental health services and the oppressive practices which disproportionately impact the lives of people from socially excluded communities. We consider the narrow focus of statutory services as well as the service user movement and the importance of understanding **intersectionality** before discussing the power of language in contributing to inclusive and exclusive practices. Finally, we explore the potential for peer support within socially excluded communities and provide some best practice guidelines to support a broader consideration of different communities in implementing peer support in mental health services.

Case Example: My Experiences of Peer Support

Shazia Ali

My journey into peer support started in 2012 after I was made redundant from a job I loved (teaching). Prior to this period my experiences of mental health services were wrapped in stigma and shame, two suicide attempts in my twenties and wellness for periods of time on and off medication. As a trauma survivor my support came mainly from friends. I began to become a more active campaigner for mental health causes when I was asked to do a piece of research on stigma in BME communities in the early 1990s as part of my role within local government. I first learned about peer support in 2008 because my partner was working in a mental health trust where peer support was being developed. I became involved in various BME user-led groups in 2009 and then became a member of a user-led organisation in 2012 where I began my peer support role in mental health hospital wards.

Living on the coast there is very little diversity, but nevertheless the community I live in is generally friendly and welcoming. While attending training with a group of people using services, I raised the issue of racism within the mental health system as well as within the benefits system, and another service user said, 'if you are not happy then go home'. It was upsetting but that had not been the first time I'd had that comment made to me. Since that time I have sat with many people using services (in my capacity as a peer support worker) who talked about foreigners taking jobs, housing and services. Sometimes they insist they don't mean me, and sometimes they look at me, as I am the only BME person in the room. I am the only BME peer support worker in both the user-led organisation and the mental health trust where I currently work.

For me, trauma lies on a continuum when you experience micro-aggression daily. We are defined as 'other' as people with mental health challenges which connects 'us' together, but I feel another layer of 'otherness' in terms of power and privilege of white-ness. Feeling that 'you don't belong here' reaffirms the power structures of not belonging.

I have felt first-hand institutional racism and discrimination in what I hoped would be a 'safe space' with people using services that I had commonalities with. This is a common experience of many black people with lived experience (Kalathil, 2011) and, more recently, the hostility towards Eastern Europeans since Brexit has felt as if it has legitimised racism and contributed to the rising of racial attacks. 'Eastern Europeans' and refugees are invisible groups within BME and LGBT and within mental health peer support provision.

From my background in user-led campaigning, I have taken on a more formal role as a 'Peer Support Specialist' within a Mental Health Foundation Trust. I have found ways to bring together the jarring of the medical and the recovery approach, and working with others I have tried to embed principles of peer support into a structure that supports 'what's strong' rather than 'what's wrong'.

Of course I have concerns around peer support being overtaken by professionals/services just as I am concerned that intersectionality can be inhabited by the dominant discourse. Learning and understanding of the values and principles of peer support into a way of working would benefit employees in a mental health trust setting. Culture change is difficult to shift if all employees, including clinicians, do not share the values and principles of peer support.

Background: Socially excluded identities in mental health services

People that experience emotional and mental distress can also belong to other socially excluded groups. In this chapter we focus specifically on the intersections of multiple identities such as race, ethnicity, class and/or sexuality *and* mental health. We argue that these add layers of complexities of privilege or disadvantage and are critical to understanding a person's needs, the challenges of accessing appropriate services, power imbalances, psychiatric labels and disempowerment.

We know approaches such as peer support save lives and save money, yet these need to be embedded within mental health systems that include a much clearer understanding of the social and cultural context than is currently on offer. An example is that, for several decades, BME communities have been subjected to heavy-handed and harsh treatment from mental health services relative to white British service users. A report by the National Institute for Mental Health in England, *Inside Outside: Improving Mental Health Services for Black and Minority Ethnic Communities in England*, acknowledged this and confirmed that the 'ethnicity agenda' within mental health services has tended to become either marginal-ised or ignored' (The National Institute for Mental Health in England, 2003, p. 5).

The research also recognised that the first step is to acknowledge the problems of mental health care that exist: 'We must begin by acknowledging the problems of mental health care as it is experienced by black and minority ethnic groups' (p. 7). It goes on to identify three clear issues of concern:

1. An over-emphasis on institutional and coercive models of care
2. Professional and organisational requirements are given priority over individual needs and rights
3. Institutional racism exists within mental health care.

This report highlighted ethnic inequalities embedded in mental health services which create an environment that is institutionally discriminatory. This approach has led to the over-representation of BME communities in mental health, members of which being more likely to be secluded, sectioned, restrained, and given severe diagnoses, higher dosages of medica-tion, with longer stays and more readmissions. This treatment which focuses on the medical model has led to misdiagnoses, mistreatment and even the loss of life while under the care of mental health services (Blofeld et al., 2003; Fitzpatrick et al., 2014). This has generated communities that fear mental health services (Sainsbury Centre for Mental Health, 2002). As a result members from these communities delay seeking support and are often intro-duced to mental health by way of the police service. Without a complete cultural change and acknowledgement of the problem, it is unlikely that members from these communities would be attracted to or benefit from peer support within a clinical setting.

LGBT groups are also socially excluded communities. Homosexuality was viewed as a mental disorder until it was declassified in 1973 from the Diagnostic and Statistical Manual (DSM) by the American Psychiatric Association, with the UK and the World Health Organization following in 1992. It has taken LGBT communities decades to challenge the discrimination associated with this identity. Sexual orientation is a risk factor as a conse-quence of long-held societal beliefs that still impact on members from these communities (Public Health Matters, 2017). A UK study in 2015 found that LGBT youths seriously contem-plate suicide at almost three times the rate of heterosexual youths and are almost five times as likely to have attempted suicide (PACE, 2015).

In England the move towards more personalised care as set out in the 'Think Local Act Personal' project recognised the need for co-production of services with communities and the role of Asset Based Community Development that focuses on the strengths rather than the deficits of a community. This initiative understood that strong inclusive commu-nities are the next stage of personalisation and acknowledged that the universalised care approach provided for the average citizen had inadvertently marginalised people with addi-tional needs leading to an imperative to change systems, processes, practices and cultures (Public Health England, 2014).

Finally, research on health inequalities shows that health, and access to good health-care, is impacted by wider factors such as where we live, the work we do, the education we receive as well as our age, sex, race and sexuality. There are deep levels of health inequalities for poor, working-class and other socially excluded communities. These communities are more likely to need appropriate health interventions including peer support, but less likely to receive them (Marmot & Bell, 2012).

Peer support in these communities could play a vital role in offering people a sense of safety and support through shared experiences. For this to happen there needs to be investment of resources to truly co-produce services that understand the impact of living in hostile and non-inclusive environments on the health and well-being of marginalised communities. In this chapter we identify and recommend good practice for working towards this goal.

Understanding intersectionality

First introduced to respond to the invisibility of black women within gender and 'race' discourses, intersectionality recognises that we live with multiple identities that are complex and interwoven and not separate; that these combinations impact on people who are most marginalised in society. 'Because of their intersectional identity as both women *and* people of color within discourses that are shaped to respond to one *or* the other, the interests and experiences of women of color are frequently marginalised within both' (Crenshaw, 1989, p. 139).

Intersectionality emphasises the importance of recognising, validating and accepting each aspect of an individual's identity and their intersection. It is a framework for understanding health disparities for people from historically oppressed groups and how multiple social identities such as 'race', sexual orientation and disability intersect at the level of individual experience to reflect interlocking systems of privilege and oppression such as racism and heterosexism at the social-structural level (Bowleg, 2012).

While we use these broad terms such as BME and LGBT and refer to them as marginalised and socially excluded, intersectionality reminds us that there are differences and privileges within these two communities of race, gender, class, disability, religion and immigration statuses that need to be recognised and acknowledged. The experience of a lesbian woman using mental health services who has white, able-bodied and middle-class privilege is different from that of a black lesbian woman who is working class or a white gay man with a disability. We cannot fully understand these identities on their own, but rather need to see how they intersect.

Exercise

Think about your own identity including your race/ethnicity, gender, class and sexuality. Take a sheet of paper and make a list of all your identities that you can think of. Which ones do you use to define yourself by? Which ones are most important to you? Are any of these identities invisible and not addressed when accessing services?

This idea of intersectionality is hugely relevant to the service user/survivor movement. The US survivor movement was informed by an acknowledgement of these multiple identities within civil rights and human rights movements while the UK's service user/survivor movement developed out of the disability rights movement. Although these movements emerged out of these diverse communities, nevertheless they focused on having one singular message: uniting under one shared service user/survivor identity. Other complex identities such as ethnicity and mental health were ignored and denied a voice.

Black and Asian minority communities' experiences of racism in many guises permeate the psychiatric experience. 'The fact that they are less represented in the service user/survivor movement implies that philosophy of empowerment in some aspects may have been constructed in line with dominant white values, and many black users may prefer alternative routes to having their voices heard' (Fernando, 1995, p. 89).

In more recent times other views suggest that 'the main call to "generalise" involvement is from statutory bodies and mainstream non user-led voluntary sector rather than from service users themselves' (Kalathil, 2011, p. 16).

Exercise

Revisit the list you have made of your different identities. How do each of these identities oppress or privilege you? Does society's approval or disapproval cause you to behave in any way? From these exercises you will recognise how identities are rich and complex but are also intertwined with societal judgement that if disapproved of can impact on an individual's or a community's mental well-being.

Peer support and the importance of belonging

It is essential that socially excluded communities are represented in the history of peer support and well-being in the UK. Peer support services at their best are empathetic and rooted in shared cultures and identities. The value of peer support is in the process of feeling validated, and sharing with others that have similar experiences and identities. During this process we discover that recovery is possible.

> *Having someone who understands you, where you come from and recognise the stigma we face in our own communities is most powerful connection. For me receiving peer support from another black person demonstrated that they understand the triple edged stigma and discrimination faced "within" community, and within the services, we cried and laughed together. Sometimes what is needed is to have a peer support worker inspire hope and is someone "who is just like me".*
> (BME peer support student)

Belonging to one or more marginalised groups fundamentally alters a person's identity, and colours their experiences of distress and recovery. Lived experience describes not only mental distress or service use, but also the experience of oppression, stigma and barriers to health opportunities, access to learning, community integration and accessing safe appropriate care services.

Mind released a strategy which included the objective that 'Everyone in England and Wales with mental health problems can access peer support by 2016' (Faulkner, 2013, p. 5). The report highlighted that peer support in socially excluded communities 'may be one of the key gaps in the provision of mental health peer support across the country' (p. 28).

The absence of marginalised issues was also identified by Together, identifying that a shared experience or context of mental distress is often not enough to address the specific needs and concerns arising from experiences of marginalisation (Faulkner & Kalathil, 2012). The report explored the diversity in which peer support takes place and included a survey of people from peer support and voluntary sector projects. More than half of the respondents said that peers should be people who shared characteristics, experiences or communities. These include gender, ethnic background, sexual orientation, age groups and religion or faith. Sixty-six per cent of respondents from BME communities felt that a shared ethnic and cultural background would be important in a peer.

Informal peer support is commonplace in communities where appropriate services are not available. BME and LGBT communities informally support each other in groups and in one-to-one settings using peer support principles, such as listening, validating and supporting each other. In this environment peer support offers opportunities for shared multiple identities and stories to be valued, embracing all parts of the authentic self. Embracing a person's whole identity should be the essence of peer support, rather than reducing them to their experiences of distress. 'There is a need for a more sophisticated understanding of the nature of peer support where it concerns people with experiences of marginalisation' (Faulkner & Kalathil, 2012, p. 46).

BME and/or LGBT communities have in the past provided support for each other, as we understood what it was like to feel multiple oppressions. I (Shazia) remember the 1980s when I opened up about feeling suicidal it was within a black women's health group. Though mental distress was not on the agenda, as there was no understanding then of the connection between physical and mental distress, I was able to disclose in the safety of other black women. I was listened to and received empathy. This enabled other women to open up about their depression, anxiety and the stigma faced within our own families. Mental health was no longer just about my lived experience; other members of the group began to share their stories. Later, I was able to join other black survivor movements. This was at a time when 'race' and class were fragmenting the women's liberation movement and the emergence of grassroots black women's groups were growing.

The stigma and structural discrimination faced by some communities may present difficulties in an individual's journey to become a peer support worker. BME and LGBT communities are wary of bureaucratic structurally discriminatory mental health services, where building a trusting relationship is challenging. Because of this, employing BME or LGBT people into formalised peer support roles might be difficult. Yet people from marginalised communities would benefit from peer support services.

The Together research emphasised the need for initiatives that are member-led, and arising from a community's interests and needs. Again 'organisational take-over' was a key concern when peer support was placed within professional or non–user-led organisations.

Exercise

Think of a mental health team you are aware of. Does it employ BME and LGBT peer support workers? What might help to embed them into mental health teams?

Barriers to peer support

In order for all communities to benefit from peer support and recovery, there needs to be a cultural shift, in terms of both the way organisations offer a recovery-focused environment and the way that they actively include all communities in service planning and provision. We have now looked at a range of research and policies that have identified the need for cultural change. It is clear from these reports that knowledge and awareness of these issues are growing; however, what appears to be lacking is the will, commitment and resources to make fundamental changes. Without a transcultural approach that sets the foundation of equality, diversity and inclusion expressed in meaningful co-production with all communities, barriers to being included in the recovery movement representing an inclusive bottom-up approach will remain. People from socially excluded communities are recognised as having additional needs that have not been taken into account within current conceptualisations of recovery. Several barriers to peer support have already been discussed including prejudice, xenophobia, institutional racism, intersectionality and the marginalisation of users' voices within clinical settings. Further barriers to peer support are discussed in the sections that follow.

Language and communication

Words have the power to hurt or to inspire, and can affirm a group as valuable contributors to society or as marginalised – defined as living on the fringes of society, powerless, without influence, and not worthy of empathy. The language choices we make express our culture, communicate our belief systems and values, and can create solidarity or drive discord. Thus understanding the language and the way we communicate in relation to socially excluded groups is critical in creating a safe environment that is hopeful, easily accessible and where people feel valued.

Language also has the power to define communities, and expresses whether they are valued or not. The universal 'one-size-fits-all' approach to services promotes a hierarchy based on class, race, sexuality and gender, and is evident when socially excluded communities are defined as 'disadvantaged', 'deprived', 'hard to reach' or depicted as 'scroungers' when relying on benefits. These labels/stereotypes are damaging, offensive and represent a political world view that is bereft of empathy for any group at the lower end of the hierarchy.

Shaped and compounded by systemic, structural inequalities, marginalisation within society, in mental health, and within the service user movement, impacts on how marginalised groups access peer support. Being labelled 'hard to reach' embeds the belief that there is a problem with these communities, rather than with organisations that need to review and address whether their services are appropriate and accessible. 'Hard to reach' removes responsibility from organisations, holding the communities responsible for being 'hard to reach'. The perception fuels on both sides mutual distrust arising from institutional discrimination (Kalathil, 2011, p. 19).

Groups seen as 'hard to reach' are less likely to be involved in consultation, planning and developing projects. Lack of involvement in the development of new projects makes it less likely that these groups will get involved at a later stage.

Replacing the term 'hard to reach' with 'socially excluded' may be more accurate, although the struggle continues to find words that are inclusive of BME and LGBT groups/ communities while honouring and respecting differences. Peer support is based on the assumption of strength and so language that focuses on the strengths of the community is needed.

Invisibility

Mind (Faulkner, 2013) and Together (Faulkner & Kalathil, 2012) reported that there was a lack of BME and/or LGBT peer support workers nationally and identified marginalised communities as being a potential gap in current peer support provisions. Unless research is specific to these communities, they are often excluded, or are included but in a tokenistic way. The processes that exclude them are not interrogated to consider why this happens – for example, which organisations are chosen to receive funding, who sets the criteria and time frame for the research, and how the researchers are chosen. DiAngelo (2018) suggests that invisibility is a form of misinformation as it denies the marginalised group's experiences and history, and its interests, needs and perspectives are minimised or absent. By not creating an environment that opens the process to ensure equal access, it becomes acceptable to exclude and then to mistreat.

Lack of funding/resources

There is very little investment in developing the infrastructure to support the development of BME community projects (The Sainsbury Centre for Mental Health, 2002). Although there is a small amount of funding for LGBT groups, there are still inconsistencies within. For example, black, lesbian/trans groups are seen as less valuable by the dominant group, and lack of funding is justified.

Lack of trust

Lack of trust is the inevitable conclusion for, 'As long as Black people are not engaged in defining the service agenda or at least are able to influence this process, they cannot be expected to trust mainstream services and engage with them' (The Sainsbury Centre for Mental Health, 2002, p. 68).

Stigma/poverty

Stigma and discrimination associated with mental health are particularly exacerbated in working-class communities due to poverty, lack of appropriate housing, education, and a lack of quality healthcare and further suffering. Shame and guilt of poverty, without choice and opportunities, contribute to stress and emotional and mental distress.

Culturally insensitive approaches to support

Western approaches to mental health are assumed to be universal and often unhelpfully applied to other cultures. These beliefs prevent or block having open dialogues, asking questions and learning how to work with people from different cultures.

Meeting 'someone like me' who can share experience of discrimination and oppression is fundamental to mutuality. Having a BME- and LGBT-specific service in the community can create safe spaces for us to share with others that can validate and empower each other.

Exercise

Are there aspects of yourself that you do not feel safe to share? What would help you to feel safe to share these parts of yourself? What could you do to help others feel safe to share their authentic self?

Case Example: Implementing Culturally Competent Peer Support: My Experiences

Eleanor

My background is in community development and, through taking redundancy in 2002, I became distressed to the point that it was difficult to get out the house. I detail this experience in Sewell (2013).

As the coordinator of a voluntary organisation, we delivered a project to gather information from BME users about their mental health experiences for an NHS Trust. We had full autonomy in putting together the project, and interviewed 15 people. There were a few key themes: first, not being allowed to tell their story, being told staff were too busy. Second, the perception that everything revolved around diagnoses and the use of medication, specifically high and severe medications and dosages. A third theme was lack of cultural awareness on the part of staff which would quickly escalate an issue that led to coercive treatment of restraint or being physically held down to be injected with a needle. There was a general anger, distress and distrust in most of the interviews.

This experience in 2008 reported by BME interviewees was shocking and surprising given the then recent Independent Inquiry into the death of David Bennett, a young African-Caribbean man who died as a result of restraint in a medium secure psychiatric unit. The Inquiry called for mandatory cultural competence training for all staff and a maximum of three minutes' restraint in the prone position as well as the development of a black and minority ethnic mental health strategy.

I was able to use the experiences of community development and emotional distress to work in an NHS mental health service with BME communities. This role contributed to bridging the gap between mental health services and BME communities by supporting the development of groups, and delivering training in well-being to communities and recovery and equality to NHS staff. Although I found the work exhilarating, exciting and hopeful, I noticed that working with socially excluded groups has a profound impact on workers who work with these communities and who are themselves marginalised.

Being able to apply and go through the first cohort of peer support training in East Sussex, I felt empowered by the US Recovery Innovation training, as one of the main tenets identified 'love' as the key to accessing recovery pathways. This clarified to me that empathy is the necessary component to recovery and well-being in which self-love and self-discovery is a pathway to recovery, well-being and equality and a way in which people who use mental health services are able to take their power back and redefine who they are.

I went on to become an accredited facilitator to deliver the peer support training, and have gone on to train over 100 peers in peer support. Based on this approach, I designed a BME Peer Support training focused on the Recovery Innovations definition of recovery as 'remembering who you are and using all your strengths to become all that you were meant to be'.

Best practice guidelines and examples

Independent BME/LGBT user-led peer support community intervention projects need to be funded and supported by community development to develop long-term sustainability. In the additional reading at the end of this chapter are some examples of successful community services.

The recovery-focused environment is essential in peer support and has to be central to any peer support service. BME/LGBT users of mental health services need to be involved in the development of intersectional peer support frameworks that prioritise the needs of BME and LGBT communities – to place intersectionality at the heart of co-design; to ensure co-production throughout every facet of peer support projects, from the development of the project to working together to create job descriptions; to identify good practice; and to develop policies and processes to support and retain new staff.

Where peer support services and peer support roles are advertised, inclusive principles need to be adhered to. Peer support roles should be advertised within BME/LGBT communities and adverts should consider the language used to reduce further barriers to BME/LGBT people applying.

Below are best practice approaches that we have developed through our work in introducing peer support in a way that is meaningful to BME and other developing communities:

Get to know and value BME/LGBT communities

- To harness the potential for peer support in socially excluded communities these communities must first be understood, valued and respected for their contribution. Making contact with peer-led groups, and proactively researching and reaching out to develop relationships with excluded communities, is vital.
- Develop relationships with communities including refugees, LGBT, BME, service user-led groups and be inclusive of the experience of many different stories of recovery and intersectionality.

Promote the value of BME/LGBT communities

- Promote the role and value of peer support to commissioning groups, highlighting the importance of funding a wide range of models of peer support, including those that are peer-led within BME and other communities
- Communicate an understanding that 'lived experience' is not a single identity in order to develop strategies that appreciate the impact of multiple oppressions on recovery, self-discovery and well-being
- Include BME/LGBT members in co-production and co-facilitation of training courses and service development.

Develop peer support that is sensitive/specific to BME/LGBT communities

- Peer-led community groups/hubs to prioritise the needs of BME and LGBT communities and offer spaces to work on well-being using specific cultural understandings. This can act as a preventative measure for people and offer safe community spaces to explore experiences
- Commission peer support services from a variety of providers (rather than the same group/s that are not reaching these communities) with a range of approaches, including organisations offering or developing peer support within BME, LGBT and other communities as well as organisations that have an understanding of an intersectional framework and encourage the embracing of intersectional identities
- BME/LGBT peer support workers need to be employed within services and Recovery Colleges
- Recruitment criteria of peer support workers need to take into account a broadness of 'lived experience' to understand the interrelating of oppressions and its impact on the individual.

Seek out ways to 'even the playing field' for BME/LGBT peer workers

- Develop a peer support equalities framework with peers to select, recruit and retain people from BME/LGBT communities
- Ensure BME/LGBT people have access to peer support training to enable them to become peer workers. This includes promoting peer support to BME/LGBT people within services and supporting them to take up opportunities
- Training for staff within services is needed to demonstrate how protected characteristics of gender, race, class, ability and sexuality intersect with mental health and how they impact on quality of care
- Mental health sectors and community groups should reassess whether their policies and strategies are anti-oppressive, going beyond recognising differences to understanding the multiple stigmas faced by people with intersectional lived experiences
- Different levels of training should be developed by and for BME and LGBT people
- Access to learning needs to consider safe spaces for individuals and/or groups through trust agreements and setting clear ground rules.

Exercise

How can you be an ally? Looking at the best practice set out above, how can you support the development of peer support in/for socially excluded communities?

CONCLUSIONS

BME/LGBT communities are over-represented in mental health services yet are under-represented in peer support services. Peer support is based on mutuality, inclusivity, empathy and listening, and these values could support these communities whose experiences have been largely based on a coercive medical model of care.

There needs to be greater awareness of how protected characteristics of gender, 'race', class, ability and sexuality as well as socioeconomic status intersect with mental health and how they impact on quality of care and health outcomes. The language used to describe these communities needs to stop shifting the problem onto these communities as dysfunctional and move to mental health reform.

Inequalities in health have dramatic implications, especially for people from socially excluded communities, yet there is very little recognition of the problem. An appropriate service based on individual need has not yet materialised for BME/LGBT communities. Groups supporting each other in these communities are invisible to local services and commissioners, as peer support does happen on an informal basis without support and funding.

A review of current peer support practices in collaboration with socially excluded communities would ensure that it is relevant and accessible to a wider range of groups. Practices need to reflect the needs and cultures of the people peer support is being offered to, so that it is inclusive and not a barrier. Organisations need to positively recruit peer support trainers and workers from diverse backgrounds.

While work has been done in recent years to implement peer support within mental health services, there is still some way to go before this peer support reflects the diversity of the communities it offers support to. This work needs to start with a more nuanced understanding of identity, culture and language.

In order for peer support to be accessible to everyone, barriers need to be acknowledged and removed; and new ways of work based on valuing and respecting the communities' knowledge should be developed. This needs to begin with the recognition that these groups are not hard to reach, but are reached through different approaches. Making peer support accessible will enable BME and LGBT communities to develop trust and work more closely with a range of mental health services.

A community development approach tailored to the needs of socially excluded communities requires co-production, co-design and co-delivery of peer support approaches. Peer support in marginalised communities is a powerful means of offering hope and connection to people who feel alienated, isolated, lonely and forgotten by mainstream services. Culturally competent peer support takes into account the different facets of a person's identity, including race and sexuality, as well as their lived experience of emotional distress.

FURTHER READING AND RESOURCES

Kindred Minds – a unique user-led group for people from BME communities living in and around the borough of Southwark:

- http://www.together-uk.org/southwark-wellbeing-hub/the-directory/9191/kindred-minds/

Canerows – a peer support group based at Sound Minds for people from BME backgrounds:

- http://www.canerows.co.uk/

MindOut – a mental health service run by and for lesbians, gay men, bisexual, trans and queer people. They offer a number of services including counselling, advocacy and peer support:

• https://www.mindout.org.uk/

Kimberlé Crenshaw's TED Talk, 'The Urgency of Intersectionality':

• https://www.ted.com/talks/kimberle_crenshaw_the_urgency_of_intersectionality

REFERENCES

Blofeld, J., Sallah, D., Sashidharan, S., Stone, R. and Struthers, J. (2003). *Independent Inquiry into the Death of David Bennett.* Cambridge: Norfolk, Suffolk and Cambridgeshire Strategic Health Authority.

Bowleg, L. (2012). The problem with the phrase women and minorities: Intersectionality – An important theoretical framework for public health. *American Journal of Public Health,* 102(7), 1267–1273.

Crenshaw, K. (1989). *Demarginalizing the Intersection of Race and Sex: A Black Feminist Critique of Anti-discrimination Doctrine, Feminist Theory and Antiracist Politics.* Chicago: University of Chicago Legal Forum.

DiAngelo, R. (2018). *White Fragility: Why It's So Hard for White People to Talk about Racism.* Boston, MA: Beacon Press

Faulkner, A. (2013). *Mental Health Peer Support in England: Piecing Together the Jigsaw.* London: MIND.

Faulkner, A. (2014). *Ethnic inequalities in mental health: Promoting lasting positive change: A consultation with black and minority ethnic mental health service users.* London: National Service User Network (NSUN).

Faulkner, A. and Kalathil, J. (2012). *The Freedom to Be, the Chance to Dream: Preserving User-Led Peer Support in Mental Health.* London: Together for Mental Wellbeing.

Fernando, S. (1995). *Mental Health in a Multiethnic Society.* London: Routledge.

Fitzpatrick, R., Kumar, S., Nkansa-Dwamena, O. and Thorne, L. (2014). *Ethnic Inequalities in Mental Health: Promoting Lasting Positive Change.* LankellyChase Foundation, Mind, The Afiya Trust, and Centre for Mental Health. https://lankellychase.org.uk/wp-content/uploads/2015/07/Ethnic-Inequality-in-Mental-Health-Confluence-Full-Report-March2014.pdf [Accessed 23 October 2018].

Kalathil, J. (2011). *Dancing to Our Own Tunes: Reassessing Black and Minority Ethnic Mental Health Service User Involvement.* London: National Survivor User Network and Catch-a-Fiya. [Accessed 20 March 2018].

Marmot, M. and Bell, R. (2012). Fair society, healthy lives. *Public Health,* 126, S4–S10.

The National Institute for Mental Health in England (2003). *Inside Outside: Improving Mental Health Services for Black and Minority Ethnic Communities in England.* Leeds: Department of Health.

PACE (Project for Advocacy Counselling and Education). (2015). *The RaRE Research Report: LGB&T Mental Health – Risk and Resilience Explored.* London: PACE.

Public Health England (2014). *Think Local, Act Personal: Developing the power of strong, Inclusive Communities.* https://www.thinklocalactpersonal.org.uk/_assets/Resources/BCC/Report/TLAP_Developing_the_Power_Brochure_FINAL.pdf [Accessed 1 August 2018].

Public Health Matters (2017). Mental health challenges in the wider community, Public Health Matters (blog): https://publichealthmatters.blog.gov.uk/2017/07/06/mental-health-challenges-within-the-lgbt-community/ [Accessed 5 July 2017].

Sainsbury Centre for Mental Health (2002). *Breaking the Circles of Fear: A Review of the Relationship between Mental Health Services and African and Caribbean Communities.* London: SCMH.

Sewell, H. (2013). *The Equality Act 2010 in Mental Health: A Guide to Implementation and Issues for Practice.* London: Jessica Kingsley Publishers.

7 | Peer Support for Family and Friends: Carers Supporting Each Other

Karen Machin, Sara Meddings and Jacqueline Clarke-Mapp

Chapter Summary

- In this chapter, **'carer'** refers to the informal support network of family, friends and neighbours. While the term 'carer' is used in policy and to access support, it is not unproblematic. This language, as well as the language of peer support in this context, is explored in this chapter and highlighted as one of the fundamental barriers to carers' support

- Support for carers is relatively new and carer peer support worker roles are newer. Carers' own needs are considered alongside the development of support groups and carers' peer support

- There is recent policy to support carers – including carers' own recovery

- Challenges and barriers for peer support include the invisible nature of emotional support compared with physical care, and encouraging and enabling carers to consider their own support needs

- Carers have historically sought help from each other and this suggests an appropriate use of peer support

- This chapter includes sections from carers who are involved in specific initiatives as well as the anonymous voices of carers who are part of support groups

Introduction

This chapter explores carers supporting other carers to progress their own recovery. It raises the question 'who is a peer?', with specific emphasis on including family and friends as peers.

It includes reflections on the development of peer support from carers support groups through to paid peer support roles. Other roles for carers, such as peer trainers, are mentioned to illustrate a range of involvement opportunities, although these do not offer the full mutuality and reciprocity of peer support.

Language

The word 'carer'

Although 'carer' is the official term used in UK services and policies for people who support their family and friends, the term itself can lead to confusion. Colloquially, in the media, and in some official documents, 'carer' is also used to describe the paid care workers who provide vital support in the community for people who need additional help with daily tasks, including personal care. Carers' organisations, such as Carers UK and the Carers Trust, emphasise the difference between these paid workers and the family and friends who provide informal and unpaid support for their relative or friend. The government fact sheet for the Care Act (2014) defines a 'carer' as:

> someone who helps another person, usually a relative or friend, in their day-to-day life. This is not the same as someone who provides care professionally or through a voluntary organisation. (Department of Health, 2016)

There are mixed opinions about the term from both carers themselves and the people they support. It can infer a one-way relationship with one person giving care to the other, ignoring emotional, financial or social reciprocity. Both emotional distress and the associated caring role can feel invisible and hidden, adding another barrier to identifying carers, for the family themselves as well as for support services. Physical or personal care can be more readily witnessed than the emotional care and support for people experiencing distress. Additionally, young people may not recognise their own role as carers; parents may be reluctant to identify a young person as their only source of support; some languages do not have a direct translation of the word or concept of the role (Carers, 2011).

There are challenges associated with the residential and legal aspects of some mental health support. Family and friends of people in long-term care such as forensic (secure) mental health services may regard themselves as visitors rather than carers (Ridley et al., 2014), reinforced by some definitions which imply that carers must live with the person they support. Staff may be familiar with communicating with the nearest relative under mental health legislation, but this person is not always the primary carer.

However, while the word itself may involve these challenges, in the UK it is an identity that gives access to a range of carers services including carers centres, carers assessments and financial support such as carers allowance. If people do not identify, or are not identified, as carers they can be excluded from this vital support.

This chapter refers to the support network of family and friends who are not paid to be there, but may be available 24/7, may have complex emotional ties with the person and may have known the person for a length of time often preceding the onset of distress. Where we use the word 'carer' we mean this network of informal support around the person. We understand 'family' in its broadest sense to include friends, allies and relatives. We acknowledge that, for some people, these relationships may be non-existent or negative, and may include a history of trauma.

Exercise

In your own life in what ways have you provided informal support for a friend or relative? How might you use this experiential knowledge to identify and support carers in your work?

Who is a peer?

The word 'peer' also creates challenges in the context of family, friends and carers. Carers' own needs are, on the whole, not included in the traditional peer support literature. With descriptions such as 'peer leaders' and 'peer trainers' alongside 'peer supporters', we need to ensure that the term 'peer' does not become used as an alternative to 'service user'. We need to ask the question 'peer to whom?'.

Key aspects of peer support are mutuality and reciprocity: people being in a similar position and being able to both offer and benefit from their relationship as discussed in Chapter 2. There is debate about what the 'similar position' may be, about a specific diagnosis or about cultural or other life situations (Faulkner & Kalathil, 2012). For carers, a further complexity is whether the peer relationship stems from the attributes of the person the carer supports, or from the carer's position or relationship with the person they support.

Different carers have a range of relationships with the people they support (parent, sibling, friend, neighbour). The people they support have many different diagnoses, and have used various services and for different lengths of time. It may be helpful that a carer peer is further along in their own recovery journey, but the people they support may be in a similar place. Spouses of people who have had a short period of crisis may feel they have little in common with parents caring for a son who has been using services for decades. People whose relative is in forensic services, potentially with the added discrimination or emphasis on confidentiality around speaking about index offences, may feel little in common with someone whose relative is in a mother and baby unit or uses community services.

Carers organisations acknowledge some of these differences by offering services which specify qualities of the carer such as age or relationship: groups for young carers, young adult carers, sibling carers, parent carers. Additionally, some organisations which provide support with specific issues, such as substance use or child sexual exploitation, also provide support for family members. Within each of these services, families will bring a range of backgrounds, relationships and experiences, including adoption, abuse and ethnicity. The Mental Health Foundation peer mentoring for mental health carers project found that carers they supported preferred to work with another carer in the same relational position and that this was at least as important as experience of caring for someone with a similar condition (Gallagher, 2016). However, carers of people in forensic mental health services can feel isolated from generic carers services, and prefer to speak to someone with similar service use (Ridley et al., 2014).

Carers have their own mental health needs which may bring them to need mental health services themselves. Carers (2017) report that 78 per cent of carers feel more stressed because of their caring role. Despite these stresses, 40 per cent of carers hadn't had a day off from caring for more than a year, and 25 per cent for more than five years. Conversely, many people who are seen primarily as service users may have a long, and often hidden, history of caring for a family member, including experience as young carers. These dual roles and perspectives further complicate the issue of carers peer support: are carers primarily supporting each other about how best to support their family member or about their own personal mental well-being and recovery? A carer might find a sense of connection and gain support from other carers in how to support her relative, ideas to help him with his experiences of distress and how to navigate the mental health system; and it is hoped that she also receives mutual support to think about her own needs and the impact of a caring role on her own choices.

These complexities need to be acknowledged in the literature on peer support.

Exercise

If you were to set up a carers peer support service in your local area, how would you define 'peer' in the context of 'carers'? Are there any boundaries about who you want to include in your service?

Carers' needs

Carers can be seen as very separate from service users: as two separate groups of people with different, and conflicting, agendas. This may fit with services needing to specify different beneficiaries or stakeholders, and can be reinforced by theories that place distress in the context of family history. The emphasis on 'carer burden' in the literature (Flyckt et al., 2015) does not support building positive relationships when viewed from the perspective of the person who needs that support and questions whether they are seen as a burden. Points of crisis where people naturally criticise those closest to them also cause staff to be suspicious of family relationships and concerned about confidentiality.

Conversely, there are times when 'service users and carers' are seen as one group, as if they have identical agendas. This can lead to prioritising the more urgent service user needs, something that carers often recognise and support, anticipating that with full care for their relative they will be able to take a break for themselves. However, this can mean there is not time or resources to consider carers' own needs.

The majority of families do share hopes for the future, including staying together or supporting each other to become more independent. We need to recognise *both* that people who use services and their relatives and carers are different individuals with their own needs and opinions, *and* that they care about one another and often have the same overall hopes for life and recovery. Relationships tend to be reciprocal. Families report that their relatives with serious mental health problems provide companionship, news about family and friends, listen to problems and give advice (Greenberg et al., 1994); they give practical and emotional support and enhance personal and familial development (Coldwell et al., 2011). Families who see positives in their situation use more social support, make sense of their experiences and are better able to cope (Stern et al., 1999).

Many carers do talk about these positive impacts that come from being involved in supporting a family member. At the same time, most carers also find that there are financial, social and emotional consequences of the role. The annual surveys of carers from Carers UK invariably describe long-term stresses, including the impact on emotional and physical well-being. However, carers often emphasise their concerns about the person they support, especially around discharge from services and potential reliance on the family for continued monitoring and support. This common theme, of carers prioritising support for their relative with disregard for their own well-being, is a challenge when considering carers support.

Carers need emotional support including someone to talk to, practical help including financial support, information including leaflets and signposting, and support to take a break (Gregory et al., 2006). In this, they are no different from any other person experiencing distress. Family members and carers may go through a process of their own personal discovery or recovery alongside those they care about – to accept and come to terms with what has happened; regain confidence and control in their life; and move on in their own lives towards their own aspirations (Machin & Repper, 2013).

UK legislation and policy

Government policy initiatives suggest families and carers are a priority. In England carers were first mentioned in legislation in The Carers (Recognition and Services) Act 1995 (Department of Health, 1996) which established carers' rights to an assessment and required local authorities to provide services for carers who provide regular and substantial care. The Carers and Disabled Children Act 2000 recognised that carers could have their own assessment even if the person they supported did not want to be assessed, and the Carers (Equal Opportunities) Act 2004 created a duty to inform carers of their right to an assessment that considers the carer's wish or need for employment, training and respite.

Current legislation includes The Care Act (2014) and the Children and Families Act (2014) in England; Carers (Scotland) Act (2016); Social Services and Wellbeing (Wales) Act (2014); and Carers and Direct Payments Act (Northern Ireland) (2002). All make similar statements about carers' rights to assessment, but they differ about the duties of authorities to respond to those assessments. Additionally, the Equalities Act (2010) in England, Scotland and Wales offers legal anti-discrimination rights to carers.

The contribution that families make in caring for their relatives has been formally recognised in various policies specifically for carers and also in mental health policy. For example, the National Service Framework for Mental Health (NSF) (Department of Health, 1999b) recognised the impact that caring for someone with a mental health problem can have on carers' own physical and mental health and the right to access services in their own right. However, the Five Years On review of the NSF reported that 'we have too little to report on improving the support we provide to carers' (Appleby, 2004, p. 74).

The **Triangle of Care** (Worthington and Rooney, 2010) was an attempt led by carers to improve the culture of mental health services towards carers. It has been adopted by the majority of mental health services in England, as well as being included in guidance documents. It encourages organisations to meet six key standards for carer engagement:

- Carers and the essential role they play are identified at first contact or as soon as possible thereafter
- Staff are 'carer aware' and trained in carer engagement strategies
- Policy and practice protocols with regard to confidentiality and sharing information are in place
- Defined post(s) responsible for carers are in place
- A carer introduction to the service and staff is available, with a relevant range of information across the care pathway
- A range of carer support services is available.

There is no guidance around provision of carers support groups or carers peer support workers. Guidance on involvement and participation may mention carers as an afterthought – '... and carers' – and guidance on peer support does not explicitly include carers as providing or receiving that support.

Exercise

Carers may be recognised in legislation and policy, but families frequently take many years to acknowledge that their caring role goes beyond that of a typical family relationship, and that they could therefore benefit from additional support themselves. What steps could you take to encourage early identification of carers?

Carers Support Groups

Attending carers support groups gave me the strength to carry on. I remember sharing problems with others and feeling quite humbled by their stories ... I was so full of admiration at how they coped and their tenacity in day-to-day life. This may sound like we met up for a good old moan, but it was not that at all. It was a group of desperate individuals trying to make sense of, and cope with, the extremes that mental health issues can throw on those around them ... As a consequence I would often leave feeling a little stronger and more able to face the day with a self-determination: 'If they can manage with all their difficulties ... then so can I.' While other times the group was an understanding ear, a handshake of compassion, a hug of encouragement, a shoulder to cry on and a kind, sympathetic voice. The feelings of isolation and helplessness were slowly being worn away: I was now being listened to and, more importantly, supported. So, surprisingly, I found myself looking forward to the next monthly meetings ... and oh what a lifetime of a struggle and an achievement that was to make, but make it I did ...

*You may now think that I initially went willingly to these 'tea and sympathy' groups: but this was not the case. I was one of those frightened, bewildered and exhausted carers that saw little value in meeting others: After all, what purpose would this serve? How was it going to improve, or change, my personal circumstances? My life was already chaotic and problematic enough, without having to find the **time**, **space** and **ultimately** the **courage** to attend one of these group sessions. How was I going to attend? ... I mean who would be looking after the 'service user' (cared for person) while I went out? In truth I was frozen by fear and responsibility.* (Carer)

Carers support groups are where carers' peer support has its foundation: carers supporting each other, either by themselves or with the resources and support of an organisation. There is no standard format for these self-help groups, with some providing refreshments and a sympathetic shoulder while others are more political, including supporting carer representation on boards and steering groups. There is no specific network of these informal groups, although some are linked together through affiliations to national umbrella organisations such as Rethink Mental Illness or the Carers Trust.

Carers peer support

Case Example: An Example of Carer Peer Support

Jacqueline Clarke-Mapp, Confident Carers

Confident Carers is a family and friend carer organisation that engages people to improve mental health services for people with lived experience of mental distress and their family, friends and unpaid carers. The work is varied and includes quality and service improvement, training, group and 1:1 coaching, and mentoring to people from diverse backgrounds.

OH is a long term carer for her partner who has a dual diagnosis of bipolar and personality disorder. When she was referred to us, she was experiencing low mood and was feeling very isolated. She had not pursued her sporting activities for years because when she left her partner on his own for too long, he would go into crisis, often ending up in hospital. The carer spent the first few sessions in tears in between sharing parts of her caring role. She felt that the power of being heard by a peer was crucial for her to take the courageous step of opening up. She said that her peer interpreted what she said and helped her translate it into personal development planning and practical support. She did not worry about experiencing stigma at these sessions, which was a marked contrast to her experience with family and friends. This was the first time she had spoken in such a personal way about her caring role and how she felt about it.

Over several weeks, OH continued with her 1:1 coaching sessions which she combined with our bespoke training course attended by other carers. These group sessions focused on education and development where carers learned from each other and developed skills and techniques that helped them look at their needs as individuals which went beyond being carers.

Over time OH resumed her sporting activities and started socialising more. She established regular protected time for herself away from her caring role. She had seen that, as she had developed the routine of attending coaching sessions and training, her partner had adjusted to this as well and, although he did have crises, it was not necessary for him to be readmitted to hospital. OH is more resilient and maintains a hopeful outlook. She says that the coaching and training she received 'saved her life'.

Carers have set up their own groups and organisations as described above. However, the literature and evidence lag behind these practical initiatives, with much of the literature founded in general self-help support groups that are not specific to mental health. Burnell (2009) found only six randomised controlled trials (RCTs) looking at carers peer support, where four were related to older people or people with dementia, and only two were related to adults with mental health problems (Chien et al., 2008; Pickett-Schenk et al., 2006). Chien and Norman (2009) looked beyond RCTs and found consistent evidence of immediate or short-term positive impacts for families, including increased knowledge, reduced distress and enhanced social support, although there was criticism of the quality of the studies. A recent evaluation of a mental health carers peer mentoring project in Scotland found carers receiving peer mentoring were better supported with improved coping mechanisms, better mental health and well-being; mentors had improved skills, knowledge and well-being and increased feelings of empowerment (Macgregor et al., 2018).

In addition to carers support groups that are organised in specific geographic local areas, the internet has proved to be particularly useful for carers seeking the support of other carers. Online support groups can be accessed at all hours of the day or night and can fit around caring, work and family commitments, without leaving the house. Dow and colleagues (2008) noted improvement in depressive symptoms and social isolation, with participants identifying many social benefits after using online support groups.

While carers groups are an established, informal, form of support, carers peer support, in the form of paid peer support workers or voluntary peer supporters, is still relatively rare. This could partly be explained by the novelty of peer support work itself. Services are still establishing the business case for peer support. With some NHS Trusts now several years into the process, the barriers and facilitators to progress are becoming clearer (as described in Chapter 2) and Trusts are addressing these, emphasising key longer-term targets such as wanting peer supporters in every team. Bourke and colleagues (2015) suggest that employing carers as paid workers values their 'real-life' experience in their caring occupation and it would seem worthwhile to extend the acknowledged benefits of peer support to carers. These initiatives are beginning to be extended to carers support – for example, at the time of writing, Birmingham and Solihull Mental Health NHS Foundation Trust and Sussex Partnership NHS Foundation Trust have trained and are in the process of recruiting carer peer support workers to work in mental health teams (Grainne Fadden, personal communication, 28 June 2018; Rachel Kenny, personal communication, 3 July 2018).

Case Example: The Experiences of a Peer Carer Specialist

Joy Ford, Dorset Mental Health Carers Project

I've been a paid Peer Carer Specialist since the end of 2012 in Dorset. It happened very indirectly. After being a carer to my youngest child, who at the age of 20 took his own life, I had very passionate feelings towards mental health and carers. I helped to run a carers group, where one day I met Dorset's Lead for Recovery and Social Inclusion. He was in the process of setting up a Recovery College. Hearing him talk about recovery was so inspirational and similar to how I felt things should be moving. I wanted to know how I could become involved. The Dorset Mental Health Forum (DMHF) were working with and training Peer Specialists who were helping co-produce and facilitate courses about mental health. The talk of a carers course started and I, my husband and another carer from Poole became involved in the co-production.

We three became Peer Carer Specialists and have been busy ever since, not only involved every term with the Recovery Education Centre, but talking to carers, letting staff know how carers are feeling. Since Dorset became involved with the Triangle of Care, our carer awareness co-production has increased, telling our narratives, what it feels like being a carer and how a carer can help in the recovery of their family member or friend.

Finding carers who would like to become peers is not an easy task: two more have joined recently. For some carers, peer work when things become easier, is the last thing they want to do. It is usually those who are old hands at being a carer, have a routine and are able to cope with the various challenges that show an interest.

We have had carers that want to be peers then lost them. Why? Mostly due to the fact that peers need to be trained and supported; it costs money and time. It can take too long to gather enough carers to train as peers so they move on to doing something different. We have a possible five carers being trained at the moment.

Because of the difficulty of finding carers willing to be peers, we do not have specific carers matched up to support other carers. Ideally it would be good to have a peer parent carer supporting another parent carer, or a peer who supports a person with bipolar matched with a carer supporting someone with the same diagnoses, etc. This is early days for us, so peer carers who support someone with a mental illness support another carer regardless of the relationship or the mental illness. The emotions and stresses in all carers are very similar.

That first initial contact is in the main a carer needing to be heard. The relief a peer hears from a carer when they realise they are talking to someone who has been through a similar experience tells us we are worth the time and training. A peer carer cannot change things, but they offer empathy, experience and understanding of their situation, because they have been through it themselves.

Exercise

In your own local area, what opportunities are there for carers to meet with other carers? What are your views on this type of support? How could you support family and friends to get involved?

Critical Debate – The Challenges of Developing Carer Peer Support

*How I eventually attended a carer support group was down to the intervention of a professional family support worker, who had the unenviable task of helping me and my family. We had been identified as a family in crisis and he was the "angel" that walked into our lives. Without his one-to-one support and guidance, I would certainly not have coped: for **he** saw something that I hadn't: **he** saw that I needed help ... and not just the "service user" ... you see, just like all "carers", I had become* **the support** *...* (Carer)

The professional who helped to set up our groups had been a carer and clearly understood the whole carer journey from first-hand experience. He had good advice and insight into the daunting world of mental health: a person who knew how to develop individual day-to-day coping skills and had the advantage of knowing what really matters. (Carer)

The challenges of developing carer peer support may echo both the challenges in developing peer support and the support for carers in general. But the first challenge is in enabling carers to accept that they need support at all. Services talk about the challenges they have in identifying carers, including the challenges of getting carers to complete a carers assessment. Carers themselves often swerve discussing their own well-being, recovery or self-referral for support, immediately applying any topic to the person they support.

After weeks or months of being immersed in another person's crisis, many carers lose track of their own needs, and hold on to a hope that, once there is support for their relative, then they will have time to look after themselves. Finding support for their relative is the priority, and in comparison they do not feel they need support. After months and years of this they lose perspective, such that their idea of a normal life is a level of functioning that most people would not tolerate. If family and friends do not recognise their own role, and do not consider asking for support, services need to be proactive about how they approach carers and offer support. As the carer quoted above highlights, people who have their own experiences of a caring role are well placed to be able to do this.

I had never seen myself in this way before. My whole world had been, and still was, simply devoted to the need of the "service user" and my children. This family support worker showed me the importance of caring for the carer. Well, putting it plainly and simply, if the carer should fall ill, or for some reason was unable to cope, who, or what, will be put in their place?

What a terrifying thought that was! The whole family world that I was striving to maintain could so easily be failed and destroyed ... by no one else but me ... What was I thinking of? ... I needed to look after myself. So reluctantly ... very reluctantly ... I attended those "tea and sympathy" self-help groups. I needed to look after my general well-being or the unthinkable could happen. What a life changer that was ... (Carer)

Services need to value the role of relatives, friends and carers in supporting people with mental health challenges and to value the lived expertise that peer carers bring. The history of the take-up or not of family interventions demonstrates how, even with a strong evidence base, work focusing on families is hard to develop. There remains a lack of availability of family interventions in mental health services despite strong evidence for its effectiveness (Fadden, 1997, 2015). The benefits of supporting family members may appear less direct than other, more pressing, requirements. Initiatives including 'Carer Champions' and Triangle of Care have shown that the whole organisation needs to be carer aware, rather than hoping that one member of staff can take responsibility for all carer issues. This echoes implementation guidance for peer supporters which recommends that they are never employed alone in a team (Smith & Bradstreet, 2011). Carer peer support needs to be in a context of a family-inclusive service that does not rely on isolated experts.

Case Example: Re:Connect and Time and Space Peer Mentoring Project for Carers in Scotland

Julie Cameron, Mental Health Foundation

These projects, in Glasgow and in Stirling and Clackmannanshire, were peer mentoring projects for carers of people with mental health problems which ran from 2014 to 2017 and involved over 100 people. They were a partnership between the Mental Health Foundation, Glasgow Association for Mental Health, and Action in Mind.

Peer mentors were recruited through advertising and received training over six modules. Carers who wanted support (mentees) were also recruited through advertising and self-referred to the service. They met with a volunteer coordinator to identify their interest and support needs, and were then paired with a mentor. People were looking for mentors with some similarity in the condition of the person being cared for, but also a similar age and relationship such as parents being matched with other parents. The mentoring was goal-focused and time-limited.

The peer-led evaluation found that mentees were better supported with improved coping mechanisms, confidence and self-esteem, more social connections and better mental health and well-being. Peer mentors had improved skills, knowledge and well-being, social connections and feelings of empowerment. Carers who had previously received little or no support and carers from equalities groups were better supported. Carers appreciated the value generated through shared lived experience. Mentees were able to open up to their mentors due to their shared experience of caring, which provided a depth of understanding not often available from professionals:

> *I get the sense that she understands my position and she understands the way that I respond to things. And what's good is that she always focuses on me paying attention to myself.* (Mentee)

> *You're peers, you're getting it from someone who understands the challenges.* (Mentor)

A key challenge for the project was the difficulty in identifying carers to receive support (mentees), perhaps reflecting the difficulty in carers acknowledging that they may benefit from support, with many not identifying with the term 'carer'. Suggestions for further improvement included mentees and mentors being more involved in the matching process and building in more supervision particularly around boundaries and endings. Mentors also felt there was a missed opportunity to develop a support network among mentors.

Since completion, the approach has been mainstreamed by Glasgow Association for Mental Health, who offer volunteer peer mentoring as part of their wider mental health carer support service. They have also extended the model to their young carers support teams. Action in Mind are continuing to explore potential funding to redevelop the service within the Stirling and Clackmannanshire areas.

Sources: Glasgow Association for Mental Health website: www.gamh.org.uk/project/carers-support/

The final report (Macgregor et al., 2018) is available on the Mental Health Foundation website: https://www.mentalhealth.org.uk/publications/evaluation-reconnect-and-time-and-space-peer-mentoring-projects

The mechanisms for supporting peer support workers and volunteers are being developed with services recognising the challenges of supporting people who may have other short notice demands on their time. Training and supervision are needed, including on how to maintain well-being when in a role that potentially involves sharing personal narratives which may reflect one's own situation. These are topics for all peer supporters and carer peers are no different. Consequently, every chapter in this book could apply equally to any carer peer supporter. However, there are some points which may need additional consideration. For example, carers may value being trained with a group of carers so that the learners begin to build their own peer support within the group. They may need some additional support about reflecting on their own well-being. People who use services should be familiar with the need for care plans and recovery plans which focus on their well-being, but this can feel alien to carers. Starting from a different place, carers may need additional support around maintaining their own well-being.

There may be specific challenges to recruiting and retaining carer peers which mirror the challenges of the initial identification of carers. Carers who have moved on from a caring role may not want further involvement with services, while carers who are still in a caring role may need to prioritise unpredictable family commitments. It will be interesting to see how services negotiate these challenges.

Additionally, many peer workers find themselves in roles not directly associated with support. There are many peer roles, including peer representatives, peer trainers, peer advocates and peer researchers. These roles require additional training and support. But they also require that services are ready to support and work alongside people who have lived experience. Teams may require additional training to work alongside carers.

CONCLUSIONS

This chapter has touched on the challenges of developing peer support for carers. With language as a fundamental barrier to support for family and friends, the phrase 'carer peer supporter' can easily be misunderstood. Fundamentally, it means carers helping and supporting each other. This is something carers have tended to do. The two carers quoted below emphasise the importance of making a positive difference for carers and that peer support can make this happen. We are at last seeing some carer peer support initiatives; we hope that these continue to grow.

> *It is no good inspiring and instilling hope in people (carers) without having the confidence that positive outcomes can and will be achieved: Why bother? When our group started out, we were full of hope and the belief that we could actually make a difference. That was 2003 then. It is 2017 now. Did we make the difference we all hoped we would make? It took up most of my life at the time. I look back now and I ask myself: Did we make a difference? What did we achieve for the carers we represented? Many of the gains we made, the additional services and staff, have been lost in years of redesign and austerity measures. Many of our friends have passed away over the years, the stress of caring shortening lives. But there is still the support we have given each other over the years: peer support outlasting the groups themselves as well as the professionals.* (Carer)

> *For me, discovering that there were other carers out there, like myself, was a life changer. I had, up to that crucial point, been struggling for many months: dealing with not just the all-consuming role of a "carer", but also being a mother and the "bread winner". I had found myself labelled, but not understood, and certainly **not listened** to. Knowing simply that there were other people like myself, struggling with the same day-to-day dilemmas and crises gave me HOPE.* (Carer)

ACKNOWLEDGEMENTS

Thank you for personal communications with Brian Gallagher from the Mental Health Foundation peer mentoring for mental health carers project, and Jane Lawrence from Improving Carers Experience (ICE) for their reflections on challenges and lessons learned in developing carer peer support. Thank you to Julie Cameron from the Mental Health Foundation in Scotland. Thank you to Joy Ford from Dorset Mental Health Carers Project. Thank you also to Phil Morgan and Paul Siebenthal from Dorset, and all the carers who have contributed to this chapter, but who asked to remain anonymous.

FURTHER READING AND RESOURCES

A comprehensive selection of carers stories of their own recovery and well-being:

Chandler, R., Bradstreet, S. and Hayward, M. (2013). *Voicing Caregiver Experiences: Wellbeing and Recovery Narratives for Caregivers.* Worthing: Scottish Recovery Network, Glasgow and Sussex Partnership NHS Foundation Trust.

A document from ImROC discussing how carers' own recovery could be supported:

Machin, K., and Repper, J. (2013). *Recovery: A Carer's Perspective.* London: Centre for Mental Health and Mental Health Network, NHS Confederation.

Carers of people who are detained in secure services were involved in developing this toolkit for services:

NHS England (2018). Carer support and involvement in secure mental health services: A toolkit, Publications Gateway reference 07618, NHS England.

A well-being plan document which specifically considers carers' needs:

Repper, J., Perkins, R. and Meddings, S. (2013). *A Personal Health and Wellbeing Plan for Family, Friends and Carers.* ImROC, Centre for mental health/ NHS confederation

Videos

The following animation from NHS England is about young carers but applicable to all ages, and suggests the importance of finding peers:

• https://www.youtube.com/watch?v=HZz0uU72eOo

Healthtalk series of films on the experiences of mental health carers from ethnic minorities:

• http://www.healthtalk.org/peoples-experiences/mental-health/mental-health-ethnic-minority-carers-experiences/topics

Carers from York Carers Centre offer their experiences of supporting people with distress:

• https://www.youtube.com/watch?v=9ESFg_Xtcxw

REFERENCES

Appleby, L. (2004). *The National Service Framework for Mental Health – Five Years On.* London: Department of Health.

Bourke, C., Sanders, B., Allchin, B., Lentin, P. and Lang, S. (2015). Occupational therapy influence on a carer peer support model in a clinical mental health service. *Australian Occupational Therapy Journal,* 62(5), 299–305.

Burnell, K. (2009). Peer support interventions for family carers: A review. Paper presented at the Industry Skills Council (ISC) Making a Difference Convention, Melbourne, Australia. https://www.ucl.ac.uk/shield/csp-documents/Consensus_Conference_180309/Peer_Support_Interventions. [Accessed 20 February 2018].

Carers UK (2011). *Half a Million Voices: Improving Support for BAME Carers.* London: Carers UK. http://www.carersuk.org/for-professionals/policy/policy-library/half-a-million-voices-improving-support-for-bame-carers. [Accessed 6 January 2018].

Carers UK (2017). *State of Caring.* London: Carers UK. https://www.carersuk.org/for-professionals/policy/policy-library/state-of-caring-report-2017. [Accessed 6 January 2018].

Chien, W.-T., Thompson, D. R. and Norman, I. (2008). Evaluation of a peer-led mutual support group for Chinese families of people with schizophrenia. *American Journal of Community Psychology,* 42(1),122–134.

Chien, W.-T. and Norman, I. (2009). The effectiveness and active ingredients of mutual support groups for family caregivers of people with psychotic disorders: A literature review. *International Journal of Nursing Studies*, 46(12), 1604–1623.

Coldwell, J., Meddings, S. and Camic, P., (2011), How people with psychosis positively contribute to their family: A grounded theory analysis. *Journal of Family Therapy*, 33(3), 353–371.

Department of Health. (1996). *Carers (Recognition and Services) Act 1995: Policy Guidance.* London: Department of Health.

Department of Health, (1999b). *A National Service Framework for Mental Health.* London: Department of Health.

Department of Health. (2016). *Factsheet 8: The Law for Carers.* https://www.gov.uk/government/publications/care-act-2014-part-1-factsheets/care-act-factsheets#factsheet-8-the-law-for-carers. [Accessed 6 January 2018].

Dow, B., Moore, K., Scott, P., Ratnayeke, A., Wise, K., Sims, J. and Hill, K. (2008), Rural carers online: A feasibility study, *Australian Journal of Rural Health*, 16, 221–225.

Fadden, G. (1997). Implementation of family interventions in routine clinical practice: A major cause for concern. *Journal of Mental Health*, 6, 599–612.

Fadden, G. (2015). Family interventions. In Holloway, F., Kalidindi, S., Killaspy, H. and Roberts, G. (eds), *Enabling Recovery: The Principles and Practice of Rehabilitation Psychiatry* (2nd edn). London: RCPsych Publications, 153–170.

Faulkner, A. and Kalathil, J. (2012). *The Freedom to Be, the Chance to Dream: Preserving User-Led Peer Support in Mental Health.* London: Together.

Flyckt, L., Fatouros-Bergman, H. and Koernig, T. (2015). Determinants of subjective and objective burden of informal caregiving of patients with psychotic disorders. *International Journal of Social Psychiatry*, 61(7), 684–692 .

Gallagher, B. (2016). Families as a resource for supporting recovery: Family member peer support. Presentation given at the ImROC conference, Recovering a Life in Times of Austerity, 25 February, London.

Greenberg, J., Greenley, J. and Benedict, O. (1994). Contributions of persons with serious mental illness to their families. *Hospital and Community Psychiatry*, 45, 475–480.

Gregory, N., Collins-Atkins, C., Macpherson, R., Ford, S. and Palmer, A. (2006). Identifying the needs of carers in mental health services. *Nursing Times*, 102(17), 32–35.

Macgregor, A., Cameron, J., Martin, N., Mackinnon, S., McGregor, M., Hunter, R. and Frost, R. (2018). *Evaluation of Re:Connect and Time and Space Peer Mentoring Projects.* Glasgow: Mental Health Foundation.

Machin, K. and Repper, J. (2013). *Recovery: A Carers' Perspective.* London: Centre for Mental Health and Mental Health Network, NHS Confederation.

Pickett-Schenk, S. A., Cook, J. A., Steigman, P., Lippincott, R., Bennett, C. and Grey, D. D. (2006). Psychological well-being and relationship outcomes in a randomized study of family-led education. *Archives of General Psychiatry*, 63(9), 1043–1050.

Ridley, J., McKeown, M., Machin, K., Rosengard, A., Little, S., Briggs, S., Jones, F. and Deypurkaystha, M. (2014). *Exploring Family Carer Involvement in Forensic Mental Health Services.* Edinburgh: Support in Mind Scotland. https://www.supportinmindscotland.org.uk/exploring-family-carer-involvement-in-forensic-mental-health-services. [Accessed 6 January 2018].

Smith, L. and Bradstreet, S. (2011). *Experts by Experience: Guidelines to Support the Development of Peer Worker Roles in the Mental Health Sector.* Glasgow: Scottish Recovery Network.

Stern, S., Doolan, M., Staples, E. and Szmukler, G. L. (1999). Disruption and reconstruction: Narrative insights into the experience of family members caring for a relative diagnosed with serious mental illness. *Family Process*, 38, 353–369.

Worthington and Rooney. (2010). *Triangle of Care*. http://professionals.carers.org/health/articles/triangle-of-care,6802,PR.html. [Accessed 6 January 2018].

8

Peer Support Training

Karen Machin

Chapter Summary

- Five topics are highlighted for peer support training: the background to peer support; core values of peer support; the environment and organisation; self-care; and specific skills needed to offer peer support

- Additional training before and after a course might include story sharing as well as specific requirements for the organisation

- Peer supporters value training, finding it improves their self-confidence and sense of empowerment

- Training should be co-delivered and reflect the core values of peer support

- Training needs to go beyond the peer supporters to include managers, colleagues and commissioners

- Future development of training should include leadership skills

Introduction

This chapter discusses the development of training for peer supporters. After considering the background, it provides an overview of topics for current training, including training before and after a peer support course. There is an emphasis on the core values of training provisions and how these relate to the core values of peer support itself.

Key barriers to training are discussed before moving on to look at the future of peer leadership.

Throughout there are exercises to aid learning, and highlight some of the critical debates on this topic.

Background

Peer support has been described as a continuum from the informal relationships of friends who are in similar situations through to formalised and paid roles within statutory services (Davidson et al., 2006). There is debate (see Chapter 3) about whether all activities across this range meet the original definition of peer support as mutual and reciprocal, part of an equal relationship (Penney, 2018). There are concerns that paid workers in traditional mental health services will struggle to retain the values of peer support, which were created to counter the powerlessness within the existing mental health system. Maintaining these peer support values is partially addressed by contracts, supervision and working arrangements, and this chapter highlights the important role of training, both for the peer supporters themselves and for their colleagues, managers and commissioners.

Historically, relationships built on friendship or being members of the same self-help group may have needed little formal training, with people relying on their own instincts and existing skills to seek and offer support within their own capabilities. They may choose people for this supportive relationship, naturally avoiding the people with whom they feel little rapport, and concentrating on those they find helpful. As such, their natural skills may be sufficient, with both parties doing their best while understanding the informal nature of the relationship. Alternatively, this grassroots approach may insist on being inclusive, with the whole group sharing responsibility to ensure that no person is excluded. This might involve sourcing skills development opportunities so that they can truly develop intentional support for each other.

In contrast, the rigours of clinical settings, providing formal support to much larger numbers of people, demand the assurance of training and certificates to ensure that services meet quality standards. Peer supporters, and the people using their service, value training and certificates which provide a guarantee of the standard of skills on offer, and in turn increase the confidence of both parties in the service. Peer supporters feel valued and supported by the organisation, and people using their services trust people who have met standards of knowledge and skills to support them.

Between these two offers of support, the informal and formal, there are growing numbers of peer support groups and projects, often based in the voluntary sector. The peer leaders, volunteers, group members and staff coordinators may have had a range of training to increase their skills and confidence, varying according to the requirements and resources of the organisation.

Exercise

Over the years, there have been continuing, sometimes heated, discussions about peer support: whether it should be informal or formal, natural or professional, unpaid or paid. People question whether training stifles something which should be natural. For example, some suggest that we all know how to listen, so we don't need teaching. But do we? Arguments could be made that every one of us could develop our listening skills to improve our relationships and enable us to offer each other support.

What are your views on the need for training of peer supporters? What is your current position on this fundamental debate?

Overview of current training recommendations

The formal use of peer support is at a relatively early stage in its development, and the training requirements are not thoroughly established. However, recommendations on how to employ peer workers do suggest the importance of training (Daniels et al., 2010; Gates & Akabas, 2007; McLean et al., 2009; Tse et al., 2014; Wolf et al., 2010), with various authors suggesting it is an essential element of ensuring sustainable peer support services (Bailie & Tickle, 2015; Campos et al., 2016; McLean et al., 2009; Woodhouse et al., 2012). Vandewalle and colleagues (2016) note the converse: that inadequate training is viewed as a challenge for such services.

In the UK there are as yet no national standards for the certification requirements for peer workers in mental health, other than the Care Certificate which may be part of a standard induction process once a peer worker is employed in a post. Guidelines for the employment of peer supporters offer some indication of the skills and training requirements of the role (Repper, 2013; Smith & Bradstreet, 2011). However, there is no single job description or role definition for peer support, with different organisations employing peer supporters across a range of duties and responsibilities. Peer support is still developing, and as such training courses are responding to local needs and international developments. For example, an early review of training available in the USA included a common suggestion that peer supporters should be trained in suicide prevention (Woodhouse & Vincent, 2006), which has not been included in more recent national certification (Grantham, 2016); recommendations from Canada (Sunderland & Mishkin, 2013) have been taken up in Australia (Hodges et al., 2016).

Common themes are emerging across a range of peer support training courses (Hodges et al., 2016; Kaufman et al., 2016; Naughton et al., 2015; Peer2Peer Project Partners, 2015; Repper, 2013; Smith & Bradstreet, 2011; Sunderland & Mishkin, 2013; Woodhouse & Vincent, 2006). Although some may emphasise one theme over another, the following are considered to be useful within training:

- Understanding of the background to peer support including service user activism, recovery and social justice
- A grounding in core values of peer support including using lived experience, being strengths-focused and non-directive

- Awareness of the settings for peer support including the general needs of the specific organisation as well as wider community resources
- An understanding of self-care including well-being planning, boundary setting and safe disclosure
- The skills needed to offer peer support including active listening, using personal experiences and managing challenging situations.

There may also be a need for additional training before and after a peer support course. Peer supporters may have been out of the job market for some time or may have lost jobs because of their distress. They may need support with preparation for work, including searching and applying for jobs as well as careers guidance. Some organisations encourage peer supporters to attend a range of Recovery College courses, where available, before attending a peer support course, as an introduction to the learning environment as well as learning on a range of topics.

Courses such as story sharing are particularly relevant where people have not had previous opportunities to share their story on their own terms. There is a myth that peer supporters must share their life story: this isn't the case, although peer support may involve sharing small details of a person's experience to illustrate points and build trust (Watson, 2012). Story sharing courses offer an opportunity to make sense of experiences before moving on to develop these peer support skills. They allow personal stories to be heard and valued in a supportive environment, and enable participants to listen to each other, a potentially powerful opportunity for becoming aware of shared experiences as well as the range of experiences which may lead to distress. This may be the first time someone has shared their story, and participants may need support around setting boundaries, and the impact such sharing may have on themselves and others.

Additionally some organisations encourage learners to make the most of placement opportunities to find out more about the role. These can help people to decide if this is the job for them, or whether they are looking for a peer role with another emphasis, such as training or research. The realities of working within an organisation may differ from expectations; placement opportunities offer a chance to understand the reality of the role and environment.

Once in post, there may be induction requirements of standard training. Further training opportunities relevant to a peer support role may include specific topics in more depth such as suicide prevention, advocacy, diverse experiences within the mental health system, or group facilitation skills. Courses in facilitating learning or research methods support the skills for a wider range of peer roles. Support to be involved in a Community of Practice may exist within organisations or externally and can be an essential part of personal development.

'Peer support' has become the term used across a wide range of initiatives beyond mental health remits, including other health conditions, workforce requirements and ages. These have common areas of expertise, with training requirements that are identical: all peer supporters value opportunities to practise listening skills, for example. The only difference is that the trainers and facilitators may adapt their language and delivery to suit specific audiences, which starts to create bespoke courses, such as those provided for young people (Lambert et al., 2014).

In contrast to this thorough list of potential training, the Side by Side Research Consortium (2017), looking at peer support in voluntary groups, recognise the limitations for projects and people with limited resources, time and funding. They note that training could delay the start of the project or limit access to people with the time and capacity to take up training opportunities. Their suggested process of group reflection leads them to ask if there is a need for training, although it is not clear how such training would be accessed.

Exercise

Reflect further on your own opinions of peer support training. Consider the issue from the perspective of a peer supporter, someone using peer support services or someone working in a team which includes peer supporters. How much training do you think is needed? Is the list of topics above excessive or is anything missing?

Shery Mead is one of the international leaders of peer support practice. Her Intentional Peer Support highlights the development of relationships: finding someone to connect with, someone who will listen and ask hard questions. In the case example below she describes their training.

Case Example: A Training Provider

Shery Mead and Beth Filson, Intentional peer support

Intentional Peer Support (IPS) training explores dialogue that invites mutually transformative relationships. Trainees learn to be in relationships that foster seeing their experiences from new angles, develop greater awareness of personal and relational patterns, and support and challenge each other in trying new things.

IPS training operates out of three principles (the values) and four tasks (carrying out the values).

The three principles are:

1. Shifting the focus from helping or problem solving to learning about how each other has come to make sense of their experience. Helping has often meant responding to the 'told' story which may or may not address the real needs of the person. When we learn more about each other, stories open up and we see other possibilities.
2. Shifting the focus from the individual to the relationship. IPS is essentially a relational practice. It doesn't seek to fix an individual, but rather by getting to know each other, and some of our traps and patterns, we both have the possibility of changing.
3. Shifting the focus from fear to hope and possibility. Too often, the mental health system has responded to us out of fear, leaving us feeling coerced, powerless and out of control. If we pay attention to what's possible (even in challenging situations), we create alternative routes.

The four tasks are:

1. Connection builds the foundation for all our interactions. It is the starting place for building trust and honesty.
2. World view explores how we've come to make sense of our experience and, through conversation, unbinds our past from our present and allows us to make new meaning.
3. Mutuality is the practice of shared vulnerability and shared responsibility. With a focus on mutuality, relationships don't get stuck in stagnant roles.
4. Moving towards rather than away from. Many of us have spent whole lifetimes moving away from what's not working (e.g. 'getting better', losing weight, etc.) but few of us have been encouraged to use our relationships to see possibilities that grow out of the first three tasks.

The IPS five-day core training is highly interactive using real examples to stimulate dialogue. We learn about a task a day and on the last day we go through the process of co-reflection (or holding ourselves accountable to the practice). Participants are also invited to show their understanding of IPS through a creative project.

Peer supporters' views on training

Where peer supporters are asked for their views about training they have received, evidence is frequently based on the formal provision of peer support, from funded projects which may be part of research initiatives. While this may bias results, silencing the voices of informal peer supporters, this can offer some indication of the expectations and requirements of people who provide peer support.

In a 2015 survey 82 per cent of the 131 participants who had received or provided peer support suggested that specific peer-to-peer training would help peer services be more effective (Flegg et al., 2015). A later study involving 147 peer supporters in UK statutory and voluntary services (Burke, 2017) clarified the value placed on training with consensus reached on the statement that peer supporters should have been through specific training for the role. The study revealed the wide range of competencies deemed essential to the role and which would likely require training as well as experience and supervision. Training was part of a recommendation for organisational support to mitigate the personal costs to the peer supporter (Burke, 2017).

Training has been described by learners as 'life-changing' (Watson et al., 2016) and 'valuable, challenging, yet positive' (Simpson, et al., 2014). A service evaluation of one training offer has shown it to improve levels of empowerment and reduce internalised stigma (Pyle, 2017).

Training is something that peer supporters value. It increases their confidence and contributes to them feeling valued, improving their quality of life and supporting their recovery.

Critical Debate: Is Accreditation Necessary for Peer Support Training?

Critics suggest that an accredited certificate is irrelevant to the practical work of peer support, and that many potential peer supporters are deterred by the thought of returning to academic study. Providers of accredited training would argue that their training reflects the values of peer support and is flexible to the needs of the organisation. They also highlight the personal achievement felt by learners who accomplish a written assignment, and that accreditation shows that learners are valued.

ASM has recently been on a peer support training course. In the case example below she describes her own experience.

Case Example: A Student Peer Mentor

ASM, student peer mentor

One summer seven years ago I began hearing voices. They told me that I was being hunted by secret agents and that I would die a horrible death from being poisoned. I did not believe them, but I did not seek help either. I continued to work two jobs and just chalked it up to stress. Then a week after I started hearing voices the delusions set in. I genuinely believed that my co-worker was trying to kill me so confronted him about it. Suffice to say I didn't last long there: I was fired on the spot.

After I was fired, I began to seek help. That delusion had gone away, but I was embarrassed about what I had I done. I went to my GP and she referred me to the Early Intervention Service. This was the beginning of my lengthy battle with Schizoaffective disorder, a condition categorised by delusions, hallucinations, and terrible mood swings. I was sectioned more times than I can count in the years that followed, and I heard voices every day. But one day, seven years after I had my first psychotic break, I felt better. This lasted for several months and I started looking for volunteering opportunities to boost my CV. My Community Psychiatric Nurse told me about peer mentoring with a local voluntary organisation. For the first time in a long time I felt like I had a chance to give back to my community and help people like me recover as I had done.

The organisation provided me with the training needed to become a qualified peer mentor. The tutors were brilliant teachers and I learned a lot from them about peer support and the concept of recovery too. Before I started the training, I had poor listening skills and low self-esteem compounded by years of not working or studying. Through the training I learned valuable listening skills, improved my self-esteem by gaining a good grade on my essay, and learned what was required of a peer mentor.

There are eight core principles of peer mentorship and the one I felt resonated with me the most was that peer mentorship is mutual. Before the training I thought that as someone who had recovered and was going to be a mentor that I would be the one guiding or leading the mentee. I learned that this is an unhelpful way to think of a mentee and that it could be damaging to the relationship.

> All in all, the training did amazing things to my life, for the first time in seven years I felt that I had accomplished something. Months later, I still feel proud of myself and I hope to one day become a qualified mental health advocate.

Exercise

Some organisations suggest they should advertise for peer supporters and then train the successful candidates. Other organisations invite a group to be trained in peer support and then interview them for roles. What are the benefits and disadvantages of each approach? How could you minimise any disadvantages?

Core values of peer support training

It is important to highlight here that there are differences in how peer support training is offered. Some are provided by external training organisations with expertise in training while others are developed internally within an organisation to meet their own needs. Repper (2013) suggests that the most effective way of retaining the essence of peer practice is to ensure that training reflects core values such as mutuality and reciprocity, being strengths-based, inclusive and non-directive. Just as peer support can slide away from these core values, training providers need to make efforts to hold to them, as well as enable exploration of the tensions and challenges involved.

Peer support training for mental health should be at least co-delivered by people with personal experience of mental health challenges. They can role model the skills of developing mutual and reciprocal relationships (Mead & MacNeil, 2005), including relevant sharing of experience. Co-facilitation should also go beyond personal experience of the distress to include the factors that brought people to this experience. People from excluded groups, who are disproportionately affected by mental health distress yet disadvantaged in finding suitable services, must be involved in developing and delivering training so that experiences such as racism and homophobia are fully included. Peer support training needs to be complemented by open and frank discussion of such topics, enabling all peer supporters to learn from the range of experiences they bring to the role.

Case Example: Peer Support Training for Black African Caribbean Men in Secure Care

Emachi Eneje, Michael Humes, Sandra Griffiths and Anita Kumari, trainers from a project to develop peer support for Black African Caribbean men in secure care

When I think of peer support, I am reminded of the Nina Simone refrain, 'Birds Flying High, You Know How I Feel', and I start to notice all the different kinds of birds. This is because the range of experiences, circumstances and settings in which people can benefit from peer support is so varied that peer support could be likened to the entire class of birds – not just one type.

Sure, all species of bird share common characteristics, but the variety emerging is great. Think of all the colours. Think of all the habitats. Think of the shapes. The sizes. And, of course, think that some birds fly, some birds swim, yet others were born to run.

This analogy of peer support frames the challenge of interest here: Can a flamingo teach a fallen eagle how to once again fly? It's true that all birds have a 'birdness' alike and share a common bird experience; however, if Nina had sung 'Eagle in the sky, you are where I hope to once again be', then you'd have to give that question some real consideration.

Our real consideration is how to deploy peer support to help address the racism and health inequalities experienced by black men in secure mental health care. These deeply damaging experiences have been long appreciated, yet no solution has yet to rid us of that problem. In 2016 NHS England Mental Health Secure Care Programme supported the work of the Black Voices Project – that travelled around England hearing the experiences of black men in secure care – the outcome of which are pilot solutions to tackle the problems experienced. One pilot solution is peer support specifically for black men in the secure setting.

The approach the peer support pilot has taken responds to the aforementioned question with 'No. It is the once fallen eagle high in the sky that best supports other eagles recovering their flight.' This is a need expressed during the Black Voices Project; the impact of racism is so profound that knowing how it feels, viscerally and psychologically, is criteria for peerness in this case.

However, it seemed that the infrastructure to produce peers working in a way that remedies challenges experienced by black men in secure care did not exist or simply was not visible, which in itself captures two themes in the black experience: black capacity building and black services accessing the marketplace.

To get us moving, the pilot built upon the training developed by the Peer Training team at the Institute of Mental Health (IMH) whose training is solid, tried and tested. The IMH training was adapted to reflect more specifically the black experience – this co-design process was integrated into training the black trainers, who would train the black peers, who would then work in secure environments. Black men who have experienced secure services were involved at all stages which satisfies the criteria of 'knowing how it feels'. This also builds black capacity and ensures authenticity and credibility.

True co-design and co-production, alongside a wholehearted commitment to the values of peer support, ensures that lived experience is at the heart of the curriculum (Watson et al., 2016).

Exercise

Reflecting on peer support, what would you consider to be the core values and principles of any peer support training?

What's missing?

A key struggle in developing and providing training concerns the resources available. Training budgets are often some of the first to be decreased in times of austerity. Training for people with lived experience may not be as valued as training for professionals who may have needs around registration as well as expectations around continued professional development. People who are familiar with living and working on restricted budgets can find it difficult to build a case for training, and mental health systems that have traditionally been led by clinicians are likely to prioritise clinical training. The consequences are that training for peer supporters can struggle to be resourced and is likely to be under-valued.

Similarly additional training, beyond core skills, struggles for resources. Peer supporters' requests for training around specific subjects may not always be achievable within limited resources. There is also the challenge of which to prioritise: increasing numbers for core training or advanced training for a few.

Where an organisation understands the potential of peer support and values its staff, it is likely to promote training to enable safe, innovative practice. Employing peer supporters has been described as 'the single most important factor contributing to changes towards more recovery-orientated services' (Repper, 2013, p. 1). For this to happen it is important that the environment is suited to their employment or they will struggle, being the sole holder of a recovery-focus, trying to influence teams from a position of powerlessness.

Training other staff has been suggested as an essential precursor and support for employment of peer supporters (McLean et al., 2009; Repper, 2013). Managers, supervisors, colleagues and commissioners are all needed to support peer supporters, to develop in their roles and adapt to the working environment. To do this effectively the whole team needs to understand the role, and the barriers and facilitators to its successful implementation. They need space to air concerns, which may include issues around confidentiality and boundaries, alongside concerns for their own jobs. Where staff have only witnessed people in crisis, they can lose hope of recovery. Even staff who may intellectually believe in peer support can express instinctive reactions to sharing confidential information with people who still use the organisation's services. Staff who are knowledgeable about peer support are in a position to use their understanding of its values to ensure that peer support remains distinct and is not diluted into a support worker function (Berry et al., 2011).

Critical Debate: Training of Peer Supporters Should Be Developed within the Organisation

An organisation may consider developing its own training for reasons of cost or to ensure that the training meets their specific needs. They may have expertise in training within the organisation, such as in a Recovery College or a Learning Resources department. This disregards the challenges of ensuring that the training, and hence the organisation, retains the values of peer support and is linked into initiatives elsewhere.

Marissa Lambert is the lead for the peer support training team at the Institute of Mental Health in Nottingham. The team has delivered the training in a wide range of settings including perinatal services, police forces and housing associations as well as mental health services. Here Marissa describes their work with wider staff teams.

Case Example: Working with Organisations

Marissa Lambert, Peer Support Lead, Institute of Mental Health, Nottingham

A key part of our service delivery is the priority we place on reflective practice and knowledge sharing, with learning integrated and disseminated across any project to all those involved. We believe that training of peer supporters is just one element of the work needed to develop and implement this new offer of support.

Delivering a series of workforce-wide 'What is peer support?' training days forms an important part of workforce development, and offers an opportunity for learning across the service, as well as ensuring support and understanding for the peer supporters themselves. A package of 'team readiness' workshops provides an opportunity for effective ground work to ensure that they are not just 'parachuting in' peer supporters to a professional team, or risking losing the uniqueness of peer support.

Staff are provided with the space to explore and understand the theory, as well as the content and delivery method of our peer support training. The workshops also provide a space to explore the challenges and fears, as well as the hopes and aspirations, of staff teams through a balance of appreciative enquiry.

Team readiness supports the team to co-create and identify where peer supporters might fit on a realistic pathway, such as helping to manage transitions in an integrated, co-ordinated care service. Peer supporters offer the potential to act as a 'trusted bridge' between individuals, teams and services. Providing a specific role for peer supporters helps everyone concerned to understand the added value and boundaries of the peer support role.

With this environment and shared understanding in place, the organisation is more equipped to take forward their vision for peer support. However, our involvement continues beyond the training. By offering annual masterclasses and ongoing supervision groups, we can support teams to remain true to the values of peer support.

One interesting recommendation we have repeatedly heard in our training comes from the peer supporters themselves who suggest that the accredited peer support course would be valuable for all staff. Members of staff who support the learners agree that the courses are a welcome opportunity for them to hear about a range of views on recovery, to learn about peer support, to refresh their listening skills and to reflect on their own roles. The courses are necessarily inclusive of a range of learners, with no hierarchy accorded to prior learning or to specific experiences of distress. By creating a welcoming and equal learning environment, everyone is enabled to take a strengths-based approach to role model the offering of mutual and reciprocal support. This encourages existing staff to witness and experience the benefits of peer support, knowledge that they can then take back to their colleagues. It is this 'ripple effect' that promotes peer support practices through an organisation.

Exercise

Family, friends and carers of people who experience distress could work as 'carer peer supporters', drawing on their own experiences to provide mutual support to other carers. How would you arrange their training? Are there any differences in their training to the training which might be provided for other peer supporters?

Training for peer leadership

As potential peer supporters are trained in the background of recovery and social justice, the core values of peer support, self-care, peer support skills and organisational requirements, they have the potential to become leaders within an organisation. However, without training for their colleagues, their newfound confidence can feel challenging to healthcare professionals who may not have had such opportunities for learning, and who may feel personally disadvantaged by this new emphasis on lived experience, to the extent of believing that 'The only way to be sure of getting a job these days is to say you have a mental health problem' (Repper, 2013, p. 8). This myth does a disservice to all concerned, but also has an impact on peer supporters as they discover the potential challenges of working within the existing mental health system, challenges which had been a part of the historical motivation of peer support.

Starting as a protest movement, the service user/survivor movement has existed since at least the 1970s (Chamberlin, 1988). Acknowledging the strength to support each other, this movement has always shared stories, building the new knowledge required to create change (Faulkner & Basset, 2010). This informal peer support has been instrumental in encouraging a move towards recovery and peer support, such that survivors have been critical when these words are used tokenistically by a mental health system without real change (Wallcraft, 2012). This history underpins peer support. However, people new to the mental health system may not have the same understanding of the motivation for change at the heart of peer support.

People who use mental health services today face a very different experience to activists and survivors of the asylum and the move to community care (O'Hagan, 2010). Previously, people became defined by their service use, and were told that they would remain in services for the rest of their lives (Chamberlin, 1988; 1998; Deegan, 1988; Wallcraft, 2003). But times have changed. In England relatively few people use inpatient units. Services are commissioned to provide specific support followed by discharge to primary care, and people with low to moderate needs wait in queues for short interventions in the push to get back to work promptly. Many newer, and perhaps younger, service users have different motivations for providing peer support than their earlier counterparts, talking about 'giving something back' or seeing it as the first step on a career path in health and social care: all very different from the original motivators of groups such as Survivors Speak Out or the national reaction of involvement strategies to support 'nothing about us without us'.

However, as noted above, peer support training directly encourages leadership by people with direct experience, as well as an ability to work alongside people with a range of expertise. This leadership could be an important driver, supportive of the latest initiatives around co-production, turning it from a buzzword into something more practical and effective.

Such leadership could involve people newer to mental health services with diverse interests and expertise. Recognition of these possibilities within peer support, developing it with opportunities for peer leadership, would ensure that organisations build on the fundamental values of empowerment and equality.

Future opportunities for training, as they build on these suggestions, should include leadership development, alongside service innovation, to inspire new generations of leaders.

Exercise

How could you encourage a move from 'peer support' through to 'peer leadership'? Is there anything about such a development that would make you concerned?

CONCLUSIONS

This chapter has touched on some of the challenges of ensuring that peer supporters have access to suitable training and skills development. Emphasising the importance of training the whole workforce including managers, colleagues and team members, it has presented the possibilities for peer leadership, taking the skills of peer supporters to transform the provision of mental health services.

ACKNOWLEDGEMENTS

With thanks to Shery Mead Intentional Peer Support, and Beth Filson; A.S.M., student peer mentor; Emachi Eneje, Michael Humes, Sandra Griffiths and Anita Kumari, trainers from a project to develop peer support for Black African Caribbean men in secure care; and Marissa Lambert, Peer Support Lead for the Institute of Mental Health, Nottingham.

FURTHER READING AND RESOURCES

A film about the Institute of Mental Health peer support training:

- https://vimeo.com/108467328#at=2

Intentional peer support training in the USA:

- http://www.intentionalpeersupport.org/trainings/

Peer Support training resources:

- https://www.scottishrecovery.net/resource/new-free-peer-support-training-resources/

REFERENCES

Bailie, H. A. and Tickle, A. (2015). Effects of employment as a peer support worker on personal recovery: A review of qualitative evidence. *Mental Health Review Journal*, 20(1), 48–64.

Berry, C., Hayward, M. I. and Chandler, R. (2011). Another rather than other: Experiences of peer support specialist workers and their managers working in mental health services. *Journal of Public Mental Health*, 10(4), 238–249.

Burke, E. (2017). Providing formal mental health peer support: What does that mean for peer supporters? Doctoral dissertation in Clinical Psychology, University of Manchester.

Campos, F., Sousa, A., Rodrigues, V., Marques, A., Queirós, C. and Dores, A. (2016). Practical guidelines for peer support programmes for mental health problems. *Revista de Psiquiatria y Salud Mental (English Edition)*, 9(2), 97–110.

Chamberlin, J. (1988). *On Our Own*. London: Mind.

Chamberlin, J. (1998). Confessions of a non-compliant patient. *Journal of Psychosocial Nursing*, 36(4), 49–52.

Daniels, A., Grant, E., Filson, B., Powell, I., Fricks, L., and Goodale, L. (eds) (2010). *Pillars of Peer Support: Transforming Mental Health Systems of Care Through Peer Support Services*. www.pillarsofpeersupport.org [Accessed 24 October 2018].

Davidson, L., Chinman, M., Sells, D. and Rowe, M. (2006). Peer support among adults with serious mental illness: A report from the field. *Schizophrenia Bulletin*, 32(3), 443–450.

Deegan, P. (1988). Recovery: The lived experience of rehabilitation. *Psychosocial Rehabilitation Journal*, 11(4), 11–19.

Faulkner, A. and Basset, T. (2010). *A Helping Hand: Consultations with Service Users about Peer Support*. London: Together.

Flegg, M., Gordon-Walker, M. and Maguire, S. (2015). Peer-to-peer mental health: A community evaluation case study. *The Journal of Mental Health Training, Education and Practice*, 10(5), 282–293.

Gates, L. B. and Akabas, S. H. (2007). Developing strategies to integrate peer providers into the staff of mental health agencies. *Administration and Policy in Mental Health and Mental Health Services Research*, 34(3), 293–306.

Grantham, D. (2016). *Under the Microscope*. Mental Health America. Washington, DC: NACBHDD. https://www.mentalhealthamerica.net/sites/default/files/looking%20glass.pdf [Accessed 24 October 2018].

Hodges, T., Downing, H. and Townsend, E. (2016). *FNQ Peer Workforce: Valuing lived experience*. Queensland: FNQ Mental Health Alliance.

Kaufman, L., Kuhn, W. and Stevens Manser, S. (2016). *Peer Specialist Training & Certification Programs: National Overview 2016*. Austin: Texas Institute for Excellence in Mental Health, School of Social Work, University of Texas at Austin.

Lambert, M., Matharoo, R., Watson, E. and Oldknow, H. (2014). Supporting transitions in child and adolescent mental health services: A rough guide to introducing peer support. *The Journal of Mental Health Training, Education and Practice*, 9(4), 222–231.

McLean, J., Biggs, H., Whitehead, I., Pratt, R. and Maxwell, M. (2009). *Evaluation of the Delivering for Mental Health Peer Support Worker Pilot Scheme*. Edinburgh: Scottish Government Social Research.

Mead, S. and MacNeil, C. (2005). *Peer support: A systemic approach*. https://pdfs.semanticscholar.org/5985/cf53401a53bb4506c67945c38385fc5d3418.pdf [Accessed 10 July 2018].

Naughton, L., Collins, P. and Ryan, M. (2015). *Peer Support Workers: A Guidance Paper* (Vol. 10). Dublin: National Office for Advancing Recovery in Ireland and HSE: Mental Health Division.

O'Hagan, M. (2010). Leadership for empowerment and equality: A proposed model for mental health user/survivor leadership. *International Journal of Leadership in Public Services*, 5(4), 34–43.

Peer2Peer Project Partners. (2015). *Vocational Training Course*. http://p2p.intras.es/ [Accessed 24 October 2018].

Penney, D. (2018). *Defining 'Peer Support': Implications for Policy, Practice and Research*. Advocate for Human Potential Inc. http://ahpnet.com/AHPNet/media/AHPNetMediaLibrary/White%20Papers/DPenney_Defining_peer_support_2018_Final.pdf [Accessed 24 October 2018].

Pyle, M. (2017). Evaluation of peer support training: Impact on empowerment and internalised stigma. Paper presented at the Refocus on Recovery conference, Nottingham, 18 September 2017.

Repper, J. (2013). *Peer Support Workers: A Practical Guide to Implementation*. London: Centre for Mental Health & Mental Health Network, NHS Confederation.

Side by Side Research Consortium (2017). *Developing Peer Support in the Community: A Toolkit*. London: Mind.

Simpson, A., Quigley, J., Henry, S. J. and Hall, C. (2014). Evaluating the selection, training, and support of peer support workers in the United Kingdom. *Journal of Psychosocial Nursing and Mental Health Services*, 52(1), 31–40.

Smith, L. and Bradstreet, S. (2011). *Experts by Experience: Guidelines to Support the Development of Peer Worker Roles in the Mental Health Sector*. Glasgow: Scottish Recovery Network.

Sunderland, K. and Mishkin, W., Peer Leadership Group & Mental Health Commission of Canada (2013). *Guidelines for the Practice and Training of Peer Support*. Calgary: Mental Health Commission of Canada. http://www.mentalhealthcommission.ca [Accessed 10 July 2018].

Tse, S., Tsoi, E. W. S., Wong, S., Kan, A. and Kwok, C. F.-Y. (2014). Training of mental health peer support workers in a non-western high-income city: Preliminary evaluation and experience. *International Journal of Social Psychiatry*, 60(3), 211–218.

Vandewalle, J., Debyser, B., Beeckman, D., Vandecasteele, T., Van Hecke, A. and Verhaeghe, S. (2016). Peer workers' perceptions and experiences of barriers to implementation of peer worker roles in mental health services: A literature review. *International Journal of Nursing Studies*, 60, 234–250.

Wallcraft, J. (2003). *On our Own Terms*. London: Sainsbury Centre for Mental Health.

Wallcraft, J. (2012). Consumer models of recovery: Can they survive operationalism? *World Psychiatry*, 11(3), 166–167.

Watson, E. (2012). One year in peer support: Personal reflections. *Journal of Mental Health Training, Education and Practice*, 7(2), 85–88.

Watson, E., Lambert, M. and Machin, K. (2016). Peer support training: Values, achievements and reflections. *Mental Health Practice*, 19(9), 22–27.

Wolf, J., Lawrence, L. H., Ryan, P. M. and Hoge, M. A. (2010). Emerging practices in employment of persons in recovery in the mental health workforce. *American Journal of Psychiatric Rehabilitation*, 13(3), 189–207.

Woodhouse, A., Biggs, H., O'Sullivan, C., Bowie, J. and McLean, J. (2012). *Developing Peer Support for Long Term Conditions*. London: Mental Health Foundation.

Woodhouse, A. and Vincent, A. (2006). *Mental Health Delivery Plan: Development of Peer Specialist Roles: A Literature Scoping Exercise*. Scottish Development Centre for Mental Health. https://lx.iriss.org.uk/sites/default/files/resources/Mental%20Health%20Delivery%20Plan%20Development%20of%20Peer%20Specialist%20Roles%20A%20Literature%20Scoping%20Exercise.pdf [Accessed 10 July 2018].

9

All Mental Health Professionals Using Lived Experience

*Sara Meddings, Phil Morgan
and Glenn Roberts*

Chapter Summary

- Significant numbers of mental health professionals have lived experience of mental health challenges

- People who use services often find it helpful when mental health professionals share their lived experience as part of their work

- There are differences, and similarities, between peer workers and other mental health professionals stemming from their primary roles and training

- As professionals sharing lived experience, it is helpful to consider what, when and how to share for the benefit of the person using services, and to reflect on whether it is okay for us as practitioners

- Professionals can use their lived experience in other ways such as in teaching and supervision or to develop services. We can draw on our lived experience without necessarily sharing it

- Organisations can create cultures where lived experience is valued as an asset

Introduction

Society has a long history of seeing people with mental health challenges as 'other' which has led to a culture of separation in mental health services too. This established view of 'us' and 'them' has been associated with an inhibition or even prohibition of practitioners sharing their personal lives with those they support, particularly their own mental health difficulties.

In the 1990s the Pathfinder User Employment Service, developed by Rachel Perkins at South West London and St George's NHS Trust, pioneered the creation of jobs where lived experience of mental health challenges was valued, advocating the benefits of such experience for all mental health professional roles (Rinaldi et al., 2004). They created peer roles where lived experience was essential and also recruited people with lived experience into existing positions such as nurses, psychiatrists and psychologists. Recently, there has been a drive within mental health services to recruit peer workers (Shepherd et al., 2010). However, there has been less focus on other mental health professionals with lived experience, and how they may use this in their roles. It is possible that employing peers and experts by experience has inadvertently hidden the lived experience of professionals, increasing the 'them and us' divide (see Huet & Holttum, 2016).

Approximately half of mental health professionals have lived experience of mental health challenges. A survey of all staff working in one NHS mental health Trust found that 43 per cent of respondents reported personal experience of mental health problems, with more than half of these having experienced services or treatments; 61 per cent had experience of supporting someone close to them; one-third had not been able to be open about this, largely due to fears of stigma, misunderstanding and rejection (Roberts et al., 2011). Another Trust found 53 per cent of staff self-identified as having lived experience of mental health problems and 39 per cent had experienced stigma and discrimination from colleagues or managers (Morgan & Lawson, 2015). Therefore, while many services in the UK have seen the value of lived experience with the development of peer worker roles, this has not necessarily cleared the way for all mental health professionals to share their experiences nor reduced the stigma surrounding mental health.

Stigma among mental health professionals and self-stigma of people using services might be reduced if staff were more open about their own experiences. The best way to reduce prejudice and stigma about people with mental health challenges is through contact with people who have received mental health services and who are productive members of the community (Corrigan & Matthews, 2003). This may also create a working environment that promotes openness and supports staff well-being.

Gradually, mental health professionals have been publicly challenging stigma by publishing their own narratives – for example, psychiatrists Dan Fisher, Linda Gask and Glenn Roberts; psychologists Pat Deegan, Rachel Perkins and Rufus May; and nurses Julie Repper and Debbie Cleaveley (see 'Further reading and resources' at the end of the chapter). These professionals have pioneered publicly that you can be *both* an accomplished mental health professional *and* someone who uses mental health services.

We write this chapter jointly as practitioners from different mental health professions (clinical psychology, occupational therapy and psychiatry) who have struggled with our own personal and family mental health experiences but learned to value this as insight and inspiration in our work. With their permission, we draw on personal communications and quotes from colleagues and people we have worked with. In this chapter we review the literature on mental health professionals sharing lived experience. We debate potential distinctions between peer workers and other professionals sharing lived experience. We then consider how to do this in practice: what factors mental health professionals might take into account when deciding whether or not to share lived experience; and how NHS Trusts and other organisations can support staff to use their lived experience.

Is there value in sharing lived experience of mental health challenges?

Wouldn't it be great if some of the nurses here had been admitted to a psychiatric ward themselves (person during inpatient stay)

There is a significant literature on use of self, wounded healers and self-disclosure within therapy and mental health. Research asking clients to recall therapy sessions suggests that the most helpful aspects of therapy were when therapists *infrequently* disclosed information about themselves, and especially when they shared personal information from the past (Hill et al., 1988; Knox et al., 1997). Clients thought it was more helpful than did therapists, reporting that they experience therapists who self-disclose as warmer, friendlier and more human and real; it reduces power imbalance between client and therapist, yet therapy roles remain differentiated; clients gain more insights and new perspectives, feel reassured that they are not the only one and feel more able to share with their therapist (Audet, 2011; Knox et al., 1997).

In their review of the literature on therapist self-disclosure, Henretty and Levitt (2010) suggest self-disclosure has a positive impact on clients: clients perceive therapists who self-disclose as warmer and are more likely to recommend them to a friend. However, disclosure of significant inadequacies can reduce the client's perception of the therapist's competence. Clients may see them as less expert which might be positive or negative. If the disclosure is incongruent or meets the needs of the therapist rather than the client, clients could feel protective of the therapist, and boundaries could become confused or violated (Audet, 2011; Roberts, 2005). There is a difference between disclosing an inadequacy and skilled sharing of processed experience and the learning from it.

The US Substance Abuse and Mental Health Services Administration (SAMHSA) report (Hyman, 2008) focuses on sharing lived experience of mental health challenges and how this can increase hope and reduce stigma. They cite psychiatrist Beth McGilley: 'I've asked many of my patients what it has meant for them to know about my history, and there is one resounding refrain: HOPE!' (Hyman, 2008, p. 19). Morgan and Lawson (2015) report on focus groups with mental health staff and people who use services, finding that sharing lived experience, especially that of mental distress, promoted a recovery-oriented ethos, offered hope, challenged stigma and discrimination, could break down 'them and us' perceptions, enhanced practice and offered the opportunity for a more inclusive humanistic mental health service. However, concerns were raised about possible exploitative relationships and whether people using services wanted staff to share their personal experiences.

Mental health professionals report that they feel greater understanding and empathy with the people they work with as a result of their own lived experience of mental distress and that they are able to bring hope (Gilbert & Stickley, 2012; Huet & Holttum, 2016).

However, this does not mean that other people are less empathic or understanding. Personal experience, the translation of this into qualities and expertise, and sharing the experience may be separate related processes.

Two recent studies have asked the views of people who use services (de Vos et al., 2016; Lewis-Holmes, 2016). A study of 205 service users of a Dutch eating disorders clinic, where staff routinely recounted their lived experience of eating disorders, found that 97 per cent of people using the service reported advantages to the use of lived experience in therapy – 82 per cent felt more recognised and heard (empathy), there was more equality, and the therapist appeared more knowledgeable, open and honest; whereas 11 per cent reported disadvantages such as forming negative comparisons and not enough distance (de Vos et al., 2016). Therapists reported greater helpfulness *and* greater disadvantages than did service users.

Lewis-Holmes (2016) carried out qualitative interviews with people using mental health services about staff with lived experience. People experienced increased empathy towards and from the practitioner, as well as increased hope, trust and feeling less alone, and they saw the staff as more human with less power imbalance. However, they also expressed concerns that practitioners might over-identify and bring their own experience too much. They worried about triggering the practitioners, needing to support them and whether information was confidential. This might be less likely when sharing experience-based capabilities rather than experience-related vulnerabilities. It may also be influenced by expectations about professionals and whether it is surprising to hear about their lived experience.

Beyond academic research, a Twitter survey of 2,673 people found that 69 per cent of people would feel comforted to know their mental health professional had their own experience of mental illness or distress, 21 per cent were not bothered and 6 per cent said they would feel uneasy (Emma @Little_Em, 2016).

There may also be risks associated with *not* sharing or being open about lived experience. People receiving support report disclosures by mental health professionals twice as helpful as non-disclosures and non-disclosures twice as unhelpful, mostly due to the effect on the relationship and equality. For example, people felt invalidated if their therapist did not answer questions about who they were (Hanson, 2005). How each was experienced was affected by how skilfully the disclosure or non-disclosure was made. Not disclosing at all can negatively impact therapeutic relationships (Henretty & Levitt, 2010). Remaining silent is not a neutral position; within our society, it tends to be assumed that mental health professionals do not have lived experience of mental health challenges unless this is disconfirmed.

Someone I (Sara) worked with assumed that all staff were happy and worked full time and she said she felt useless in contrast. She found it surprising and helpful to learn that I worked part time because I was self-managing a disability. This enabled her to feel recovery was possible and take steps towards part-time work.

In addition to the evidence for the benefits of using lived experience, peers and other staff use lived experience due to values which see ourselves as connected by shared humanity. By all staff connecting with and using their lived experience, there is an opportunity for a more humanistic approach to healthcare and a breakdown of the 'them and us' culture. The values of peer support, outlined in Chapter 2, can be shared by all staff. 'If any service is to promote the recovery of those whom it serves then it must develop relationships that recognise our common humanity. This can only be achieved if staff share something of themselves' (Perkins, 2016, p. 8).

> ### Case Example: Diana's Experience
>
> #### Diana Byrne
>
> I once had a nurse who was amazing and brilliant, in the way she worked with me. She was very empathic – the first person to talk from the heart. I was intrigued to know how she was able to empathise and understand exactly how I felt. I asked her how was it that she really understood the struggle I was experiencing. She told me she had had her own mental health struggle and had overcome it. She inspired me and gave me hope that I could have a better life. I thought: 'If she can do it I can. If she can get over it I can learn to cope and there must be a way out of this.' She helped me begin my long and sometimes difficult, painful Recovery Journey.
>
> My advice to mental health professionals is choose who you disclose to and if you think it will help them to share some of your story then do. Always question yourself as to why you think it'll be helpful.

Exercise

Diana's account from the perspective of someone who uses mental health services illustrates aspects of sharing lived experience:

- Connecting – 'talked from the heart' 'very empathic'
- Responsive – 'I asked .. she told'
- Measured – 'she told me of her own mental health struggle' (not all the details)
- Identification – 'if she can do it I can'

Think about these four domains in your own work and life. How has it felt when you or someone you are talking with had demonstrated these?

Critical Debate: The Roles of Peer Support Workers and Other Mental Health Professionals Sharing Their Lived Experience

In this chapter we argue that it is beneficial to both people using services and staff if all staff connect with their whole selves and use their lived experience in their work. In other words, if they see themselves as sharing some points of identification with the people they support. This is a core skill of a peer worker. So what, if any, are the differences between peer workers and other staff?

There may be an argument that if professionals or support workers shared their lived experience of mental health problems, peer workers would not be needed. Conversely, we understand peer work as a specialism, with clear values and which requires particular training and supervision around sharing lived experience and how to maintain personal well-being while doing so.

Peer workers may be perceived to have more equal status with the people they support than other mental health professionals. A professional sharing their lived experience is not equivalent relationally to a peer worker: mental health professionals with mental health challenges still have status, certain legal powers, hierarchy and specific knowledge.

Perkins (2016) suggests that different roles have different primary functions and bring different expertise: mental health professionals are defined by and primarily utilise their qualifications and work experience; peers their lived experience of recovery and mental health challenges. However, people in each role bring their resources in relation to recovery and coping, life experience and professional skills and knowledge in ways that enhance their role. Some become skilled in all of these.

The expectations of people using services is for mental health professionals to primarily offer their specified expertise and this may affect how they perceive sharing. Staff need consider the impact of sharing in the light of these expectations; it might be more surprising and impact differently to hear of a psychiatrist's experiences compared with a peer's.

As peer roles develop and other staff increasingly share their lived experience, we can build our understanding of how sharing lived experience, whether by professionals or by peers, can enhance people's experience of accessing and working within mental health services.

What to consider when sharing lived experience

While sharing lived experience means moving away from traditional divides, it remains important to maintain professional boundaries. Professional guidelines discuss the importance of professional boundaries and of avoiding actions which might cause harm and affect the reputation of the profession. These guidelines are beginning to discuss sharing lived experience. The Royal College of Psychiatry (RCPsych) discusses the risks of excessive or inappropriate disclosure, raising the need for psychiatrists to use care and supervision and to ensure their own needs are met elsewhere (Royal College of Psychiatry, 2013). Despite these cautions, psychiatrists must challenge discrimination and promote positive images of mental health in the media (Royal College of Psychiatry, 2014) and several presidents of the RCPsych have spoken about their own lived experience. Nursing standards for competence state 'mental health nurses must practice in a way that focuses on the therapeutic use of self'; 'They must be aware of their own mental health, and know when to share aspects of their own life to inspire hope while maintaining professional boundaries' (Nursing and Midwifery Council, 2014, pp. 17, 19). Some therapeutic approaches such as narrative systemic therapy and dialectical behavioural therapy encourage sharing lived experience as part of the approach.

Shepherd and colleagues (2008) suggest standards or ten top tips for skilled recovery-oriented practice, adopted by many NHS and voluntary sector organisations, including: 'After each interaction, the mental health professional should ask her/himself, did I ... identify examples from my own "lived experience", or that of other service users, which inspires and validates their hopes?' (p. 9).

Drawing on our own experience, the literature on sharing lived experience and Lewis-Holmes' (2016) research into if and how people who use services would like staff to share their lived experience, we can begin to develop guidelines for considering sharing our lived experience. There are two guiding questions that we have found to be central:

- Is this for the benefit of the person I am working with?
- Is it okay for me that I share this information?

These questions may be relevant both when we think it might be helpful to share information and in response to questions from people we are working with.

Case Example: Sharing Lived Experience as a Clinician

I am employed as a clinical psychologist to use the expertise from this training. The kind of psychologist I am is influenced by my own life experiences. I have close relatives who have used mental health services and I have experienced periods of distress and accessed services in adolescence. I also manage a long-term health condition.

In my clinical work I primarily use the skills I am trained in. I also find people value my briefly sharing lived experience. For example, I have shared that I too can have intrusive thoughts. I have found it useful to share examples of how I have coped with difficulties, especially when these also fit with the evidence base. Clients have told me that hearing I have had past struggles and need to manage my well-being helps them feel understood and that there is hope for recovery. I let them know that I am okay and that I have my own supervision and support so they need not worry. I sometimes hear from team colleagues what people have taken from my sharing – this helps me monitor the usefulness of sharing and is a reminder that what I share is not confidential.

I work in different contexts. In co-facilitating hearing voices groups and Recovery College courses, I share more information more frequently than in psychological therapy sessions. I also use my lived experience indirectly. My experience as a relative has helped me develop insights into what it's like to be a relative when loved ones go into crisis and how services have been helpful and unhelpful. This has fed my passion to improve services for carers and family members.

My peer colleagues are invaluable. We are supportive allies and they help me to think about what and when it is helpful to share. I only share what I am comfortable with – this tends to be information I have processed over time and which feels more resolved.

Areas for consideration

What to share

People who use services talk about the importance of the lived experience shared by others in a therapeutic context being relevant to them (Lewis-Holmes, 2016). It may be helpful to hear how a practitioner has coped with anxiety, but, for example, if the practitioner's anxiety was mild and exam-specific, whereas the person they're working with felt constantly anxious and unable to leave the house, this might be too different and create further distance.

Experiences may be less equivalent than they first seem due to inequalities such as poverty, class, sexism, homophobia and racism, which create additional challenges to recovery and further divisions between practitioners and people who access services. We all carry privilege and biases, often unconsciously, which affect any interactions but are particularly relevant in the context of the existing power imbalance of provider and recipient. Instead of offering hope, feelings of inadequacy might be reinforced by comparisons with this person with the same diagnosis who has become a successful professional.

People who use services find it helpful to hear about past struggles that have been successfully resolved (Knox & Hill, 2003). However, it cannot be assumed that what worked for one person will work for another (Lewis-Holmes, 2016). Roberts (2005) recommends sharing dilemmas and how it was to grapple with them rather than suggesting solutions which may not fit.

When to share

Sharing lived experience may be more helpful in certain contexts, such as when the relationship has developed, than others. People want to know that the practitioner they are working with is competent, well trained and stable (Lewis-Holmes, 2016). Alongside particular experiences, it may be helpful to share that you are well supported and have supervision and that they do not need to worry about you.

> *My therapist shared that she had been divorced in a way that was helpful for me. I had been talking about how my partner and I had recently separated and were getting divorced. I was feeling shame about the relationship failing and felt quite isolated as all my friends were in long-term relationships and only one had ever been divorced. It was helpful for me to know that my therapist, who I respected and found helpful, had also been divorced. However, had she told me in an earlier session or gone into the details of her own divorce this would not have been helpful.*

Why – reasons for sharing

Information may be shared to help foster a therapeutic relationship; bring hope or model recovery; to normalise problems or reduce feelings of being alone; or to dispel assumptions.

> *I shared with a client with psychosis about having a long-term condition that meant I sometimes had to take periods of time off sick. The team and I worried that otherwise she would think that it was her causing me to become unwell as she believed that she had the power to poison people.*

It is also useful to reflect on potential unconscious motivations such as whether sharing gratifies your own needs to reduce your insecurities, seek approval or work through your own problems.

How to share

People using services report valuing sharing which is short, infrequent and retains focus on their needs and goals. A full disclosure or announcement which includes many details about the practitioner's lived experience may feel like role reversal, shifting focus to the practitioner, and is not helpful (Lewis-Holmes, 2016). Brief sharing of information with a recovery frame and reassurance about the practitioner's own support and well-being is preferable. Further brief information could then be given in response to questions.

> *When I was struggling with my sleep and feeling bad about this I found it helpful that my worker said she also sometimes struggled with sleep. I felt she understood and I was not alone. Hearing her dilemmas about following what was meant to work helped me trust her as we focused on strategies I could use to improve my sleep.*

When sharing, it is important to be tentative and notice the impact this has. We have found it helpful to check with the client and ask them how they experienced the disclosure. When working with a family, consider how it affects each member of the family. It might be helpful for one member of a family to hear a personal experience, but make another member feel more distance.

Your well-being

Finally, it is important to consider what it is like for you to be sharing this, not only with this client, but with others they might share it with; and how you would feel discussing this with colleagues or in supervision. Information you share with clients is not confidential – it puts your personal information in the public domain. While sharing your experiences, it is important to monitor how you feel and moderate what you share accordingly (Table 9.1). The impact the sharing has on you will affect how it is received. We use supervision to reflect on the experience of sharing for us and clients. We have found it is usually more helpful to share information where there is more distance through time or space to process it in supervision, life or our own therapy. Sometimes we use our experiences indirectly to reflect on questions to ask or offer empathic responses. In order to develop skills in using lived experience, training and supervision are needed in a supportive organisational context.

Exercise: For Mental Health Workers

All mental health professionals bring:

- Expertise by training
- Life experience, which may include lived experience of mental distress and recovery.

Think about what life experience you bring to your work and what, when, why and how you might or might not consider sharing this with people you work with in mental health services. How could you transform your experience into expertise of value in your work and how could you check this was of benefit to those you work with and okay for you too?

Table 9.1 Considerations for mental health staff when sharing lived experience

	Does it benefit the person you are sharing with?	Is it okay with you?
What	Is this the kind of information which people often find helpful? Is it a similar experience? Is it about coping and recovery?	Are you happy to share this? Are you happy that it might be shared with other people and be in the public domain? Is this something you have largely processed or resolved? Are you happy to be asked further about it? Have you had any training on how to share your experiences?
When	Is this the right time in your relationship with this person? Is this the right time to be sharing this particular information with this person? Does it fit with their present focus?	Is this the right time for you? Do you have adequate support and supervision? Are you feeling okay today?
Why	Why are you sharing this information? What is the likely benefit for the person you're working with?	Are there any possible unconscious reasons why you might want to share this which might not be for the benefit of the person?
How	Are you sharing small things at a time? How will you check how the client experiences this?	How are you experiencing it?

Different ways of using our lived experience

Although the focus of this chapter is on how staff might share our lived experience with the people we work with, we might also share with colleagues and supervisees, when delivering training and developing services. This may challenge expectations that as a mental health professional we would not also have lived experience of mental distress.

The GP Dr David Shiers spoke openly about his family's struggle to cope with and get appropriate care for their daughter who was diagnosed with psychosis from an early age (Shiers, 1998). His experience motivated him to create a campaign which led to international collaborations and a national development programme for first episode psychosis services across the UK. David led these developments as national co-director for early intervention services and was awarded an OBE for his services to vulnerable people.

We might also use lived experience to inform our practice without disclosing it. One of us suggested routinely sharing our notes and letters about clients with them. This was influenced by personal experience of seeing a psychotherapist, wondering what he was saying and requesting to read his notes. Lived experience also affects our relationship with mental health legislation if we think that this could be me or my relative (see Roberts et al., 2008).

Case Example: Using Lived Experience to Reflect on Mental Health Legislation

Being detained under mental health legislation and treated against your will is possibly the most traumatic expression of psychiatric care people ever experience. It commonly leaves long memories and other scars. It is also difficult for the staff involved and we often lean heavily on professional detachment to cope. But it is here that our humanity counts the most.

I found it bewildering when my mother was detained and treated in this way. I was called out of a ward round I was leading on an inpatient rehab unit to speak firstly to the assessing social worker and then to my very distressed mother. It was such a collision between my personal and professional lives and a considerable lesson too. People subject to mental health legislation are often overwhelmed, firstly by their own experience and then by the service response to their predicament. They need their humanity, individuality and personality to be seen, heard and respected. The person involved could be our mother, brother or ourselves. If we can sustain a sense of kinship and common humanity to mobilise our empathy and focus our professional skills on sustaining a sensitive personal relationship in these most difficult of circumstances we are so much more likely to offer care with compassion. We may then use mental health legislation, as intended, to support recovery rather than be complicit in delivering an additional dehumanising, traumatic impediment.

How organisations can support staff to use their lived experience in their work

A key element to sharing lived experience is support, supervision and training. This provides organisations with an opportunity to embed a culture that places shared humanity at their heart and listens to and learns from lived experience. The Francis report (Francis, 2013) highlights that healthcare organisations can be the opposite of compassionate, yet in order for lived experience to be valued, people need to feel safe and have space. There needs to be organisational commitment to staff sharing their lived experience with a culture of openness, sharing life experiences and valuing diversity. This can be reinforced by the executive team and should run through the whole organisation, from recruitment, team cultures, leadership, learning and development, supervision, clinical engagement, staff well-being, human resources and occupational health.

Many healthcare organisations have embraced peer workers and overseen shifts in how lived experience is valued. However, this can situate lived experience within the peer workforce and not translate into changes to the experience or practice of all staff.

In order to support this culture change some organisations have developed networks for staff with lived experience. These can build alliances with other staff networks that support staff who also may experience stigma and discrimination, for example Disability, BAME, LGBT.

One such example is the Dorset Hidden Talents Project.

Case Example: Dorset Hidden Talents

In 2010 the Dorset Wellbeing and Recovery Partnership (a partnership between Dorset Healthcare and Dorset Mental Health Forum, a local peer-led organisation) set up a project called Hidden Talents. The project was developed as part of the recovery agenda. While peer worker roles were being developed existing staff in traditional roles started to ask about how their lived experience could be utilised. Staff reported that they felt that they could not be open about their experiences as they felt they would be stigmatised.

The Hidden Talents project aims to challenge stigma, increase understanding of how lived experience can be used to improve people's experience of services and promote the well-being of all staff.

Central to the success of Hidden Talents is the combination of top-down permission giving and bottom-up ownership and development of the project. It was originally launched by the chief operating officer sending out an email to all staff stating that the organisation 'valued lived experience as an asset'. The chief executive and the board have publicly and regularly endorsed the project.

The main thrust of the work has been developed by the staff involved in Hidden Talents, who self-identify as having lived experience and work across a range of clinical and administrative roles across the Trust. The group have produced booklets and a film aimed at challenging stigma, valuing the lived experience of all staff and promoting the project. The group runs monthly peer support groups, have developed a course on sharing lived experience; been involved in updating policies and guidance for staff accessing mental health services and sharing personal information; and worked with human resources and occupational health to raise understanding of people's experiences.

While progress has been made over the past five years, it has been challenging and has involved significant courage from those involved being pioneers in being open about their experiences. There is still much to do in building a culture that truly values lived experience, but the development of the group and their passion has been impressive and the continued commitment of the organisation has been encouraging.

In order to create a humanistic recovery-focused culture which values lived experience, a clear vision and action plan are needed which involves all aspects of the service. Human resources and occupational health can support staff well-being and the recruitment and retention of a diverse workforce. Narratives build emotional engagement alongside research evidence. Managers, professional leads and professional bodies can give people confidence to share experiences and act as role models. Clear policies, guidelines and protocols support and empower staff to share lived experience.

Staff also benefit from training in using lived experience, and opportunities to discuss this in supervision. This might be a reflective practice group around using lived experience or might involve including it in regular supervision. Managers and supervisors therefore might also benefit from training in this area.

Exercise

The importance of a supportive team and/or organisation is key in being able to safely share lived experience. Reflect on your experiences of working in a team or organisation: (e.g. at work, college or sports club)

- What are the elements of your team/organisation that would support sharing of lived experience?
- What are the elements that would make it difficult?
- What things could be done differently to cultivate the sharing of lived experience?

Learning points for building organisational cultures supportive of staff using lived experience:

- Recognise the value and create opportunities for staff to learn how to transform their personal life experience into expertise of use in their work
- Form staff networks to offer mutual support and develop a vision and plan
- Ensure senior staff give clear messages about lived experience being an asset
- Share narratives that illustrate the value of lived experience
- Articulate the relationship and role similarities and differences with peer workers within the organisation
- Build alliances and networks that share and support the value of lived experience and how this may improve the well-being of all staff as well as improving the experience of people who access services and their families.

CONCLUSIONS

Lived experience of mental health challenges is common among all mental health professionals and not only designated peer workers. All staff using their lived experience as well as their expertise by training is potentially one way of valuing this experience and breaking down 'us and them' divides, changing the culture of mental health services. We have shown how all staff may use their lived experience to benefit people using services and how organisations can support this. It may be transformational for both workers and people using services if all staff own and express our experience with shared humanity:

> *Not to use lived expertise is a waste* (Alex Garner, Participation Lead, Sussex Partnership NHS Foundation Trust)

ACKNOWLEDGEMENTS

With thanks to Diana Byrne and Alex Garner, and to those who contributed experiences to this chapter and remain anonymous.

FURTHER READING AND RESOURCES

Five mental health professionals write about their lived experience:

Deegan, P. (1996). Recovery as a journey of the heart. *Psychiatric Rehabilitation Journal*, 19(2), 91–97.

Gask, L. (2015). *The other side of silence: A psychiatrist's memoir of depression.* Chichester: Summersdale Publishers.

May, R. (2000). Routes to recovery – the roots of a clinical psychologist. *Clinical Psychology Forum*, 26, 35–41.

Perkins, R. (1999). My three psychiatric careers. In Barker, P., Davidson, B. and Campbell, P. (eds), *From the Ashes of Experience.* London: Whurr Publications.

Roberts, G. (2012). Recovery for practitioners: Stories to live by. In McManus, G. and Carson, J. (eds), *From Communism to Schizophrenia and Beyond.* London: Whiting and Birch.

Videos

Rachel Perkins talking about using lived experience:

- https://www.youtube.com/watch?v=T_Ialloj1Hs

Debbie Cleaveley discusses her recovery:

- https://www.youtube.com/watch?v=QGDzdssv6qs&NR=1&feature=fvwp±10.0....0...1.1.64.psy-ab.2.11.861.6.0j35i39k1j0i131k1j0i67k1.Zf4qPQxtVLU

Video introducing Dorset Hidden Talents:

- https://www.youtube.com/watch?v=R-PNy5oqdbY

REFERENCES

Audet, C. T. (2011). Client perspectives of therapist self-disclosure: Violating boundaries or removing barriers?. *Counselling Psychology Quarterly*, 24(2), 85–100.

Corrigan, P. and Matthews, A. K. (2003). Stigma and disclosure: Implications for coming out of the closet. *Journal of Mental Health*, 12(3), 235–248.

de Vos, J. A., Netten, C. and Noordenbos, G. (2016). Recovered eating disorder therapists using their experiential knowledge in therapy: A qualitative examination of the therapists' and patients' views. *Eating Disorders*, 24(3), 207–223.

Francis, R. (2013). *Report of the Mid Staffordshire NHS Foundation Trust Public Inquiry.* London: The Stationery Office.

Gilbert, P. and Stickley, T. (2012). 'Wounded Healers': The role of lived-experience in mental health education and practice. *Journal of Mental Health Training, Education and Practice*, 7(1), 33–41.

Hanson, J. (2005). Should your lips be zipped? How therapist self-disclosure and non-disclosure affects clients. *Counselling and Psychotherapy Research*, 5(2), 96–104.

Henretty, R. and Levitt, H. M. (2010). The role of therapist self-disclosure in psychotherapy: A qualitative review. *Clinical Psychology Review*, 30, 63–77.

Hill, C.E., Helms, J.E., Tichenor, V., Spiegel, S.B., O'Grady, K.E. and Perry, E.S. (1988). Effects of therapist response modes in brief psychotherapy. *Journal of Counseling Psychology*, 35, 222–233.

Huet, V. and Holttum, S. (2016). Art therapists with experience of mental distress: Implications for art therapy training and practice. *International Journal of Art Therapy*, 21(3), 95–103.

Hyman, I. (2008). *Self-Disclosure and Its Impact on Individuals Who Receive Mental Health Services.* HHS Pub. No. (SMA) -08-4337. Rockville, MD: Center for Mental Health Services, Substance Abuse and Mental Health Services Administration.

Knox, S., Hess, S. A., Petersen, D. A. and Hill, C. E. (1997). A qualitative analysis of client perceptions of the effects of helpful therapist self-disclosure in long-term therapy. *Journal of Counseling Psychology*, 44(3), 274–283.

Knox, S. and Hill, C. E. (2003). Therapist self-disclosure: Research based suggestions for practitioners. *Journal of Clinical Psychology*, 59(5), 529–539.

Lewis-Holmes, E. (2016). 'They've been there, they know.' How mental health service users think about mental health staff with lived experience. Unpublished doctoral thesis, Royal Holloway, University of London.

Morgan, P. and Lawson, J. (2015). Developing guidelines for sharing lived experience of staff in health and social care. *Mental Health and Social Inclusion*, 19(2), 78–86.

Nursing and Midwifery Council (2014). *Standards for Competence for Registered Nurses.* London: Nursing and Midwifery Council.

Perkins, R. (2016). Finding other ways of enabling people using services to access support from others who share their experience. Keynote paper, Peer Worker Critical Debate, 1 June, Nottingham, ImROC.

Rinaldi, M., Perkins, R., Hardisty, J., Harding, E., Taylor, A. and Brown, S. (2004). Implementing a user employment programme in a mental health trust: Lessons learned. *A Life in the Day*, 8(4), 9–14.

Roberts, J. (2005). Transparency and self-disclosure in family therapy: Dangers and possibilities. *Family Process*, 44(1), 45–63.

Roberts, G., Dorkins, E., Wooldridge, J. and Hewis, E. (2008). Detained – what's my choice? part 1: Discussion. *Advances in Psychiatric Treatment*, 14, 172–180.

Roberts, G., Good, J., Wooldridge, J. and Baker, E. (2011). Steps towards 'putting recovery at the heart of all we do': Workforce development and the contribution of 'lived experience. *Journal of Mental Health Training, Education and Practice*, 6(1), 17–28.

Royal College of Psychiatry (2013). *Vulnerable Patients, Safe Doctors: Good Practice in Our Clinical Relationships.* London: Royal College of Psychiatrists.

Royal College of Psychiatry (2014). *Good Psychiatric Practice: Code of Ethics* CR186. London: Royal College of Psychiatrists.

Shepherd, G., Boardman, J. and Burns, M. (2010). *Implementing Recovery: A Methodology for Organisational Change.* London: Centre for Mental Health.

Shepherd, G., Boardman, J. and Slade, M. (2008). *Making Recovery a Reality.* London: Centre for Mental Health.

Shiers, D. (1998). Who cares? Personal view. *British Medical Journal (Clinical research ed.)*, 316, 785.

10 | Employing and Supporting People with Lived Experience in Peer Support and Other Roles

Clare Ockwell and Howard Pearce

Chapter Summary

- Peer support is based on equality and involves mutual sharing of lived experience. Other roles for people with lived experience should avoid using the term 'peer' as they are not based on the same principles and values as peer support

- Things to take into consideration when employing anyone with lived experience include:

  - Recruitment policies that avoid intimidation and that promote applications from people with lived experience who may be just re-entering the workforce

  - Consideration of benefits issues

  - Training, support and supervision

  - Openness to making reasonable adjustments

  - Preparing non-peer workforce/organisational issues

Introduction

In its purest form peer support in mental health has existed for as long as people living with such issues have met with each other. At this informal level peer support has generally been a popular and therapeutic means of seeking support. However, in recent years peer support has been formalised. This raises a number of issues for organisations of all kinds, including:

- How people who are at various stages in their own recovery journeys can be supported to maintain their well-being at work
- How to keep peer support authentic within organisational structures that work traditionally and are not used to peers and that are still developing their recovery ethos.

'Peer' is first defined as 'an equal' (*Chambers Dictionary*) and while peer support is yet to reach the dictionary it has been defined many times over in literature and practice, usually underpinned by principles and/or values. Chapter 2 explores some of these definitions and values of peer support.

For the authors, some of the key factors in working in a 'peer' role are keeping the power balance as equal as possible and ensuring the supported peer retains autonomy. However as Beales and Wilson (2015, p. 315) point out, 'It is often mistakenly assumed that everybody who experiences mental distress is a peer supporter' and it is important that temperament, aptitude and well-being are all given careful consideration prior to encouraging anyone to follow this as a career pathway.

Where, for organisational reasons, people with lived experience are employed in roles which do not require them to offer peer support or uphold the values of peer working, the title 'lived experience worker' might be more appropriate.

However it should not be forgotten that at any given time, one in six of the workforce might be experiencing mental health difficulties which affect their ability to function (Lelliot et al., 2008; explored further in Chapter 9). So it is certain that within any large workforce in the NHS or third sector there will be a large number of lived experience workers who should equally be afforded appropriate support in their employment. Planning for a lived experience workforce should teach lessons that are of benefit to the welfare of all staff.

In this chapter we explore the methods used in different working environments to support people from lived experience backgrounds, and what best practice might look like when it comes to employing peer support and other lived experience workers in different organisations. We draw on the experience of a variety of local and national organisations, which have developed their lived experience workforce using peer supporters and/or in other roles.

We also explore different models of supporting lived experience in the workforce and consider how these fit with current thinking on co-production and peer support. In particular, we use case examples from two peer-led organisations in Sussex, the CAPITAL Project Trust and Recovery Partners to demonstrate differing but strong models of peer employment. We also include an experience of a peer worker within the NHS.

We go on to discuss some of the challenges and benefits for non–peer-led organisations, particularly NHS Trusts, as they progress towards embedding peer workers within their teams. In the course of this, questions will be posed to help those setting up peer support services to consider some of the pitfalls and how to embed best practice into their plans.

We also consider some of the problems that can arise when employing people with lived experience, such as the issue of working part time while claiming benefits, the risk of excessive stress, the possible recurrence of mental health symptoms and stigma from mental health professionals. Also some of the economic factors for the employing organisations, such as the prevalence of short-term contracts, financial insecurity and convincing funders that employing people with lived experience can provide value for money.

Recruitment, occupational health and HR (human resources)

In general, work is good for mental health and long unemployment leads to mental health difficulties (Warr, 1987; Mental Health Foundation, 2012). However, there are many barriers to employment for those with a mental health history, including stigma, discrimination and poor expectations from employers (Centre for Mental Health, 2013). Mental health professionals also have low expectations and underestimate skills and abilities. Nearly half of people with mental health problems in paid employment have previously been advised by their mental health professionals not to work (Rinaldi et al., 2008). Provided recruitment processes are positive and support networks are available, working in peer support can bypass these problems because a mental health history is one of the qualifications.

For many peer workers, taking on a peer role may be their first step into the world of work for many years, and merely applying for work requires a huge leap of faith. It is therefore sensible to make the processes of recruitment as straightforward as possible. However there are also barriers at this stage, including occupational health assessments and criminal records checks or **Disclosure and Barring Service (DBS)** checks.

Most employers want to see a conviction-free history and may be wary of employing someone with a criminal record. However, it is to be expected that on occasions DBS checks will turn up some incident in the past. This should lead to a sensitive discussion about the circumstances of the criminal behaviour. These conversations might include supervisors, service managers and members of HR to discuss the nature of the offences a person has committed and the likelihood that this will negatively impact on their current role. In most cases it should not be a problem; indeed, in some cases it is an advantage. For example, someone with several convictions for drunkenness or drug possession in the past may be a role model for clients who are struggling with addiction. Peer workers and their managers may want to think through a relapse or safety plan to identify circumstances where there is higher risk of problems reoccurring so that the staff member and employer can plan for this, for example by the peer worker gaining extra support, a change in duties or time off when there is greater risk.

Occupational health assessments are also a routine part of the employment process in larger organisations. They are designed to assess the health needs of new employees and, where needed, offer support for them to fulfil their role. They can be unhelpful or stigmatising experiences for peer workers in some large organisations, including the NHS, if the person doing the assessment is not aware of the nature of peer support or the value of lived experience. The authors have heard examples of people being refused work because they have a mental health diagnosis, despite the nature of peer support requiring this experience. Reviews show that there is little relationship between diagnosis or severity of illness and employment outcomes – the best predictors of work outcomes being recent employment history, motivation and self-efficacy: 'Wanting to work and believing that you can are the best predictors of work outcomes' (Rinaldi et al., 2008, p. 51).

The first question on some occupational health forms may be 'How many days off sick have you had in the past two years?' One of the authors truthfully wrote in response 'Every single one of them.' Fortunately, the occupational health department were aware of the situation and approved the application. Smaller organisations, especially those that are fully or partially staffed and run by people with lived experience are generally much better in this respect. Larger organisations which do not specialise in peer support may need to work closely with their HR and occupational health departments to develop a shared understanding of the peer worker role and a clear process for supporting people with lived experience into work.

In addition, people new to or returning to work may need extra information to understand the recruitment processes; they may benefit from help with application forms and interview practice, perhaps by being signposted to an Individual Placement Support (IPS) employment service (see Rinaldi et al., 2008). A simple and efficient recruitment process is helpful to all employees, and peer workers are no exception. Over-complicated systems with long delays might cause people to lose self-confidence and cause financial issues where the benefits system is being navigated alongside a person's employment.

Exercise

Consider the recruitment and selection procedures currently used by the organisation you work in or one you are familiar with. Identify ways in which they might be improved to enable people with lived experience to feel more comfortable and empowered to apply for posts. Using your knowledge of local resources, how can people best be supported to apply for peer worker roles and by whom?

Training, support and supervision

Although peer support has always happened on an informal basis it would be wholly inappropriate to parachute anyone into a formal role without receiving training. Meeting people with mental health issues and listening to their current problems or past traumas or abuse can affect the peer worker. They may have similar experience of trauma or abuse and find themselves affected by difficult memories. Things could happen while supporting clients that trigger past difficulties or cause peer workers to wobble in their own mental health.

Even if there are no triggers, the peer worker may take on some of the problems of their clients and be upset by them long after their time with the client has finished. Mourra and colleagues (2014) suggest that one important function of training and supervision for peer workers is to support them to undertake the emotionally involved process of peer support while protecting their own well-being.

Training should be provided to enable peer workers to maintain their well-being by planning ways to reduce the risk of being triggered or triggering others by what they share and hear being shared (see Chapter 8). Training also ensures that peers understand issues such as safeguarding and confidentiality. Consideration should be given to offering peer workers accredited training as this will not only enhance their status within staff teams but also allow peers to demonstrate competence at a recognised level to future employers.

Like all professional groups, to reduce the impact of mental health triggers, recurring memories and client problems affecting the peer worker, it is important to provide good support and supervision. It is best if support and supervision is provided by someone who has experience of working as a peer, preferably a trained peer supervisor, or maybe a fellow peer worker. This is a well-established approach within the peer support literature, where, particularly within non–peer-run organisations, it is essential that supervision and performance appraisals should be facilitated by other peer workers (Ashcraft & Anthony, 2007; O'Hagan et al., 2010). Supervision with other peers supports them to reconnect with the values that underpin their role and they can experience mutual, reciprocal relationships which they can use as a template within their work. Similarly to peer support relationships, peer supervision should be underpinned by the values of learning together, self-reflection and mutuality (Mead, 2001).

An advantage to the peer worker of working in peer support, especially in a peer-led organisation, is that they will have support from their peers in learning the skills required for peer support and starting work – something that can often be very stressful, especially for people who have been out of work for years – as well as continuing support while working. Support while working is the single most helpful support in terms of finding and keeping work according to a survey of employment for people with a diagnosis of schizophrenia (SANE, 2013). Guidance on employing peer workers often suggests that more than one peer should be employed at any one time (e.g. Repper, 2013). This provides non-peer staff with a broader understanding of peer support, removes pressure from a single peer worker and affords each peer worker the support of the other person as they navigate their new roles.

Like all staff working in supportive roles, every peer worker needs supervision at least monthly and more frequently if there are particular challenges. Additionally, the importance of peers meeting regularly outside of supervision, both formally and informally, should not be underestimated. This creates opportunities for peer support, reflective practice and team training, enabling them to have reflective space for everyone to air any difficulties and share possible solutions. Similarly, one person may want to share a good outcome, or the success or failure of certain techniques, so that everyone can reflect on best practice.

In addition to regular supervision, peer workers, like all staff members, should be aware of the ways that they can access urgent support within work if they need to – for example, after a peer worker has seen a client and traumatic memories were triggered; or if a supported peer needs an urgent solution, maybe to avoid a client becoming homeless or losing custody of a child.

There are advantages to working in peer support. Peer workers are able to use their mental health experience as a bonus in their work, as an asset. For some people, peer support may be the only work they could contemplate, because many employers would be reluctant to employ them, even if they have excellent qualifications. There is also the satisfaction that comes from helping other people along their recovery journey, seeing their successes as they progress towards something they previously thought impossible.

Peer support work may be the stepping stone to other positions. With experience and confidence gained, many former staff from both Recovery Partners and CAPITAL are now working full time or in more senior jobs in the NHS and other organisations.

Reasonable adjustments

The Department of **Work and Pensions** (DWP, 2017) gives some guidance on employing people with mental health conditions:

- Offering flexible working patterns, including changes to start and finish times and adaptable break times
- Changing their working environment, for example providing a quiet place to work
- Working with them to create an action plan to help them manage their condition
- Allowing them leave to attend appointments connected with their mental health.

While these are helpful and constitute reasonable adjustments, they fall short of what could be provided by an employer who is familiar with mental health needs. Other reasonable adjustments may include:

- Additional support with personnel procedures, for example completing timesheets, booking holiday – particularly initially
- Promoting self-management, including taking the odd day's absence to support well-being
- An appreciation of where behaviour is caused by declining health and flexibility to intervene to prevent this spiralling beyond what can be tolerated and support the worker's well-being.

Reasonable adjustments are illustrated in the first case example and again at the end of the second case example.

Exercise

What reasonable adjustments might improve working conditions for peers and other lived experience workers?

Case Example: Community Peer Support – Supporting Peer Workers at Recovery Partners

Recovery Partners (http://recovery-partners.co.uk) is a non-profit peer-led mental health organisation operating mainly in East Sussex. Everyone in the organisation has mental health lived experience and some are also carers. It was set up in 2011 to provide peer support in Sussex. Since 2011 Recovery Partners has employed between 10 and 20 part-time peer workers. Work has included one-to-one peer support, drop-in sessions and training for service users, carers and professional staff, attending mental health planning and other meetings in the county, assisting with the support plans of people with mental health needs, suicide prevention and the operation of a Place of Calm for people at risk of suicide (see Chapter 11).

According to a 2013 survey by SANE (2013) only about 8 per cent of people with a diagnosis of schizophrenia are in employment, although more than half of the people with the condition would like to work. However, in peer support a diagnosis of schizophrenia can be an asset because it gives the person a common experience with some clients.

Marie (not her real name) has worked at Recovery Partners for several years. At her initial interview we asked her a question that is not often used in job interviews: 'Do you hear voices?' 'Yes I do as a matter of fact.' 'Oh good, we've had a special request for someone who hears voices.' Adapting the recruitment process increased her confidence through valuing her lived experience.

Working with people with similar experiences can be triggering. Marie was offered additional supervision sessions and found it helpful to research ways to support people with a diagnosis of schizophrenia from the Mind website as it provides good advice without being too drawn into the fears the condition produces. She was also supported to understand how to complete computerised timesheets.

Supporting peers helped Marie to feel well even when she was having a bad day. Recovery Partners has enabled her to structure her working life around her moods – her working day was reasonably adjusted to focus on the mornings as her good times are in the mornings.

Marie had a history of alcohol abuse and after some time in the job she relapsed and took some months off. With support from other staff she was encouraged to return to work and learn coping strategies:

When I started working in Peer-Support I was so unsure of myself. But I quickly settled in and found I was able to find ways to relate to everyone I tried to help. Having suffered trauma at a young age and having mental health problems throughout my school life; I had experience in understanding how people came to rock bottom, feeling they didn't want to live anymore.

My previous jobs were often unsuitable and unfulfilling. Recovery Partners has been the total opposite of that: meaningful and rewarding. I have never stuck in a job over 3 or 4 years, and Recovery Partners is the longest I have worked anywhere

Preparing the non-peer workforce

Authentic peer support is very different from clinical helping relationships within mental health services. Because of this, it is important to take time to explain the peer support role to clinical staff before peer workers are introduced to teams. It is important that teams are given the opportunity to address their concerns about this new workforce. Such concerns may range from 'What happens if they get unwell?' to 'Why are you paying former patients just to sit and talk to people?' This space is essential both to enable staff to talk frankly about their feelings about this new project and to enable them to understand the difference in approach that should work as a bridge between people using the service and staff. The process of working with teams and wider stakeholders to develop a peer support role is described in the following case example.

Exercise

Reflecting on what you have read, list the improvements your organisation will need to make to provide a more welcoming environment for peer workers.

Case Example: Inpatient Peer Support, CAPITAL Project Trust

The CAPITAL Project Trust (http://capitalproject.org/) was founded in 1997, initially as a training for trainers project to offer people with mental health issues the skills they needed to offer experience-based training to mental health professionals. It fairly soon diversified into other areas, including research, consultation and group advocacy. What also began to happen very early on was informal peer support. Members offered one another the support they needed to achieve. This ranged from a core belief in each other's abilities to enabling someone to deliver a training session by travelling with them.

Today CAPITAL has over 300 members, many of whom offer each other a wide variety of peer support. It is a peer-led organisation with its entire staff comprised of people with lived experience. We began to provide formal peer support in 2010 when we were contracted to offer it to inpatients on acute mental health wards across West Sussex. In this context we had to push to be able to employ people properly, as initially the assumption was made that people would like to do this as volunteers. Although, arguably, much of our business up to that point had already been about peer support, employing people in a dedicated role for this took considerable preparation:

> For peer support to be authentic and useful, it must be service user led, based on supporters and clients being of equal value with mutuality of benefit and joint responsibility for outcomes and finally, peer support services must be the result of genuine, service user led co-production between staff, peer supporters and people accessing the service. (Beales & Wilson, 2015 p. 316)

To this end we did the initial work to develop what the role should look like with hospital inpatients at Meadowfield Hospital in Worthing. This significantly informed the development of the peer support role description. We also worked closely with Sussex Partnership NHS Foundation Trust and local commissioners to ensure we were building something that would satisfy all stakeholders.

As we did not want to set anyone up to fail, a key part of the preparation was taking time to introduce the peer support role to all the other staff on the ward. We developed a short training session that could be taken up by lead staff, following our initial introductions, so that it was cascaded to everyone working on the site.

Staff members are encouraged to take occasional 'well-being days' as reasonable adjustments to promote self-care and prevent longer-term sickness. Additionally, we have a bank of relief peers who will step in to fill the gap should someone need to take time out. Our sick pay allowances allow for increased need to take sick leave for mental health issues (see https://fitforwork.org/employee/taking-a-leave-of-absence/causes-of-absence/mental-health-problems/). None of our staff need fear repercussions for taking the time they need to maintain their mental health. In one recent instance a post has been held open for almost two years. Bank staff are also eligible for rolled-up sick pay should they need it. We also have an established principle of the 'sanity break', a paid break of up to 15 minutes to be taken as time out when things get stressful.

To ensure our peer support workers have appropriate skills we have developed our own peer support training which is accredited to Level 4 by the University of Middlesex. It was devised specifically with the needs of people with mental health issues in mind, aiming to balance sufficient academic rigour with maintenance of a relaxed approach that builds confidence among the students. Much of the evidence for the award for the course is drawn from shadowing working peers and observed practice.

Case Example: Employment as Peer Support Specialist in the NHS

Tom (not his real name) has mental health issues and saw many psychiatrists and other professionals for years. His mental health is now much better and he has been employed as a bank peer support specialist by a mental health trust for several years. For much of that time there was little work available from the trust and some years none at all. The most significant work is part time in an assessment and treatment team at a local mental health centre.

He was the first peer worker at the centre and the first that many staff had met. Some staff accepted him immediately, recognising that he would relate to patients easily. However, it was four months before he had his first referral for one-to-one peer support and it was nine months before he had a reasonable portfolio of clients. These nine months involved a steady process of educating the team members about peer support. He met with other peer support staff in the same mental health trust and found that some had similar experiences. However, in other teams in the trust things were very different, and peer support specialists performed a whole range of tasks that he was not allowed to do, and some were on a higher pay scale.

Previously Tom worked in an NHS mental health residential home. Some residents were sectioned; others were voluntary patients. Once again he was the first peer support worker there, and some staff were unsure how to make use of him or how to integrate him into the team. He was rapidly accepted by the residents when they learned he had been in the mental health system for some years.

Some residents were given their medication before going into the dining room for the evening meal. One evening Tom joined the residents for the meal and took his own medication. Another member of staff was horrified and later told Tom 'You can't take your medication in front of the residents.'

Exercise

Consider the issues raised in Tom's case example – and discuss the following questions:
- What could have been done to prepare this team for a peer worker joining the team?
- Was Tom right to take medication while sitting with residents?
- Was the other member of staff right to criticise him?

Barriers that may affect all peer support workers, paid or voluntary

Gillard and colleagues (2014) highlight key barriers to effective adoption of peer worker roles:

- *A lack of shared understanding of the role* may put it at risk of being eroded beyond recognition with insufficient respect being given to the distinctive role so that it becomes eroded by expectations to perform too many generic tasks
- *Undermining peer identity* so peers become over-professionalised and too similar to other staff, including using professional jargon, so peers can be distanced from the people they support
- *Lack of role-specific support* including management and supervision that acknowledges the specific nature of the role, and training that gives peers the skills they need to share lived experience. It is also important not to disempower peers with an over-medicalised reaction to any relapses
- *Reshaping the peer role to fit existing organisational structures* rather than these being allowed to evolve may dilute the peer role, and lose its distinctive qualities
- *Cultural inflexibility within the organisation*, for example strict adherence to clinical boundaries, as opposed to 'peer' boundaries. There may be a reluctance to be open about mental health issues within the team, implying that peer expertise is not valued.

In addition to these barriers, we have experienced some other challenges which may affect peer workers.

Benefits issues

In our experience most peer workers are employed part time, and may be on bank contracts that do not include regular sick pay or holiday pay. This means that if they are off work for any reason, including sickness, they will not be paid. This adds to the uncertainty of their situation.

Many potential peer workers will want to take on these roles as 'permitted work' so peer roles should be structured accordingly. From an employer's perspective this is not an ideal model as it means more work, adding to costs; however, it is vital to ensure that peer workers are well supported and able to reacquaint themselves gradually to the world of work.

Many people with mental health issues are, or have been, on disability benefits such as **Employment Support Allowance (ESA)** and other benefits. If they start paid work in peer support and this is treated as permitted work while they continue to receive ESA, then they have to ensure that they work less than 16 hours a week and earn less than an amount that is usually 16 hours at the national minimum wage for over 25s (currently £7.50 an hour). They will then be able to continue to receive ESA and be credited with **National Insurance** contributions. They will need to let the Department of Work and Pensions (DWP) and the local authority know if they are also claiming any means-tested benefits such as **housing benefit**, parts of universal credit, **council tax benefit** or child tax credit, because their earnings will affect how much of the means-tested benefits they are paid.

Most people getting disability benefits such as ESA are reassessed by the DWP periodically. This is necessary because people's health may improve or deteriorate over time. There is the concern that they may be reassessed because the DWP learn that they are working or volunteering. For most people, the arrival of a letter from the DWP is a worry. For people with mental health issues such as anxiety the worry can be much worse, and has been known to cause peer support workers to stop working for several months until their benefit entitlement is certain.

If a paid peer worker is not receiving ESA or another income replacement benefit then depending on how much work they do they may not earn enough to pay National Insurance. This could affect the amount of state pension they will receive when they retire. Again their earnings could affect the amount they receive of any means-tested benefits including working tax credit, statutory sick pay and maternity benefits as well as those noted above.

It is advisable for prospective employers to facilitate specialist benefits advice for prospective and current employees.

Job security

Short-term contracts and short-term funding are the norm for many charities and other third sector organisations. It is unusual for any contract to be for more than three years and many are for one year or less. This means that at the end of the contract the work may have to change to the requirements of a new contract. Or funding may stop altogether, leaving paid staff and volunteers redundant. Loss of funding is happening for many mental health organisations across the country, causing them to have to close down, partly as a consequence of the general squeeze on finances. The NHS has historically offered the potential for more stable permanent contracts, yet even in the NHS most peer support workers are on short-term, part-time contracts. Only a few have substantive posts with job security.

Long-term conditions and disabilities

Additional support provided to peer workers is part of the reasonable adjustments that need to be made when employing someone with a disability. While this may be second nature to some organisations, for others having open conversations about how best to offer support to employees might be less familiar. Every person's experience of distress is different. What is a 'trigger' for one person may not be for another, and how each person copes with these is also different. For people with lived experience to be truly supported, an honest conversation about distress and well-being is essential. These conversations could take the form of a well-being plan that is shared with a peer worker's supervisor (or their wider team if they are comfortable with this). A well-being plan could include:

- Areas which might create difficulty for the peer worker – these might be broad areas, for example early mornings, IT systems, or very specific and related to personal experience, such as having to do basic life support training
- How the peer worker might react – for example, feeling anxious, feeling unable to come into work, or over-working
- What the peer worker will do for themselves in this situation – for example, taking some time out, using annual leave, asking for support from an identified colleague
- What the peer worker needs from the people around them – for example, a quiet space to eat lunch or meditate, a text message, permission to go home early
- What is not helpful in these situations – for example, speaking on the phone, physical contact like a hug, people asking a lot of questions.

Well-being plans such as this help to build a picture of why a person might react in unexpected ways to situations and enables support to be provided based on this shared understanding. Regularly reviewing these is important, especially for peer workers who are new to work and may still be learning what areas they find difficult within the workplace. Attention may also need to be given to the partner or family of the peer worker. They may have fears for their family member about whether they can cope with work or whether it might lead to a relapse.

Working with risk

Peer support can be offered in many places, including psychiatric hospitals, mental health centres, third sector organisations, community venues such as coffee shops and parks, or at the person's home. It is often necessary to have some form of risk assessment done before meeting a client. In many cases this is already available from the NHS, for example when meeting a patient in a hospital or mental health centre. However, in other cases there is no risk assessment available and in these circumstances it may be necessary to be cautious about meeting the person, especially when meeting them for the first time.

Some clients experience severe anxiety and rarely or never leave their home because of this. In these circumstances it is necessary for the peer worker to visit the person at their home. As with any member of staff, working alongside another colleague in this situation is helpful and peer workers should work within the same lone working processes as anyone else within an organisation to ensure their safety.

CONCLUSIONS

There are huge potential benefits to any mental health service in having peer workers employed, either through an independent organisation or directly. However, peer support services should be established with due consideration to the potential challenges it could pose to the worker, to the organisation and potentially to the peers they are working with. It is a general principle that demoralised and disempowered workers are unlikely to be effective and are likely to be prone to work-related stress and this may be a particular risk to peer workers. Therefore it is important to think through potential challenges and meet them with any necessary cultural change, including proper preparation of teams prior to peers being placed there and to establish and maintain appropriate support mechanisms. Consideration should always be given to whether there is appropriate expertise within an organisation to do this effectively or whether it is better to approach a peer-led organisation to offer consultancy and supervision.

All workers should be encouraged and supported in their roles, but there should be dedicated thinking about how to support peer workers who use their lived experience to get alongside and enable the peers they work with to reclaim control of their lives.

FURTHER READING AND RESOURCES

A practical guide to employing and supporting peer workers by ImROC:

* https://imroc.org/resources/7-peer-support-workers-practical-guide-implementation/

Mind's wellness at work guide for employees:

* http://mindfulemployertensteps.co.uk/resources/mind-guide-for-employees-wellness-action-plans.pdf

REFERENCES

Ashcraft, L., Anthony, W. (2007) Adding peers to the workforce. Tools for Transformation, 27(11), 8-12. Tools for Transformation, 27(11), 8-12.

Beales, A. and Wilson, J. (2015). Peer support – the what, why, how and now. *The Journal of Mental Health Training Education and Practice*, 10(5), 314–324.

Centre for Mental Health (2013). *Briefing 47 Barriers to Employment: What Works for People with Mental Health Problems.* London: Centre for Mental Health.

DWP (Department for Work and Pensions). (2017). *Employing Disabled People and People with Health Conditions.* London: DWP. https://www.gov.uk/government/publications/employing-disabled-people-and-people-with-health-conditions [Accessed 8 July 2018].

Gillard, S., Edwards, C., Gibson, S., Holley, J. and Owen, K. (2014). New ways of working in mental health services: A qualitative, comparative, case study assessing and informing the emergence of new peer worker roles in mental health services in England. *Health Services and Delivery Research*, 2(19).

Lelliot, P., Boardman, J., Harvery, S., Henderson, M. and Knapp, M. (2008). *Mental Health and Work.* London: Royal College of Psychiatrists. (https://www.gov.uk/government/uploads/system/uploads/attachment_data/file/212266/hwwb-mental-health-and-work.pdf)

Mead, S. (2001). *Peer support and a Socio-Political Response to Trauma and Abuse.* https://www.intentionalpeersupport.org/articles/ [Accessed 24 October 2018].

Mental Health Foundation. (2012). *Employment is Vital for Maintaining Good Mental Health.* Mental Health Foundation. https://www.mentalhealth.org.uk/blog/employment-vital-maintaining-good-mental-health [Accessed 8 July 2018].

Mourra, S., Sledge, W., Sells, D., et al. (2014). Pushing, patience and persistence: Peer providers: Perspectives on supportive relationships. *American Journal of Psychiatric Rehabilitation*, 17, 307–328.

O'Hagan, M., Cyr, C., McKee, H., & Priest, R. (2010). Making the Case for Peer Support. Mental Health Commission of Canada. Available from: https://www.mentalhealthcommission.ca/English/document/445/making-case-peer-support [Accessed 8 July 2018].

Repper, J. (2013). *Peer Support Workers: a practical guide to implementation.. ImROC Briefing Paper No. 7*, London: Centre for Mental Health and Mental Health Network, NHS Confederation.

Rinaldi, M., Perkins, R., Glynn, E., Montibeller, T., Clenaghan, M. and Rutherford, J. (2008). Individual placement and support: From research to practice. *Advances in Psychiatric Treatment*, 13, 50–60.

SANE (2013). *Schizophrenia and Employment: Putting the Lived-Experience of Schizophrenia at the Heart of the Employment Agenda.* London: SANE. http://www.sane.org.uk/uploads/schizophrenia_employment_web.pdf [Accessed 8 July 2018].

Warr, P. (1987). *Unemployment and Mental Health.* Oxford: Oxford University Press.

FOUNDATIONS OF
MENTAL
HEALTH
PRACTICE

11 Peer-Led Services: Doing It Ourselves

Mirika Flegg and Anna Stratford

Chapter Summary

- This chapter defines peer-led service providers as organisations or independent groups where those with lived experience of mental health challenges have control over resourcing and decision-making processes. This suggests that peer-led provisions may be distinct from current conceptualisations of peer support and patient public involvement

- We provide a number of strategies and tools to identify and categorise peer-led provisions and examine their limitations. We suggest what tools may be most appropriate for evaluating peer control within service evaluations, sustainability planning and research activities

- Peer-led providers work in partnership with statutory services via collaboration and delegation pathways and we discuss the risks and benefits of each approach

- We argue that peer-led provisions can be bolstered through increased supports to national third sector organisations, providing the infrastructure to nurture locally based peer-led networks, groups and individuals

- Stigma negatively impacts the uptake of peer support services, minimises peer leadership opportunities and negatively impacts wider organisational cultures. We recommend a number of strategies to address stigma at a systems level such as career progression opportunities for those with lived experience, the promotion of peer-led/survivor research and the introduction of anti-stigma training for non-peer providers

Introduction

This chapter adopts the term 'peer-led' to refer to services, organisations and structures where those with lived experience of mental health challenges have control over the design, development, delivery and evaluation of the service. Those with lived experience have historically provided services and support to one another independently and in partnership with statutory services (Mowbray et al., 2005; Wilson, 2015). Recently a wave of global research has investigated services run specifically *by* and *for* those with experiences of mental health challenges (e.g. in the UK: Parmenter et al., 2015; in Canada: O'Hagan et al., 2010; in New Zealand: Doughty & Tse, 2005; in the USA: Jones, 2015). Across contexts, peer-led provisions improve patient outcomes, provide increased employment and social integration opportunities, challenge stigma surrounding mental health, and improve statutory services. Peer-led provisions may be hard to identify and categorise due to various ways these approaches are considered. This poses challenges when identifying how they can be supported.

Policy and guidelines have articulated two pathways to support those with lived experience to have control over service design and provision. These include the delegation of services to independent peer-led providers and increased collaborations with service users within professional services. Delegation agendas have been articulated for example by the World Health Organization (WHO, 2005) and the NHS (2014). Collaboration or Partnership approaches have been articulated across a number of UK reports (e.g. NHS, 2014, 2016; Tattersall, 2002). Delegation, or the contracting out of services to independent providers, has long been seen to be the most inclusive way to support those traditionally seen as less powerful (Leana, 1987). It increases their control over decision-making processes and develops their leadership potential (Leana, 1987). Control can be considered in terms of knowledge power, where those with experience of mental health make decisions about service design or delivery. It can also be considered in terms of financial power/autonomy over provisions (see Lund et al., 2016). Independent peer-led providers have raised concerns of professional task-shifting to the third sector without needed financial and systems supports (Evans & Fisher, 1999; Flegg et al., 2015). They have also expressed concerns that the influence of professional services may taint the 'essence' of peer-led approaches (Williams, 2011).

Many have suggested that partnership approaches are problematic because the philosophical position inherent within peer-led services is at odds with the often disease-focused model driving statutory services (Doughty & Tse, 2005; Mowbray et al., 2005; O'Hagan et al., 2010; Parmenter et al., 2015). This divide has been explored in many UK evaluations of peer involvement (e.g. Ramon, 2003), social work (Repper & Breeze, 2007), education (Newton et al., 2013), service provision and research (Flegg, 2017). Collaboration processes rely on those in power to relinquish control (Leana, 1987) and may be seen as tokenistic depending on the individuals involved (Evans & Fisher, 1999; Repper & Breeze, 2007). Currently, UK public services in health, education and research frequently involve those with lived experiences in service provisions. However, the evidence suggests that their influence is limited (Flegg, 2017; Newton et al., 2013; Ramon, 2003; Repper & Breeze, 2007). Stigma associated with mental distress is stated to be a primary reason for why partnership initiatives fail. The ability of collaborative approaches to address stigma remains a critical debate (e.g. Bockting et al., 2013; Verhaeghe et al., 2008).

This chapter reports what is known about peer-led provisions globally and within the UK. It explores key terms and discusses the level of control those with lived experience of mental distress have over decision making and resource allocation. Key challenges are explored such as how these organisations and services can be identified, categorised and supported. Through case studies and a review of relevant literature, it reports benefits and challenges of peer-led provisions as a community engagement intervention to treat and prevent mental health challenges. Recommendations are made in consideration of peer-led provisions at both grassroots and system levels.

How do we identify peer-led provisions?

Reports generated from both professional and peer providers have recognised that challenges in defining and identifying peer-led provisions have made it difficult to evidence, understand and support them (O'Hagan et al., 2010; Parmenter et al., 2015). The absence of clear definitions may also prevent independent peer providers from accessing funding (O'Hagan et al., 2010). Strategies currently used by the NHS that seek to categorise patient and public involvement may be insufficient to assess peer-led provisions. This is because they may not consider peer decision making across areas of service (Litva et al., 2002) nor adequately consider financial power (Simpson & House, 2003). The section that follows explores key terms associated with peer-led provision and identifies strategies that consider peer control over decision-making and resource provisions.

Key terms associated with peer-led provisions

Various terms have been associated with peer-led provisions, yet these have been inconsistently defined (Litva et al., 2002). Peer-led services have often been associated with terms such as 'self-help', 'mutual-help', 'service user-run', 'service user-led', 'user-run' or 'user-led' and 'consumer-run' (Doughty & Tse, 2005; Mowbray et al., 2005; Wilson, 2015). Mowbray and colleagues (2005) suggest the term 'consumer-run' refers to formally provided peer-based services where governance and staff have lived experience and which 'operates as a business' (p. 278). Mowbray and colleagues' (2005) definition suggests these provisions are autonomous in terms of resourcing and decision making. Most definitions, however, primarily suggest autonomy is associated with decision making. The terms 'service user-run' and 'service user-led' usually refer to services or organisations where the initiating and decision making of services lies with those with lived experience (e.g. Doughty & Tse, 2005; Parmenter et al., 2015). Terms such as 'peer-run' and 'peer-operated' have similarly been introduced (Solomon, 2004, p. 393). In addition, the term 'user leadership' has been used to refer to an organisation or service where the majority of decisions at every level are made by those with lived experience (Together & NSUN, 2014, p. 2). The case example explores the complexities associated with assessing peer control.

Case Example: The Sussex Place of Calm – The First 24/7 Peer-Supported Crisis Support Service in the UK

The Sussex Place of Calm was a crisis prevention service piloted from June 2015 to March 2017 with support from East Sussex County Council and Sussex Partnership NHS Trust (Finlay, 2016; Briggs et al., 2016; Recovery Partners, 2017b). It was the first peer-led suicide prevention service in the UK to provide 24/7 crisis support.

Initial funding for the Place of Calm came from East Sussex Public Health who committed to piloting a 'non-statutory place of safety' as part of their suicide prevention strategy (Finlay, 2016). The funding came from professional services, yet the Place of Calm was staffed by those with lived experience of mental health and managed by two third sector organisations: Recovery Partners, which is a peer-led organisation that provides peer support in mental health (Recovery Partners, 2017a), and Sussex Oakleaf, which provides peer mentoring and other recovery-based mental health services (Sussex Oakleaf, 2017). Evaluations of the pilot showed statistically significant improvements in mental health (Briggs et al., 2016). Support from peers was associated with better outcomes and was reported to be non-stigmatising (Briggs et al., 2016). Follow-up surveys showed that 94 per cent of individuals reported that the service had 'saved their life'. Hospital admissions were reduced and cost-benefit analysis suggested that £6.00 health and social care spending could be saved for every £1.00 spent on the Place of Calm (Recovery Partners, 2017b). Other peer-led crisis provisions have shown similar cost-benefits (e.g. Williams, 2011, p. 7). Owing to funding pressures, the Place of Calm was closed following the pilot. However, an online petition to save the service received almost 40,000 signatures from UK residents and global supporters (Save Sussex Place of Calm Suicide Prevention Service, 2017). Recovery Partners continues to provide peer-led services in other areas.

Exercise: Case Example Review

Would you define the Place of Calm as a peer-led service? Why or why not?

How do we categorise peer-led provisions?

As the case example suggests, identifying peer-led provisions can be challenging. To be defined as peer-led requires those with lived experience to be placed at the highest level of decision making and across all areas of service (design, development, delivery, evaluation and management). Strategies currently used to categorise user/peer involvement in services are likely insufficient to assess peer-led provisions because they do not sufficiently consider control over decisions and resources. As such, existing research in patient/public involvement and peer support may not be transferable to understanding peer-led organisations.

In terms of identifying levels of service user involvement, the most frequently applied strategy used by the NHS has been Arnstein's (1969) Ladder of Citizen Participation (Collins & Ison, 2006; Tritter & McCallum, 2006). However, this does not categorise participation in different stages such as service design, development, evaluation and management

(Collins & Ison, 2006; Tritter & McCallum, 2006). Within peer-led education a Ladder of Participation by Goss and Miller (1995) is frequently applied to identify and assess these provisions (Repper & Breeze, 2007). However, it has similar limitations. Some authors have rather created tools to categorise the level of peer control over the decision-making process at various stages and in relationship to professional affiliations (Emerick, 1990; Mowbray et al., 2005; Parmenter et al., 2015; Schubert & Borkman, 1991; Together and NSUN, 2014). These strategies may be useful for those wishing to identify literature surrounding peer-led approaches and within service evaluations.

Peer-led providers may seek a strategy that uses plain language (see Lockey et al., 2004) and considers user involvement in decision making (Simpson & House, 2003; Litva et al., 2002). Together and the National Survivor User Network (NSUN) offer a tool to determine where services/organisations sit on the 'Service Leadership Spectrum' based on three categories: 'Beginnings of Service User Involvement, Good Service User Involvement and Service User Led' (Together and NSUN, 2014, p. 5). Other strategies have been created in partnership with those with lived experience and consider dependency on external resources and the extent services internally value experiential knowledge (e.g. Schubert & Borkman, 1991; Mowbray et al., 2005). These may aid in sustainability planning and thus be most appropriate from a commissioning and programme management perspective. Other strategies (e.g. Emerick, 1990) are more geared towards helping professionals identify appropriate peer partners.

Caution must be considered when using such strategies to categorise peer involvement levels. First, they may be limited in their ability to assess hierarchies within peer-led provisions. As Mowbray and colleagues (2005) suggest, power differentials can exist even when the entirety of staff are comprised of those with lived experience. Current debates in peer support literature often centre on how long one remains a 'peer' when employed as a peer provider and/or how peer-led provision can retain their integrity where services are increasingly professionalised (Williams, 2011). These challenges have been identified across reviews of peer-led service provision (e.g. Doughty & Tse, 2005; Jones, 2015; O'Hagan et al., 2010; Parmenter et al., 2015).

Second, peer-led provisions may not necessarily focus on mental health per se, but rather may take the shape of arts or action-based groups (Harris et al., 2015; O'Hagan et al., 2010). Individuals who experience mental distress may also experience additional health challenges (Mutsatsa, 2015) and exclusions from education, employment and social connections (Webber et al., 2015). As was found in Canada, defining peer-led services exclusively around the concept of mental health may exclude holistic, minority and cultural programmes, precluding them from accessing funding (O'Hagan et al., 2010). Too narrow definitions may be why minority provisions have been excluded from existing reviews of peer support within the UK (e.g. Faulkner, 2013). Many providers may not explicitly promote themselves as being peer-led (Flegg et al., 2015; Harris et al., 2015; O'Hagan et al., 2010) and may not have the resources to publicly promote services (Flegg et al., 2015). This makes these groups hard to identify and engage with. In a review of community-based peer provision, Harris and colleagues (2015) recommended engaging with local leaders to identify and support peer-provisions within minority or traditionally excluded groups.

Third, most literature identifies those with lived experiences as operating outside of statutory services. Yet statistics suggest that those with experience of mental health conditions are employed *within* public services. One in four adults will experience mental distress (McManus et al., 2009), with a higher than average proportion of these individuals employed in the NHS (Roberts et al., 2011) and within higher education (Wilson, 2015). Historical evidence of those in leadership positions who experienced mental illness includes UK monarchs, prime ministers, scientists, and entertainers (Ghaemi, 2011). Yet there is a notable absence in the literature that considers these individuals as peers, thus fragmenting the peer community through an 'us' (service users) and 'them' (professionals) approach (see also Chapter 9 on lived experience of all staff). Cultural shifts within organisations are required to appreciate and strengthen peer leadership pathways. This may begin with supporting staff in senior positions to disclose their experiences of mental health challenges and providing career progression opportunities for peer support workers.

Lastly, policies and funding guidance may demand peer engagement in service provision and research (e.g. Lockey et al., 2004). However, inconsistencies in reporting structures make comparing their impacts against those that are professionally led challenging (Lockey et al., 2004; Mowbray et al., 2005). Advocating for academic journals to include patient and public involvement in structured abstracts and/or contacting individual authors to request more information may, therefore, be required (Flegg, 2017).

The essence of peer support is about mutual respect, relationship building and social support (Mead & MacNeil, 2006). As such, evaluations led by those with experiential knowledge of peer-led provisions may aid in identifying and addressing these limitations.

Exercise: Identifying Peer-led Services

Imagine you are doing a best practice review of peer-led services. How might you identify services and literature to include in your review?

Case Example: Mothers Uncovered

Mothers Uncovered (2017) was established by Maggie Gordon-Walker in 2008 as a project under the charity Livestock. Maggie had just given birth to her second child and wished to find a service to support her more holistically. She found most of the services that existed focused their attention on the child or, alternatively, used a postnatal depression model. When she could not find a service that suited her needs, she started her own. Mothers Uncovered is not just about helping prevent postnatal depression, but about giving all women a chance to process the experience of becoming a mother. While the group supports mental health implicitly, it does so in a way that sees mental well-being as only one part of the person. Nine years on, Mothers Uncovered is a creative support network, with group gatherings run by past participants of the programme. They aim to create a safe space where mothers can talk about their successes and challenges with one another. This involves activities like arts, drama and cooking. They also get together to support the wider community such as by giving to charity and by sharing research and practice knowledge.

> ### Exercise: Defining and Understanding Peer-led Services
>
> Would you consider Mothers Uncovered to be a mental health service?
> Why or why not?
>
> What benefits do you see for peer-led programmes that promote themselves as holistic support services and how might this also hinder them?

What supports peer-led provision?

Within the UK peer-based provisions are currently supported in policy yet there are inconsistencies in their provision and evaluation (Newton et al., 2013; Repper & Breeze, 2007; Williams, 2011). These inconsistencies may be due to the differences associated with delegation and partnership agendas. In 2005, at the first WHO European Ministerial Conference on Mental Health, a joint commitment was made to support the development of **non-governmental organisations** *run by* and *for* those with experiences of mental distress (WHO, 2005). The NHS Five Year Forward View explicitly pledged commitment for the support of services provided by 'independent peer-to-peer communities' (p. 12). The collaboration agenda has long been pushed by the UK's Department of Health (DH, 2010; Tattersall, 2002). By 2016 the Five Year Forward View for Mental Health explicitly recommended that 'co-production with experts-by-experience should be a standard approach to commissioning and service design' (p. 20). The section that follows considers system supports that may enable peer-led provisions operating independently of, and in partnership with, statutory services. These may include the support of national third sector groups and peer-led networks that aim to reduce stigma and provide further support to local groups.

System supports: National groups and networks

Much of the UK-based research has considered front-line peer support services (e.g. Parmenter et al., 2015; Repper & Breeze, 2007), yet most have not considered the systemic structures that enable these services to flourish. Jones (2015) outlines interwoven systems and structures in the USA that promote peers to have control over leadership decisions and resourcing. She outlines state-level divisions of mental health that fund national and international projects where those with lived experience are at the helm. These provide further support for smaller peer-led organisations, offering assistance such as a peer-run technical support line. They also provide funding for local, national and international peer-led networks such as Peers for Progress (2018). Jones (2015) credits the third sector for providing services directly and holding governments to account surrounding funding provisions and partnership agendas. These groups, along with peer-led networks, play a unique role in addressing stigma by informing policy and best practice service improvements on a wider scale (Jones, 2015).

The importance of national groups and peer networks to support the sustainability of peer provisions and address stigma has been raised internationally (e.g. Emerick, 1990; Jones, 2015) and within the UK (Flegg et al., 2015; Harris et al., 2015; Parmenter et al., 2015). Emerick (1990) suggests that these national groups are the most likely to engage in partnership activities with professional services. Parmenter and colleagues (2015) have highlighted their importance in supporting local provisions, such as providing training. Therefore, increased provisions to UK national groups known to support peer-led providers may be considered. Multi-year funding is required to allow them to develop sustainable local programmes, with Harris and colleagues (2015) recommending independent providers be given a minimum of three years of continuation funding.

Connections between local and national groups may be accomplished through in-person and online support networking structures (Flegg et al., 2015; Harris et al., 2015; Williams, 2011). UK independent peer-led providers advocate a network approach, calling for the formation of local networks to support smaller groups, supported by national networking and advocacy organisations (Flegg et al., 2015; Harris et al., 2015). The network model suggested necessitates it be peer-led with structures to allow individuals to transition from local social networks to wider ones (Flegg et al., 2015; Harris et al., 2015). This allows smaller groups to share best practices, increase signposting and improve access to training and development (Flegg et al., 2015). The majority of existing network models within the UK include peer-led providers (see, for example, the Mental Health Network and Strategic Clinical Networks). Existing network structures that enlist those with lived experience as minority members may limit the control peers have over network decisions. However, some peer-run networks currently exist such as the Sussex Peer Support Network and the NSUN Network for Mental Health.

Case Example: The Sussex Peer Support Network

The Sussex Peer Support Network (SPSN) began in February 2015 following a community-led evaluation into peer-based mental health provisions in Sussex, UK (Flegg et al., 2015). Those who provided and received peer support services suggested that a network model would help peer-led organisations to share best practices and help with training and signposting. Thus far the SPSN has run entirely on charitable and in-kind donations from individuals and small third sector organisations. Seventy-five per cent of the SPSN leadership team must have lived experiences and experience running peer-led services. Members must have lived experience/experience running a peer-led service in order to vote. Health professionals, academics and community leaders are welcome to attend meetings; however, only those who identify as having lived experiences are entitled to vote. This structure has led to several research and partnership initiatives between network members, with many also including statutory services and academic institutions.

Exercise: Supporting Peer-led Services

How might existing networks be strengthened and/or changed to better support peer-led groups and organisations?

Reducing stigma

Those experiencing mental health challenges are stigmatised and public stigma is associated with increased self-stigma (Evans-Lacko et al., 2012). Addressing stigma involves informing, educating and providing the public with positive opportunities to have contact with those who experience challenges with mental health (Evans-Lacko et al., 2012). Peer support processes might improve stigma, yet stigma and self-stigma may also impede peer-led provisions (Flegg, 2017; Repper & Breeze, 2007). Bockting and colleagues (2013) suggest stigma in front-line peer-led provisions can be decreased if peer services are offered independently of public health services. Conversely, Verhaeghe and colleagues (2008) argue that partnerships are needed to address stigma universally. However, professionals may not be prepared to relinquish control in partnership processes (Newton et al., 2013; Ramon, 2003; Repper & Breeze, 2007).

Ramon (2003) postulates that many professionals see peer-led provisions as threatening their individual jobs and the value of their professional identities. Peers who have other skills may be seen as unrepresentative of those that experience mental health challenges. Within education, for example, Felton and Stickley (2004) found that academics question how representative peer lecturers are of people with mental health challenges if they are able to teach a class of students. Yet many health professionals and educators themselves have experience of mental distress (Roberts et al., 2011; Wilson, 2015). Repper and Breeze (2007) suggest what is needed to address stigma contexts more widely is a cultural shift towards more inclusive and explicitly peer-led practices *within* public systems and beyond:

> If the patronising culture that reportedly endures in educational institutions is to be challenged, then consumer involvement needs to be approached at a systems level; operating at all levels and in all aspects of the organisation. (p. 39)

Anti-stigma training programmes in the UK and Canada that focus on well-known leaders with mental illness have shown positive impacts (e.g. Pinfold et al., 2005). These considered anti-stigma training for young people. However, a similar approach may be taken in the education of health educators, practitioners, human resource staff and commissioners to reduce stigma and self-stigma.

In a review of peer support in the NHS, Gillard and colleagues (2015) suggest peer support workers may be most effective when they are directly employed by third sector organisations. Many may see this as evidence that partnership approaches are more effective. Considering this finding from a peer leadership perspective, however, it could be interpreted to suggest that services are most effective when they are peer-led. Jones' (2015) review of peer support in the USA supports this second interpretation. New research is required into peer-led services from the perspective of control over services prior to favouring partnership approaches. Research may also consider if statutory services that embed those with lived experiences within their leadership and employment support structure, such as within human resource departments, lead to improved peer provisions.

Exercise: Partnering with Peer-led Providers

How might stigma and self-stigma impact partnerships between peer-led and professionally led providers?

Peer-led research

One way statutory services and academic institutions can increase peer leadership within their organisations is by strengthening peer involvement in research (Flegg et al., 2015; Lockey et al., 2004). Peer-led research is often called 'survivor research' (McPin, 2017). In the UK some structures currently exist to support those with dual identities as professionals and experts by experience. These include the Service User Enterprise, a UK-based research unit known as the largest worldwide for employing researchers with lived experience of mental health (SURE, 2017). They also include the Centre for Citizen Participation at Brunel University, London (McPin, 2017). Supporting peer-led research may provide practitioners with connections to those with lived experience who hold leadership positions, providing a recovery-focused environment where peers are not asked to be the sole agent of change. It may also lead to new innovations in research and increased opportunities for findings to be critically interpreted.

Harris and colleagues (2015) recommend that all those involved in collaborating with community-based peer providers, including educators, practitioners and commissioners, should be educated on the equity context and have advanced engagement skills. Peer researchers and peer-led organisations may be best placed to undertake a review of peer leadership practices within statutory services and to address identified training and development needs.

CONCLUSIONS

Peer-led provisions can be provided within and beyond statutory services, providing they are willing and able to devolve control to those with lived experience. Prominent strategies to identify peer provisions are inconsistently used and often do not consider the level of control those with lived experiences have over decisions and resourcing. Involving those with lived experience in these evaluations may address known limitations of assessment strategies and improve the validity of future research. Peer-led providers have reported they are willing to provide services independently of statutory services yet require further control over resource allocation processes (e.g. Flegg et al., 2015; Stewart, 1990). Independent peer-led provisions may be best strengthened via increased supports for independent national providers and through the attention and subtle tweaking of existing networking structures.

Addressing the philosophical divide between peer-led and professional service provisions may involve addressing the wider stigma context. The inclusion of those with lived experience of mental health challenges in mainstream services has identified that they experience direct discrimination from professionals when they are included via collaborative processes (e.g. Ramon, 2003; Repper & Breeze, 2007). Yet professionals also experience mental health challenges. To support their own workforce and enable external service users to work in partnership with them, statutory services should therefore work to address their internal cultures to show greater appreciation of experiential knowledge. This may involve strengthening existing structures that value the lived experience of professionals. Training opportunities may be provided to health professionals and the public to address stigma more widely.

FURTHER READING AND RESOURCES

Mental Health Network:

- http://www.nhsconfed.org/networks/mental-health-network

Mothers Uncovered:

- http://mothersuncovered.com/

NSUN Network for Mental Health:

- http://www.nsun.org.uk/contact-us/

Recovery Partners:

- http://recovery-partners.co.uk/how-we-can-help/place-of-calm/

Sussex Oakleaf:

- www.sussexoakleaf.org.uk

Sussex Peer Support Network:

- https://blogs.brighton.ac.uk/sussexpeersupportnetwork/

Together for Mental Wellbeing:

- http://www.together-uk.org/

The Principled Ways of Working Conference:

- https://www.youtube.com/watch?v=KmRbb5Z0dHw&feature=youtu.be

Peer Run Respite Grassroots Wellness:

- http://youtu.be/nLcTrrWEmzY

Peer Leadership Centre (USA) includes video of Larry Fricks Interview:

- https://www.peerleadershipcenter.org/plc/Workforce.asp

REFERENCES

Arnstein, S. R. (1969). A ladder of citizen participation. *Journal of the American Institute of Planners*, 35(4), 216–224.

Bockting, W. O., Miner, M. H., Swinburne Romine, R. E., Hamilton, A. and Coleman, E. (2013). Stigma, mental health, and resilience in an online sample of the US transgender population. *American Journal of Public Health*, 103(5), 943–951.

Briggs, S., Finch, J. and Firth, R. (2016). *Evaluation of a Non-Statutory 'Place of Calm', a Service Which Provides Support after a Suicidal Crisis to Inform Future Commissioning Intentions. Final Report.* Recovery Partners. http://recovery-partners.co.uk/mailouts/Anna/PlaceofCalmFinalReport.pdf. Accessed October 2016 [Accessed 10 April 2017].

Collins, K. and Ison, R. (2006). Dare we jump off Arnstein's ladder? Social learning as a new policy paradigm. In *Proceedings of PATH (Participatory Approaches in Science & Technology) Conference, 4–7 Jun 2006*, Edinburgh. http://oro.open.ac.uk/8589/1/Path_paper_Collins_Ison.pdf [Accessed 23 October 2018].

DH (Department of Health) (2010). *Equity and Excellence: Liberating the NHS*, NHS White Paper, https:// www.gov.uk/government/uploads/system/uploads/attachment_data/file/213823/dh_117794.pdf [Accessed 23 October 2018].

Doughty, C. & Tse, S. (2005). *The Effectiveness of Service User-Run or Service User-Led Mental Health Services for People with Mental Illness: A systematic literature review*. Wellington: Mental Health Commission. http://citeseerx.ist.psu.edu/viewdoc/download?doi=10.1.1.476.9433&rep=rep1&type =pdf [Accessed 23 October 2018].

Emerick, R. E. (1990). Self-help groups for former patients: Relations with mental health professionals. *Psychiatric Services*, 41(4), 401–407.

Evans, C. and Fisher, M. (1999). User Controlled Research and Empowerment. In W. Shera and I. M. Wells (eds). *Empowerment Practice in Social Work: Developing Richer Conceptual Frameworks*. Toronto: Canadian Scholar's Press, 348–369.

Evans-Lacko, S., Brohan, E., Mojtabai, R. and Thornicroft, G. (2012). Association between public views of mental illness and self-stigma among individuals with mental illness in 14 European countries. *Psychological Medicine*, 42(8), 1741–1752.

Faulkner, A. (2013). *Mental Health Peer Support in England: Piecing Together the Jigsaw*. London: Mind.

Felton, A. and Stickley, T. (2004). Pedagogy, power and service user involvement. *Journal of Psychiatric and Mental Health Nursing*, 11(1), 89–98.

Finlay, R. (2016, April) Evaluation of the Place of Calm. East Sussex County Council. http://www. sussexpartnership.nhs.uk/sites/default/files/documents/ruth_finlay_evaluation_of_the_place_of_ calm_pecan_19.9.16.pdf [Accessed 10 August 2017].

Flegg, M., Gordon-Walker, M. and Maguire, S. (2015). Peer-to-peer mental health: A community evaluation case study. *The Journal of Mental Health Training, Education and Practice*, 10(5), 282–293.

Flegg, M. (2017) Peer Support, Quality of Life & Resilience: A systematic literature review across patient populations. Paper Presentation at the Researching Resilience Conference 1V: Global South Perspectives, South Africa, June 2017. https://ptriv.sched.com/event/ALL9/researching-pathways-to-resilience-odin-hjemdal-rhian-adams-for-suna-erigit-madzwamuse-mirika-flegg   [Accessed 10 August 2017].

Ghaemi, N. (2011). *A First-Rate Madness: Uncovering the Links between Leadership and Mental Illness*. London: Penguin.

Gillard, S., Gibson, S. L., Holley, J. and Lucock, M. (2015). Developing a change model for peer worker interventions in mental health services: A qualitative research study. *Epidemiology and Psychiatric Sciences*, 24(5), 435–445.

Goss, S. and Miller, C. (1995). *From Margin to Mainstream: Developing User-and Carer-Centred Community Care*. York: Joseph Rowntree Foundation.

Harris, J., Springett, J., Booth, A., Campbell, F., Thompson, J., Goyder, E., Van Cleemput, P., Wilkins, E. and Yang, Y. (2015). Can community-based peer support promote health literacy and reduce inequalities? A realist review. *Journal of Public Health Research*, 3, 3.

Jones, N. (2015) *Peer Involvement and Leadership in Early Intervention in Psychosis Services: From Planning to Peer Support and Evaluation*. https://www.nasmhpd.org/sites/default/files/Peer-Involvement-Guidance_Manual_Final.pdf [Accessed 5 May 2018].

Leana, C. R. (1987). Power relinquishment versus power sharing: Theoretical clarification and empirical comparison of delegation and participation. *Journal of Applied Psychology*, 72(2), 228.

Litva, A., Coast, J., Donovan, J., Eyles, J., Shepherd, M., Tacchi, J., Abelson, J. and Morgan, K. (2002). 'The public is too subjective': Public involvement at different levels of health-care decision making. *Social Science and Medicine*, 54(12), 1825–1837.

Lockey, R., Sitzia, J., Gillingham, T., Millyard, J., Miller, C., Ahmed, S., Beales, A., Bennett, C., Parfoot, S., Sigrist, G. and Sigrist, J. (2004). Training for service user involvement in health and social care research: A study of training provision and participants' experiences (The TRUE Project), *Worthing*: *Worthing and Southlands Hospitals NHS Trust.*

Lund, R., Panda, S. M. and Dhal, M. P. (2016). Narrating spaces of inclusion and exclusion in research collaboration–researcher-gatekeeper dialogue. *Qualitative Research*, 16(3), 280–292.

McManus, S., Meltzer, H., Brugha, T. S., Bebbington, P. E. and Jenkins, R. (2009). *Adult Psychiatric Morbidity in England, 2007: Results of a Household Survey.* The NHS Information Centre for Health and Social Care.

McPin (2017). Centre for Citizen Participation in University, Brunel University, London. http://mcpin.org/ resources/service-user-and-carer-groups/london/centre-for-citizen-participation-brunel-univer-sity-london/ [Accessed 19 August 2017].

Mead, S. and MacNeil, C. (2006). Peer support: What makes it unique. *International Journal of Psychoso-cial Rehabilitation*, 10(2), 29–37.

Mothers Uncovered (2017). Mothers Uncovered (website). http://mothersuncovered.com/ [Accessed 10 October 2016].

Mowbray, C. T., Holter, M. C., Stark, L., Pfeffer, C. and Bybee, D. (2005). A fidelity rating instrument for consumer-run drop-in centers (FRI-CRDI). *Research on Social Work Practice*, 15(4), 278–290.

Mutsatsa, S. (2015). *Physical Healthcare and Promotion in Mental Health Nursing.* London: Learning Matters.

Newton, A., Beales, A., Collins, D. and Basset, T. (2013). Service user leadership: Training and development for service users to take the lead. *The Journal of Mental Health Training, Education and Practice*, 8(3), 134–140.

NHS (2014). *Five Year Forward View*, London: Health Education England. https://www.england.nhs.uk/ wp-content/uploads/2014/10/5yfv-web.pdf [Accessed 10 October 2016].

NHS (2016). *Five Year Forward View for Mental Health*: https://www.england.nhs.uk/wp-content/ uploads/2016/02/Mental-Health-Taskforce-FYFV-final.pdf [Accessed 15 July 2017].

O'Hagan, M., Cyr, C., McKee, H. and Priest, R. (2010). *Making the Case for Peer Support*, Calgary: Mental Health Commission of Canada.

Parmenter, V., Fieldhouse, J. and Deering, K. (2015). *Good Practice in Peer-Facilitated Community Mental Health Support Groups: A Review of the Literature*, University of West England, Bristol. https://www2. uwe.ac.uk/faculties/HLS/ahp/AHP%20Documents/Good-Practice-in-Peer-Facilitated-Mental-Health-Groups.pdf [Accessed 23 October 2018].

Peers for Progress (2018). 'Who We Are', Peers for Progress (website). http://peersforprogress.org/who-we-are/ [Accessed 10 March 2018].

Pinfold, V., Stuart, H., Thornicroft, G. and Arboleda-Flórez, J. (2005). Working with young people: The impact of mental health awareness programs in schools in the UK and Canada. *World Psychiatry*, 4(Suppl 1), 48–52.

Ramon, S. (2003). *Users Researching Health and Social Care: An Empowering Agenda*, Birmingham: Ventura.

Recovery Partners (2017a) 'Home', Recovery Partners (website). http://recovery-partners.co.uk/ [Accessed 19 August 2017].

Recovery Partners (2017b) 'Place of Calm', Recovery Partners (website). http://recovery-partners.co.uk/ how-we-can-help/place-of-calm/ [Accessed 19 August 2017].

Repper, J. and Breeze, J. (2007). User and carer involvement in the training and education of health professionals: A review of the literature. *International Journal of Nursing Studies*, 44(3), 511–519.

Roberts, G., Good, J., Wooldridge, J. and Baker, E. (2011). Steps towards 'putting recovery at the heart of all we do': Workforce development and the contribution of 'lived experience'. *Journal of Mental Health Training, Education and Practice*, 6(1), 17–28.

Sussex Place of Calm Suicide Prevention Service (2017). 'Home', http://recovery-partners.co.uk/how-we-can-help/place-of-calm/ [Accessed 10 September 2017].

Schubert, M. A. and Borkman, T. J. (1991). An organizational typology for self-help groups. *American Journal of Community Psychology*, 19(5), 769–787.

Simpson, E. L. and House, A. O. (2003). User and carer involvement in mental health services: From rhetoric to science. *British Journal of Psychiatry*, 183, 89–91.

Solomon, P. (2004). Peer support/peer provided services underlying processes, benefits, and critical ingredients. *Psychiatric Rehabilitation Journal*, 27(4), 392.

Stewart, M. J. (1990). Professional interface with mutual-aid self-help groups: A review. *Social Science and Medicine*, 31(10), 1143–1158.

SURE (2017). The Service User Enterprise, King's College London (website). http://www.kcl.ac.uk/ioppn/depts/hspr/research/ciemh/sure/index.aspx [Accessed 10 August 2017].

Sussex Oakleaf. (2017). 'Home', Sussex Oakleaf (website). www.sussexoakleaf.org.uk [Accessed 19 August 2017].

Tattersall, R. (2002). The expert patient: A new approach to chronic disease management for the twenty-first century. *Clinical Medicine*, 2(3), 227–229.

Together and NSUN. (2014) *Service User Involvement in the Delivery of Mental Health Services*. Briefing Paper, May 2014. http://www.together-uk.org/wp-content/uploads/downloads/2014/06/Service-User-Involvement-briefing.pdf [Accessed 10 August 2017].

Tritter, J. Q. and McCallum, A. (2006). The snakes and ladders of user involvement: Moving beyond Arnstein. *Health policy*, 76(2), 156–168.

Verhaeghe, M., Bracke, P. and Bruynooghe, K. (2008). Stigmatization and self-esteem of persons in recovery from mental illness: The role of peer support. *International Journal of Social Psychiatry*, 54(3), 206–218.

Webber, M., Reidy, H., Ansari, D., Stevens, M. and Morris, D. (2015). Enhancing social networks: A qualitative study of health and social care practice in UK mental health services. *Health and Social Care in the Community*, 23(2), 180–189.

WHO (World Health Organization). (2005). *Mental Health: Facing the Challenges, Building Solutions*. Copenhagen: WHO. http://www.euro.who.int/__data/assets/pdf_file/0008/96452/E87301.pdf [Accessed 20 October 2018].

Williams, A. (2011). *Valuing Peer Support: A Review of the Literature on Peer Support in Helping People with Mental Health Issues towards Personal Recovery*. https://www.hacw.nhs.uk/EasySiteWeb/GatewayLink.aspx?alId=23955 [Accessed 20 October 2018].

Wilson, C. (2015). Lighting dark: Fixing academia's mental health problem. *New Scientist*, October 2014. https://www.newscientist.com/article/dn26365-lighting-dark-fixing-academias-mental-health-problem/ [Accessed 19 August 2017].

Conclusions: Make This the Beginning and Not the End

12

Emma Watson and Sara Meddings

In this book we have presented peer support as an approach underpinned by shared experience, shared power and emotional safety or attunement. Within each chapter the authors have built their discussion on the explicit or implicit assumption that peer support is in some way different from the support that is traditionally offered in mental health services. Some have articulated why this might be, in terms of values base, history and training, and the issue of power was revisited time and again.

Unlike traditional services, the goal of peer support relationships is not to fix a person's problems or reduce their symptoms. The focus is building a relationship which may help both people make sense out of their experiences and live meaningful, satisfying lives where what matters is personally defined. Peer support rests on the assumption that it is the person themselves who is best placed to make sense of their experiences. With this understanding, the support that is offered leaves control with a person, in terms of both how they choose to understand themselves and what course of action they choose to take. In many ways this approach inverts the power relationship that is offered within traditional services which are based on the assumption that a professional is needed to provide expertise to the patient to help fix their problems or reduce their symptoms.

It is for this reason that so many of the authors in this book have wrestled with how peer support may sit alongside or within systems which are built on such seemingly competing approaches. Some argue that peer support within medical systems will always be compromised or can never be mutual, and others describe ways of working within these systems. This is easiest where the philosophy of the system/context is more aligned to the values that underpin peer support and where there are employment and support structures in place. Peer support is competing for space in a system where everything is a competition, resources are scarce and austerity has led to services being reduced and all staff strug-gling to work within increasingly stressful environments. Peer-led services, which exist outside of mental health systems, have the ability to develop their own identity away from medical approaches. This may be where peer support is least compromised, but moving peer support away from medical or mainstream systems reduces the possibility that peer support approaches can influence the cultures that exist within them and risks being seen as an 'added luxury' without sustainable funding, reaching fewer people.

There is a sense that peer workers benefit from a considered approach to employment, supervision and training to support them in their roles and to support the peer worker with their own recovery. The processes that have been developed for peer workers often involve honest conversations about well-being in work, adjustments based on what a person needs in order to stay in work, and regular connection with other peer workers to build support networks. The processes that have been found to support peer workers would likely benefit all staff members working within mental health services. Training in values based approaches, person centred skills, employment support and open conver-sations about coping and well-being, ongoing reflective practice; these sound like universally helpful elements of employment, regardless of whether a person is in a peer role.

As peer support evolves in the UK there may be a danger of creating another 'us' and 'them' divide between peer staff and non-peer staff, where one group is treated with more compassion and understanding than another. This would be a great irony, given that peer support is based on connection and shared humanity. Perhaps the challenge of the coming years will be to understand peer support as distinct from other approaches, but not entirely separate – to take learning from peer support and apply it to other staff and vice versa without losing the identity that makes peer support so powerful.

And it is clear that peer support *is* powerful, as each chapter has provided evidence for this, whether this is still emerging or well established. Authors have described evidence that supports the employment of peer workers, the helpfulness of peer support for the people who receive it and the benefits of Recovery Colleges and peer-run services. They have also described and offered examples of best practice emerging around peer support training, peer support in socially excluded communities, with carers and for other profes-sionals who see the value of using lived experience in their role. While the evidence and best practice in these areas are often impressive, they also highlight the distance still to travel. Calls for more evidence are commonplace within peer support literature, particu-larly evidence to show that peer support brings about clinical outcomes and reduces pressure on mental health services. This may be seen as an example of the dominant model imposing its own focus on clinical outcomes on the relatively new practice of formal peer support. While it is important to 'speak the language' of outcomes so that the value of lived experience can be communicated, there is also a need to develop our understanding of peer support and the structures that are needed to make it effective.

There is a need for peer support in communities that are not always reached by services or formalised peer support, including carers, and people from socially excluded communities such as LGBT, black and minority ethnic groups and people in rural areas. The focus of peer support in recent years has meant that growth in certain areas, such as mental health teams and recovery colleges, has been rapid, but broadening the focus is now essential.

Progressing beyond the introduction of peer workers is also needed. The ongoing training, supervision and development that is most helpful for peer workers requires further thinking in order to sustain and embed what is still a relatively new way of working in formal mental health services. Alongside this, an understanding of how to support career progression for peer workers is essential. This requires the creation of more senior roles for peers – if lived expertise is genuinely valued equally to expertise by training then this needs to be mirrored in the structures of organisations which purport to hold these values. It also includes offering mentorship, management and leadership training so that peers can move into more senior roles without needing professional or clinical registration which may compromise their peer skill set.

Peer leadership, both within and outside traditional mental health services, begins to change the dominant narrative about mental health, redressing the power balance and offering an image of people with mental distress that encompasses successful leadership positions. This provides mental health services, and society, with narratives of recovery which move beyond 'us' and 'them' distinctions, and the concepts of professionalised treatments, to people, their families and communities supporting each other and understanding the positive contribution that the experience of distress can offer. Movement of this kind requires the mental health system and society to address discrimination at all levels, and to hold a vision of a radically different future in mind, both for individuals and for society as a whole. We have a vision.

Imagine if the next time you or your loved one experienced intense distress you had options; imagine you could meet with people who had been through similar things, who could offer you a safe and supportive space to explore things and to work towards your self-defined goals. Maybe you could spend some time in a peer-run respite house where the people around you followed your lead and worked with you to offer support. Perhaps if you decided to take medication a psychiatrist would be there, and if you wanted counselling or psychology that would also be on offer. Imagine if, instead of being in charge, these professionals were accountable to leaders and managers with their own lived experience. The people around you would be trained to use their experiences in a helpful way, but also to work with other organisations to help you pursue different opportunities, and offer support for those around you as well.

The support you received would take into account your whole identity and culture, not just your experiences of distress. The mutual approach to understanding risk and safety would mean that the use of restraint, either chemical or physical, would be unheard of. Imagine if, when you were ready, there would be a way for you to become involved in these services if you wished, not only as a peer worker or trainer, but in planning and commissioning services, based on your experiences of what was helpful for you and those around you. Imagine if, during this time, your positive sense of identity wasn't affected; neither you nor those around you felt ashamed for having struggled, and you didn't feel like you had failed – because you were surrounded by people who shared in the struggle with you as peers. They saw you as a human being who is finding ways to cope which they can understand. Imagine a world where the experience of mental distress was valued as an asset, where you could be employed as a chief executive of an NHS Trust or a senior manager because of and not despite this.

This vision may seem like no more than an irrelevant dream, or even an opportunity to despair at the current situation but hold hope. This vision may not be realised overnight but we all have the ability to review the power and resources we have available to us and think about how we might use them differently. How might you use your own experiences when you support others? How might you begin to think differently about risk and safety? How might you get to know what peer support communities exist around you? And finally, how might you begin to get political about mental health services? Peer support must be about more than employing peer support workers into traditional mental health services; it must aim higher. We must move beyond conversations about interventions and begin talking about human and civil rights, developing vibrant communities, celebrating human experience and bringing about social change.

Glossary

This glossary provides brief definitions for reference; however, many of the chapters explore these in more depth.

Accredited courses – accredited peer support training involves an academic component such as a written assignment that is moderated by an education provider and results in a recognised certificate.

Carers – informal support network of family, friends and neighbours. This is different from people who provide emotional or physical support in a professional role.

Co-production – doing things *with* people rather than *for* or *to* them. Co-production means designing and delivering services in an equal and reciprocal relationship between professionals, people using services, their families and communities, where everyone's assets are valued.

Council tax benefit – paid by the local authority to cover part or all of the cost of council tax.

Department of Work and Pensions (DWP) – the government department that deals with welfare benefits and pensions.

Disclosure and Barring Service (DBS) – a national scheme to check if people who work with children, vulnerable adults or certain other areas have any criminal convictions in their past.

Employment and Support Allowance (ESA) – a welfare benefit for those unable to work because of health problems.

Housing benefit – paid by the local authority to cover part or all of the cost of rent.

Income replacement benefit – a government payment for those who are not working, such as retirement pension, ESA, income support and some aspects of universal credit.

Intersectionality – the interconnected nature of different identities including gender, race, sexuality, class and mental health. The term can apply to individual people or whole groups to describe how these identities overlap to create layers of oppression.

Lived experience – personal knowledge that is gained through direct, first-hand involvement. In the context of peer support, lived experience refers to a person's experiences of distress, trauma, oppression, service use and recovery.

Lived expertise – the skills that a person has developed through processing their lived experience and transforming it into an asset.

National insurance (NI) – a tax usually deducted from a person's salary to pay for their state retirement pension or other benefits if they are unable to work.

Peer-led provisions – services and organisations where those with lived experience have control over all aspects of provisions such as service design, delivery, development, management and evaluation.

Peer support – giving and receiving support based on shared experience, culture or identity. Peer support is 'mutual' in that it is based on equality rather than power imbalance and is founded on principles of shared respect, self-discovery and emotional safety.

Peer trainer – someone with lived experience of mental health challenges or a long-term condition who is trained in teaching and in using their lived experience to help others.

Peer worker – a person who is employed in a role where they are expected to draw on their personal experience of distress and recovery to support others. Organisations use a variety of terms to describe this role, including peer provider, expert by experience, consumer provider, peer specialist, peer mentor and recovery coach. While there may be differences in the key responsibilities within each role, the use of peer support skills and lived experience is a common thread. Often these terms have been selected by the volunteers involved as ones that they feel comfortable with.

Recovery – refers to personal recovery rather than clinical recovery. Personal recovery is a self-defined unique process of building a meaningful life which may or may not occur alongside the remission of 'symptoms' (clinical recovery).

Recovery College – a college with a recovery-educational approach offering courses to increase people's knowledge and skills and promote self-management, usually about mental health or other long-term conditions, recovery and well-being. They are underpinned by principles of co-production, adult learning and inclusivity and are strengths-based, recovery-oriented and progressive.

Recovery-focused/recovery-oriented – a supportive approach which helps a person achieve their own self-defined goals and places them in control of the direction and pace of progress. It is under-pinned by hope, not taking control away from a person and helping a person connect with opportunities which they have identified as important in their recovery.

Self-directed learner – someone who is not only involved in but leads her or his own learning process.

Self-stigma – when an individual internalises feelings of external discrimination, leading to them disas-sociating from that identity and holding stigmatising beliefs about others like them.

Socially excluded communities – groups of people who are denied access to services and opportunities that are available to members of other groups, and which are fundamental to everyday life.

Strategic essentialism – the strategic coming together of people within minority groups, or with shared identities, so that they can best represent themselves. This involves the temporary disregard of strong difference which may exist between group members so that they can foreground their shared identity to achieve political goals.

Survivor – an empowering descriptive term for a person who has experienced (and survived) traumatic or distressing life events. People describe themselves as surviving the experience of mental distress and as surviving mental health services.

Survivor knowledge – a specific form of expertise derived from personal experience of mental distress, trauma, service use and recovery.

Third sector/voluntary sector/non-governmental organisations – organisations or collectives which sit outside of the public sector (government-provided services such as the NHS) and the private sector (profit-making businesses). The third sector includes independent organisations including charities, self-help services, community organisations and social enterprises and other not-for-profit organisations. These may be peer-run, such as Recovery Partners in Sussex, or not, such as Mind.

Triangle of care – a collaborative relationship between the person using services, their family member or carer and mental health professionals. It has been developed as a framework for mental health services to acknowledge the central role that carers play; it aims to support communication and partnership working and promote the recovery, well-being and safety of people using services.

Index

Printed by Printforce, the Netherlands